Nostradamus
&
Our Lady
of Fátima

Nostradamus & Our Lady of Fátima

An interpretation by

Robert Tippett

Copyright © 2013

All rights reserved. Produced in the United States of America. No part of this publication may be reproduced, or transmitted, in any form or by any means electronic, mechanical, photocopying, recording, or otherwise, without the prior written permission of the author.

ISBN 978-0-9801166-6-3

Published by Katrina Pearls, LLC

Cover Photographs

A wax display at the *Musee Grevin de la Provence,* Salon-de-Provence, France (2006). It depicts the arrival of the *Saints-Marys-of-the-Sea,* in the Camargue. Photo by Robert Tippett.

Cathars being expelled from Carcasonne (1209). This occurred during the Albigensean Crusade. (unknown artist) Source: Wikipedia.

Image of Nostradamus traveling Europe, circa 1537. His travels took place after the 1534 death of his first wife and two children. (unknown artist).

Four Horsemen of Apocalypse, by Viktor Vasnetsov. Painted in 1887. Source: Wikipedia.

Closeup of the statue at Our Lady of the Guard (*Notre-Dame de la Garde*), outside that basilica in Marseilles, France (2006). Photo by Robert Tippett.

A photostatic copy of a page from Ilustração Portuguesa, October 29, 1917, showing the crowd looking at the "miracle of the sun" (September 12, 1917). Source: Wikipedia.

Internal Acknowledgments

Partial image of one quatrain published in the 1568 Lyon edition of *The Prophecies,* made available online by Mario Gregorio. (fair use)

Image of the European Union residence permit emblem. Permission to copy under terms of the GNU Free Documentation License. (fair use)

This book is dedicated to the memory of my loving mother, who passed away while this book was still in the works. Mom has now joined the ranks of those many souls who give their full support to what I am doing, have been doing, and will continue to do with Nostradamus, although it was difficult for her to understand my efforts prior to that crossing over.

Table of Contents

Foreword
Chapter 1
    Some Background Stuff
        What's in a Name? 13
        Saints Marys of the Sea 15
        The Name Mary, as "Our Lady" 21

Chapter 2
    The Word "*Vierge*" Explained
        The First of Eight Times Repeated 23
        A Unique Redemption 26

Chapter 3
    He has Spoken through the Prophets
        The Marian Apparitions 29
        The Prophecy of Fatima 32
        The Prophecy of Malachy 38

Chapter 4
    The First "*Vierge*" Quatrain
        Quatrain II-17 41
        Gentiles in the Pyrenees 43
        The North Wind 51

Chapter 5
    The Second "*Vierge*" Quatrain
        Quatrain III-44 58
        The Animal in Man 60
        The Lightning of Evil Doing 66
        Rome and the Dilemma of Israel 69

Chapter 6
    The Third "*Vierge*" Quatrain
        Quatrain III-84 74
        A Big City Half in Ruin 75
        A Wall and a Plumb Line 81
        An Important Virgin 86
        The Power to take Peace from the Earth 91

Chapter 7
The Fourth "*Vierge*" Quatrain
- Quatrain IV-35 100
- A Light Put Out 103
- A Form of Blind Injustice 108
- A Spear of Gold with A Point of Fire 114
- The Union of Tuscany & Corsica 118

Chapter 8
The Fifth "*Vierge*" Quatrain
- Quatrain VI-35 122
- The Symmetry of Color 125
- Christianity and Latin 130
- Wanderers on the Solar Plain 136
- Hidden by a Wax Seal 144

Chapter 9
The Sixth "*Vierge*" Quatrain
- Quatrain VIII-80 156
- The Widow, Him, and the Virgin 158
- The Men Who would be Kings 163
- Drinking from the Cups of Wolves 170
- The Lampstand will be Removed 175

Chapter 10
The Seventh "*Vierge*" Quatrain
- Quatrain VIII-90 181
- When Crusaders Sense Trouble 182
- The Worship of Ba'als 185
- When Swine Trample Places Holy 188
- The End of a Lineage 195

Summary
A Church in Need
- Basic Review 198
- The Slope of Failure 203
- A Thread of Sinew 207
- Her Son's Church 213

Foreword

The language of *The Prophecies* is not like French, English, or any other language spoken by groups of people. It is a holy language, like that composing the many books of the *Holy Bible*. While its words can be translated into every known language of the world, the meaning of the words cannot be understood by any standard of syntax those languages rely on for understanding. A holy language requires a holy syntax; and because few people have learned to speak in the tongues of God that is what makes the language of Nostradamus impossible to fully understand.

In this text, I begin many chapters with the Old French text of Nostradamus, followed by an English translation of mine. That translation will be found meaningless, when first read as four lines of prose. As one goes through the chapters, one will find out how little I refer back to that initial translation. The reason is there are so many different combinations of translations possible that it is impossible to write them all out as one simplified, yet intelligible translation. My translations are made after looking at a matrix of possibilities and attempting to give the translations that offer the best direction towards the ultimate meaning. Still, that only can have impact after the whole interpretation has been presented; and even then, the translation is always found lacking when read as four lines of prose.

The impact is found by first reading each word individually, rather than as one word in a series of words, when each word is limited by its place in that series. The importance of individually reading words is how one can find the repetition of words, in the whole scope of *The Prophecies*, as significant and important. I have written one book (*The $25-Million Answer*) that focuses on the use of the one word "mountain" (as "*mont,*" "*monts,*" and "*montaigne*"), which then led to a focus on the uses of the word "antichrist." This book focuses on the use of the one word "virgin" (as "*vierge,*" "*vierges,*" and "*Vierge*").

By focusing on one word's usage, one is focusing on one cell of one quatrain, and how that relates to one cell of another quatrain, and another. Each quatrain is a cell of *The Prophecies* as a whole, and the whole also includes letters of instruction, which instruct about those cellular elements. From this level of inspection, one sees how the whole is interconnected, threaded together in complex ways, such that the whole is like a living entity. One piece is itself one piece, but each piece connects to another, and another, so that the life found in one part of the body is also reflected in several other parts, while each part is individually its own. All is connected in this way.

The same can be seen reflected in the books of the *Holy Bible*. Each book represents its own genre of writing: history, doctrine, song, prophecy, parable, etc. Still, each book relates to the theme of God and His lineage produced, through which the world would be led to God. There is also repetition of verbiage found, where new prophets quote the old words as fulfilled in new times. This is why the *Holy Bible* is called a living text, as it has meaning that applies to all times, such that simple translations often cannot allow one to see meaning extending beyond what appears to be the obvious.

The comparison of *The Prophecies* to the *Holy Bible* is due to the source being the same. Nostradamus can then be seen as a holy prophet, with *The Prophecies* being yet another holy book from God. The language of all is holy, and beyond the linear capabilities of man and his limiting syntax.

The problem with *The Prophecies* is it needs a holy interpretation, which allows others to see the depth of scope its language contains. The Apostle Paul said that the gifts of the Holy Spirit included prophecy and the ability to interpret prophecy. This book is my holy interpretation of eight elements of the body of *The Prophecies*, as led by the Holy Spirit.

Being led by the Holy Spirit is not something one can control, or something that one can master and call upon at will. The Holy Spirit comes to those who are ready, and who have prepared to receive the spirit of the body of Christ. Such people follow whispers of insight and are open to inner suggestions as to meaning. If I have been able to interpret Nostradamus through the guidance of the Holy Spirit, others can also be so led to be filled with independent understanding.

This book, as have all of the books explaining Nostradamus that I have written previously, has been written for the purpose of allowing others to understand, so that others may understand beyond what I am capable of writing. I have sacrificed to make this available, and I sacrifice willingly. I have been honored to understand the word of God, and it is an honor to share that understanding with others.

May the peace of the LORD be with you as you read this book; and may your hearts be opened so your eyes can see and your ears can hear. Your minds must be opened by the heart, where faith is ignited. Through faith, miracles of understanding will come from testing what I write, proving that God is indeed real and present within your heart. May your heart be warmed by understanding this holy language, making you fluent through the Holy Spirit.

Robert Tippett

August 15, 2013

Nostradamus & Our Lady of Fatima

Chapter 1
Some Background Stuff

What's in a Name?

In the stories of the *Holy Bible*, in particular those that are in the Hebrew of the Old Testament, one sees how names have special meanings. For instance, the father who would beget two of the world's greatest religions, Abraham (father to sons Isaac and Ishmael), his name began as Abram. The name Abram means, "exalted father."[1] The name change to Abraham brought about the meaning, "father of a multitude."[2]

There are also meanings attached to the names of places, such that the place Golgotha is explained to mean, "Place of the skull." Other names are explained as having been created because of an event that occurred at that place. For example, Isaac reopened a well of his father, but local tribesmen complained that it was their well. Because of that dispute, the well was named Esek, meaning "contention" (or "argument.").[3] The point of this is to show how names have special meaning.

Perhaps it is unrealized, but the name Nostradamus is the Latinized form of the family surname Nostredame. That name was taken by Nostradamus' grandfather, Guy Gassonet, as a fitting name for his conversion from Judaism to Christianity. He willfully converted (believed to be in 1455), taking the name Pierre Nostredame.[4]

---

[1] From NetBible – Strong – 087 (http://classic.net.bible.org/strong.php?id=087)
[2] From NetBible – Strong – 085 (http://classic.net.bible.org/strong.php?id=085)
[3] From Biblos.com, Strong's Concordance – 6230 - eseq (http://concordances.org/hebrew/6230.htm)
[4] Per the Wikipedia article "Nostradamus," under the subheading "Childhood" (http://en.wikipedia.org/wiki/Nostradamus), and repeated by other online sources.

That first name, in French, means "Stone" or "Rock," and is the equivalent of Peter, the name of the Apostle who founded the Christian Church of Rome. The given name Nostradamus' grandfather chose then honors the Virgin Mary, the mother of Jesus, who is venerated by the Roman Catholic Church. Nostre-dame (in Old French) means "Our-lady," meaning the name Nostradamus' grandfather chose made a statement about how he wished to be known as a newly converted Christian. His new name announced (in Old French), "I am *Pierre de Nostre-Dame*." That translates to mean, "I am a Rock to Our Lady."

The Old French spelling of "*nostre*" has since been modified to become "*notre*," and it is the pronoun that in English is "our." The word "*dame*" is clearly recognizable as meaning "lady." Thus, the modern spelling, as Notre Dame, is easily recognizable, if not understood by all. In America, that is the name of the famous Catholic university in South Bend, Indiana. The name is also attached to many Catholic basilicas, cathedrals, churches, and primary schools all around the world. The name is in honor of "Our Lady" of Christ, the Virgin Mary, who is officially venerated by the Church of Rome. The possessive pronoun, "Our," reflects this special adoration bestowed upon her memory by those of that Christian religion.

In the 16th century, in Europe, it was popular for the pioneers of the Renaissance to Latinize their names. Due to this movement, it was understood that Nostredame became Nostradamus, to fit a trend. While it may have been recognized as part of a fad, the Latinization of "Our Lady" holds a higher symbolism. Since Latin is the official language of the Roman Catholic Church, a name change to Nostradamus becomes a statement that Michel de Nostredame is "one personally dedicated to Our Lady," as his own statement of faith. He transcended from French to the language of the Church to make that statement, albeit without fanfare.

By recognizing the Christian element of Nostradamus' name, one can better glimpse him as one who truly lived up to his name. He was a dedicated Christian, demonstrated through his service to others as a doctor, apothecary, author, and astrologer. He also demonstrated his dedication to the Roman Catholic Church, as seen in his knowledge of Latin and the *Holy Bible* written in that language, which he quoted in his letters accompanying *The Prophecies* and in multiple quatrains. In the mid-16th century, regardless of the revolution Martin Luther began, said to have spread to France as early as 1519,[5] most of Europe only had Latin versions of the *Holy Bible*. Because Nostradamus displayed knowledge of that version, a dedication to his professed religion was shown.

Saints Marys of the Sea

One can even assume that his grandfather's conversion could have been, in some way, related to the legend of Provence, at *Saintes-Maries-de-la-Mer* (Saints-Marys-of-the-Sea). The legend holds that a raft without a sail landed there, with Mary Jacobé (the wife of Cleopas, a.k.a. "the other Mary"), Mary Salomé (the sister of Mary the mother of Jesus), and Mary Magdalene on board.[6] These passengers were followers of Jesus, and all settled in the costal area of the region known as Provence, in the present-day Department of France known as the Mouths-of-the-Rhone (*Bouches-du-Rhone*). At one time, the place of that landing was called *Notre-Dame-de-Ratis* (Our Lady of [the] Boat), but reverted to the original name in 1838.[7]

The original name of the place of that landing was *Oppidum Priscum Râ*,[8] which was the Roman name, dating from their conquests of Gaul. That name was attributed to the Celtic presence there, which would pre-date the Gaelic Wars initiated by Julius Caesar (58-51 B.C.). The Latin name means, "Ancient Boat Town," but one can also see the same words making the ancient name represent a place of the "Venerable Fortified Wood Raft," based on acceptable translations of the Latin. When the Celts are believed to have revered that site for the holy springs of a "threefold water goddess," the legend of the three Marys gains more significance. Their arrival there can be seen as fulfilling an unrecognized prophecy.

That Latin name could refer to it being a place to set sail from, as a harbor, because the place is in the *Buches-de-Rhone* department. That name

---

5   Wikipedia article "Martin Luther," under the subheading "The start of the Reformation" (http://en.wikipedia.org/wiki/Martin_luther).
6   Joseph of Arimathea, the uncle of the women and also the one whose tomb the body of Jesus was laid in, is said by some to have been on board. Also named is the brother of Mary Magdalene, Lazarus. In addition, someone revered as "Saint Sarah," a dark-skinned girl, who some believe may have been an Egyptian servant to the three Marys, was also on board. Some believe Sara was a baby, and the daughter of Mary Magdalene. Saint Sara is an attraction for a pilgrimage made by Roma gypsies, who originated from Eastern and Central Europe, as well as Western Turkey (Anatolia). Roman gypsies make a link to the migration of Easterners to southern France, who would become known as the Cathar people.
7   From the Wikipedia article "Saintes-Maries-de-la-Mer," under the subheading "Religion," referencing "Droit (1963)" (http://en.wikipedia.org/wiki/Saintes-Maries-de-la-Mer).
8   The website "Sacred Sites" says the place was, "Once a sacred site of the Celtic threefold water goddess, the holy spring was known as Oppidum Priscum Ra." In Latin, the name literally means, "Fortified wood Old-fashioned Raft."

means, "Mouths of [the two] Rhone [rivers]," and it represents where a delta exists between the main Rhone River and the smaller branch, called the Petite Rhone. The place is now only a slight rise above the silt and sediments of the swampy delta (elevation 0-20 feet above sea level), now called the Camargue;[9] but in 35 A.D., that state was probably less pronounced, meaning it could have been more port friendly (especially for flat-bottom boats).

The specific place where *Saints-Maries-de-la-Mer* is located is at the western edge of the present official region of France, known as Provence-Alpes-Côtes-de-Azur, more commonly called Provence. Michel de Nostredame (and also his father and grandfather) lived in southern France, in Provence. Michel was born in Saint-Rémy-de-Provence, and he wrote *The Prophecies* in Salon-de-Provence.

There is a yearly pilgrimage to Saints-Marys-of-the-Sea, which links Roma gypsies to a shrine there, dedicated to Saint Sarah.[10] Saint Sarah is the patron saint of the Roma, and she is also referred to as "Sara the Black,"[11] which links her history to being an Egyptian servant who accompanied the three Marys. Some believe she was actually an infant, and the daughter of Mary Magdalene.

In the book *The Templar Revelation*, the authors draw a link between the many churches dedicated to Saint John the Baptist in southern France, and to the presence of Black Madonna statues in those churches. These authors saw Saint Sarah as a direct descendant of Jesus, thus making her the center of the attention in their speculation about a bloodline of Jesus. That speculation had previously been presented in the book *Holy Blood, Holy Grail*, and would later be part of the foundation for the novel and subsequent movie, *The Da Vinci Code*.

The name Sarah thus becomes important to understand. It was the name of the wife of Abraham, given that name as a change from Sarai, after she became pregnant with Isaac. Before she was blessed with that miraculous pregnancy (she was 90 years of age and previously "barren"), Abraham had sired another son through an Egyptian servant given to him by the Pharaoh of Egypt. This means the presence of an "Egyptian maidservant" connects to the name Sarah, albeit in a round-about way.

---

9   From the Wikipedia article "Saintes-Maries-de-la-Mer," under the section "Statistics." (http://en.wikipedia.org/wiki/Saintes-Maries-de-la-Mer).

10   From the Wikipedia article "Saintes-Maries-de-la-Mer," under the subheading "Religion." (http://en.wikipedia.org/wiki/Saintes-Maries-de-la-Mer).

11   From the Wikipedia article "Saint Sarah" (http://en.wikipedia.org/wiki/Saint_Sarah)

One was given to Sarai, the wife of Abram, in her name change to Sarah, when Abram's changed to Abraham. The name change to Sarah means she went from being "My Princess," to Abram ("High Father"), to "Princess" to Abraham ("Father of a Nation of People"). The Sarah who accompanied the three Marys to Gaul is thus also a "Princess." While a maidservant, she would be the mother of what would become a new nation of people. The Egyptian maidservant given to Abram and Sarai was named Hagar, whose name also deserves the merit of research.

According to the website Net Bible, the name "Hagar" means, "flight." Still, that site also posts,

> "Hagar" allegorically represents the Jewish church (Gal. 4:24), in bondage to the ceremonial law; while "Sarah" represents the Christian church, which is free."[12]

That reference to Hagar above is found in the letter written by Paul, sent to "the churches of Galatia" (Galatians 1:2). The people of Galatia were Celtic, who lived in the region now known as Anatolia, in the Turkish peninsula (Asia Minor). The Hebrew meaning for "Agar" is said to be, "stranger." This meaning would be symbolic of one who was unknown, but received and welcomed (as Abraham welcomed the three strangers who were angels, and as Sarai took Hagar in), but then set free for "flight," to establish her own identity. That would match the synopsis above, where Hagar represented the bondage of the Jewish Temple.

That statement presents one with the ability to see how the raft bearing three Jewish women, all named Mary, along with two men who followed Jesus, also Jews, were the first seeds of Christianity in France. The symbolism of one being seen as an Egyptian, different by her dark skin, makes the above statement act as an independent acknowledgment of the landing at *Saints-Marys-of-the-Sea*, reflecting Jewish flight to a place where they would be free to worship as Christians.

The website Net Bible also states that the name Sarah means, "Princess [of the multitude]," or "My lady,"[13] thus representative of a name for the mother of the children of God. The Midrash (the Hebrew word meaning "Study") of Genesis sees Hagar as a daughter of the pharaoh, such that

---

12 From the website Net Bible page for "Hagar," under the subheading "Hagar [EBD]," where EBD stands for Easton's Bible Dictionary – (http://classic.net.bible.org/dictionary.php?word=hagar)
13 From the website Net Bible page for "Sarah." (http://classic.net.bible.org/dictionary.php?word=sarah)

she too was a princess, but one who was given into slavery.[14] The same status befell Joseph, the youngest son of Israel. Jesus, as Christ the King, likewise was given away by God, as a prince willingly sent by His Father to serve others. This says that being a servant simply means one must serves others, before serving self. As such, the female Sarah (either as an Egyptian servant or as an infant child) should be seen as one of great importance, having a royal place that predicts she is to produce a line of heirs.

The pilgrimage that the Roma see as important to their religious beliefs must then be understood as being from respect for that holy lineage. To realize that they travel each year to the Camargue, in France, means to realize how they leave their homes in the East and travel west. This makes their journey parallel the story of the Three Wise Men, who also came from the East, and travelled west to receive the baby Jesus and his Mother Mary, both strangers to them.

This similarity of pilgrimage, from the east to the west, then makes an important historical reflection. It connects to the record of eastern peoples migrating to southern France prior to the 12th century. Much of that was reflected in the mysterious rise of the Cathar people in that area, who had origins traced back to the regions of the Roma, in Eastern Europe and Asia Minor. Some of that relocation could be attributed to the Roma's reverence for Saint Sarah, which would imply there was some reason for this pilgrimage, meaning news of her being there would have had to reach back to the east.

Another possibility would be a link to the earliest Christian churches, such that many of the migrants could have been Jewish believers in Jesus as their Messiah. The first three Crusades spread from the late 11th century to the later years of the 12th century (The First Crusade ended in 1101, with the Third Crusade between 1189-1192). With so much continuous turmoil surrounding Jerusalem and Palestine, due to shifts back and forth between Christian and Muslim control, that history would give extra merit to the rising Jewish population that spread across Europe. From the Eastern Church's influence in regions of Asia Minor, where the earliest Christian churches sprang up, a significant number of the "refugees" to southern France would have been followers of Christ. By the time the 14th century brought a Roman Inquisition to France, one can see

---

14   From the Wikipedia article "Hagar," under the subheading, "Rabbinical commentary." (http://en.wikipedia.org/wiki/Hagar_(Bible))

how many Jews could find reason to convert to a religion named for belief in a Jewish Messiah.

There is no doubt that a migration of people from the east brought newcomers to southern France, including the Trouvère (1160 – circa 1300[15]), who were traveling minstrels, much like the Troubadours. Both names are rooted in the French word *trouver*, which means, "to find," or "to think." The names were from southern French dialects, such as Occitan, Catalan, and Provençal. They wrote songs that were soaked with humorous parody and political satire, designed to make their audiences think about how others sought to take advantage of the ignorant. Often, the lyrics urged the listeners to find their own religious path to Christ. The opinion that supports this view is called (Crypto-)Cathar.[16]

A theory of the disappearance of the Trouvère is based on the Roman Church finding the people of southern France a threat to the Church's influence there. That was due to the popularity attracted by the "political theater" put on by wandering troupes. They performed for many people who were known as the Cathari, or Cathars. That name was given to them by the locals they lived among, with the word for the name stemming from the Greek *katharos* (an Eastern origin), meaning "pure."

It was said, by those who observed them and lived amongst them but who were not a part of them, that they (the Cathari) were "good Christians."[17] From their Eastern origins, they settled in the regions surrounding the mouth of the Petite Rhone (to the west), which would then tie them to the pilgrims who traveled to the landing site of the three Marys. That would explain their numbers as being from those who fled the east and felt free to stay near their shrine.

Those migrating settlers could also be representative of early Christians who were not Jews believing their Messiah had come, but were from Gentile heritages. As the original churches of the Apostles were in the regions associated with the Roma, their preaching the Gospel to Jewish communities meant they welcomed the pagans who worshiped other

---

15   From the Wikipedia article "Trouvère."
16   From the Wikipedia article "Trouvère," under the subheading "Origins," number 5 hypothesis, which states: "According to this thesis, troubadour poetry is a reflection of Cathar religious doctrine. While the theory is supported by the traditional and near-universal account of the decline of the troubadours coinciding with the suppression of Catharism during the Albigensian Crusade (first half of the 13th century), support for it has come in waves. The explicitly Catholic meaning of many early troubadour works also works against the theory."
17   From the Wikipedia article "Catharism," under the subheading "General Beliefs," in the quote by Bernard Gui (1261-1331), in his work On the Albigensians.

gods. Christianity was to be spread to those who had not been raised Jewish, to convert all would-be faithful to the concept of the One God, with Christ as their link to Him.

Over the centuries, the Eastern Orthodox Church, based in Constantinople (Greece-Turkey), especially as the Byzantine Empire (395 – 1453), had provided protection for Eastern Christians. Those Eastern pilgrims to the West were often considered Gnostics (or Dualists) by Rome, as they refused to accept Roman ways and refused to profess faith to a Church (an institution), rather than direct faith in God and Christ. After the fall of Constantinople in the Fourth Crusade (1204-1261), Rome attempted to secure both their eastern and western fronts (so to speak), warring against all who were not Roman Catholic (especially Muslims and Jews). The capture of Constantinople by the Roman crusading knights is said to be the last stage of the East-West Schism (begun in 1054), when reconciliation was no longer possible. That capture led to the creation of a Latin Empire that fought against the remnants of the Byzantine Empire, eventually beginning the decline of Christianity as a force of military power in the East.

There is no doubt that the Roman Church did not appreciate the presence of the Cathars in France, as they deemed them heretics because of their beliefs that differed from Roman Catholicism. Likewise, the Romans did not appreciate the mounting presence of Jews in Europe; and the Church's favor towards the Western military order known as the Knights Templar, those dedicated to the "protection of pilgrims," had waned. The Church initiated a series of actions in France, against those groups out of favor (Cathars, then Templars), as well as Jews, as forceful persecutions of their "enemies."

The success of those actions would later embolden the Church to address their "Spanish problem," with a most terrible Inquisition (the Spanish Inquisition). That persecution would place another enemy in their sights, the Muslims of Spain and southern France (the Moors). After the Church's genocide of the Cathar people, survivors may have seen reason to convert to a religion that venerated Jesus as Savior, to elevate its ranks, rather than fight against its persecutions. One of this number could have been Guy Gassonet, Nostradamus' grandfather.

The Name Mary, as "Our Lady"

With this history remembered, one can see how it can be seen that the drifting of a small raft onto the shores of France set in motion a long series of events that would lead to tremendous changes within the Church of Rome. All could be linked back to the presence of three Jewish women setting foot upon Gaul, all with the same name. This makes understanding the name Mary important.

The name Mary comes from the Hebrew name Miriam, which means, "Their rebellion." When one knows that the angel Gabriel appeared to a young girl already named Mary, the meaning of her name should be seen as appropriate for her, as the one chosen by God to bear the baby Jesus. Mary would give birth to the one who would lead "their rebellion" against the establishment, both Roman and Jewish. When one sees how the New Testament mentions a proliferation of Mary figures (six, as stated by the website Scripture Says[18]), one can see these female supporters of Jesus (a westernized name, from Hosea, or Jehoshua, meaning, "Savior") supporting a theme of rebellion.

Those of Jerusalem denied Jesus because he did not fit the mold of warrior rebel, one who would lead a successful uprising against the Romans. As such, the Jewish establishment expected to be freed from their renewed captivity (following the domination of Babylon-Persia, then Rome) by one like Sampson or David. They would follow a leader of arms, more than a leader of words. The revolution led by Jesus was clearly not to be physical or violent, and he was more against the Jewish Temple's authority than against that held by Roman governors. Still, the revolution he began would successfully spread, while remaining "their rebellion" for those who believed and resisted changes in their faith.

This surrounds the spread of God's Savior for the world. As such, Christianity can be seen as a rebellion from the ways Judaism had morphed over the centuries; and Catharism (Gnosticism) can be seen as a rebellion against the changes that occurred within the Church of Rome. Further, the landing of an unnavigatable raft at a place previously named for a "Venerable Wooden Raft," where a "three-fold water goddess" was honored, the three Marys symbolize a feminine trinity of rebellion that would transform France (then known as Gaul) from pagan to Christian.

---

18   In answer to the question, "How many Mary's are there in the Bible?" (http://www.scripturessay.com/article.php?cat=&id=601)

All of this history makes it possible to see the name Nostradamus as being in honor of Our Lady, the mother of Christ, whose spirit is dedicated to protecting those believing in Jesus as Christ. It represents those who make up the body of that Church, which is beyond the scope of admiration held by the Church of Rome, where a church is defined as two or more coming together in the name of Jesus, where all are truly filled with the Holy Spirit.

Nostradamus, the name, can also can be seen as a personal statement about a Jewish convert's adoration for the mother of all would-be kings of France (the blood of Christ), as Our Lady Sarah.[19] Still, with Nostradamus bearing the given name Michel, which is the equivalent of Michael, the name Michel de Nostredame says he is born as one "Who is like God from Our Lady." The "God of Our Lady" is Jesus, making Nostradamus a name dedicated to being like the son, born of the one with the Immaculate Heart.

---

[19] Nostradamus' birth town is named for Saint Remigius, who was the Bishop of Reims and Apostle of the Franks. It was he who baptised Clovis I, King of the Franks, turning the entire Frankish people into Christians.

Chapter 2
The Word "Vierge" Explained

The First of Eight Times Repeated

The theory of repeated word use, relative to the word "virgin," means it is important to see if Nostradamus conclusively wrote of Mary in *The Prophecies*. By searching for the word "virgin" in his letters, one finds that Nostradamus mentioned that word only once, in his letter of explanation to Henry II. He did so as a flow from writing the name "Jesus Christ," stating Jesus was "born of the unique virgin." That indeed associates that word with the mother of Christ.

Nostradamus also wrote some form of the word, either "virgin" (lower case), "Virgin" (capitalized), or "virgins" (plural), in seven quatrains. For one to understand the meaning of those references, the systems that make understanding *The Prophecies* possible must be realized. That knowledge allows one to assume that connection to Mary, in some way, based on the explanation. The systems then allow for those seven separate references to be united, as if placed together to explain topics related to Christianity, in particular the Roman Catholic Church. When one does this, some amazing revelations come forth.

It first must be recognized how no word written in *The Prophecies* has only one meaning. This means that the same words can explain other things, while also being statements about the importance of the Virgin Mary, also known as *Notre Dame* (Our Lady). Nostradamus explained this in his preface to *The Prophecies*, when he said "nothing is ambiguous that is not amphibological." That statement is then amphibological, in the sense that the same words can also state, "everything is ambiguous if one does not see it in an amphibological light." This explanation (paraphrased here for simplicity) applies to the whole of the quatrains and the letters explaining those poems. Therefore, this rule applies to the use of the word "*vierge*."

To explain this concept, the one capitalized presence of "Virgin" is recognized in both French and Latin as referring to the constellation Virgo. "Virgo" is Latin for "the Virgin," and "*Vierge*" is the French proper name for that sign. The capitalization changes the word into a proper name, making it a word describing one having recognition as the one most important "Virgin."

In Greek mythology, this is believed to have been Dike (or *Dicé*), who was one of the three goddesses making up the Horai (or *Horae*), who left earth for the skies, becoming the stars of the constellation Virgo. The Romans saw the Virgo as the goddess of justice and fertility, mainly a goddess of the harvest. While the Roman Church has disassociated itself from any belief in mythology and astrology, the capitalization of the Latin word, Virgo, can equally be a direct statement about the one who has been given that title as "the Virgin," Mary, the mother of Christ. Thus, the same word can bear all of that history and meaning.

Any meaning relative to any word written is viable on an interpretive level because *The Prophecies* is a divine document, in which God speaks in unlimited directions. Nostradamus also explained this, and his explanations of divinity must be respected, as the author of *The Prophecies*. When the whole is proclaimed to have come from a divine source, it becomes a flawed act of mortals to deny that multiplicity is by design. Simply by allowing for each word to have multiple meanings, one can read Nostradamus' seven uses of "*vierge*" in ways that include prophetic allusions to his namesake (one dedicated to Our Lady).

The lower case spellings can equally be references to the same person, spoken from a more general perspective, and not focusing on the aspect of Immaculate Conception. The general sense places the Virgin Mary more in a light of purity, or one of *katharos* (purity). From this perspective, one must analyze these references made by Nostradamus in the light of the question, "Did Nostradamus allude to the Virgin Mary as a sign of his name being a dedication to her?"

Chapter 2: The Word "*Vierge*" Explained

In the letter of explanation that Nostradamus wrote to his king, Henry II, he wrote at one point:

> & the times of our savior,
>
> & redeemer Jesus Christ,
>
> born from the unique virgin,

The context of this series of segments (lines of text separated by marks of punctuation) fits into a story that appears in his letter to his king, explaining the meaning of *The Prophecies*. In that letter, Nostradamus wrote extensively of the lineage between Adam and Jesus, based on the timeline established in the *Holy Bible*. Immediately leading into the three segments shown above are other segments that tell about Noah, Abraham, Moses, and David. In a letter written as an explanation of *The Prophecies*, Nostradamus wrote, "Then after to enter the times of David, & the times of our savior [lower case spelling], & redeemer Jesus Christ, born of the unique virgin [lower case]".

The context then appears to be an explanation of prophecy being based on a divine lineage, since quatrains about the future cannot be explained as relating past biblical events. Those lines of thought cannot be viewed as Nostradamus attempting to retell the chronology of the *Holy Bible*, as little benefit comes from that understanding. This means that each segment of words bears its own scope of focus applicable to some explanation for the stories contained within the text of the quatrains. Without realizing the explanation amphibology, and seeing that as an intended use of words with double meaning, designed to mislead, one is expecting an explanation for *The Prophecies* to be related solely to biblical events and characters, and not also as projections of the future.

This small section of the letter to King Henry II can better serve our understanding by our seeing it stating recognition of how *The Prophecies* is a story about the return of "our savior," who is Jesus, as Christ. The statement, "& the times of our savior," is emphasized by the presence of the ampersand introducing that statement of explanation.[1] The focus of importance is on "the times," which then leads ones focus "to, from, of, and with" (the directional preposition "*de*") "our savior." In the lower

---

[1] The systems say ampersands introduce important elements, upon which significant focus should be placed. The examples of ampersands shown demonstrate both (1st & 2nd segment) is preceded by a comma. The systems say a comma states a point of separation, as a mark that is syntactically redundant when preceding an ampersand (as ", &"), as normal syntax has those marks imply the words, "and and."

case spelling of "savior," the importance of "the times" is then relative to us ("our") acting "to save" ourselves from those "times." We are to "save from the times," which we will have embraced.

A Unique Redemption

Another ampersand then separately places import focus on how "our salvation" will be reflected in our future, as it has been in the past. The are always three "times" to consider, relative to "our times" (past, present, and future). This then emphasizes when there will be "one to deliver" us a personal understanding of Jesus as Christ. This relates to the word "*redempteur*" following the ampersand and preceding the name Jesus.

In Old French, the word "*redempteur*" meant, "A redeemer, a ransomer, and/or a deliverer." As a lower case word, it is not fully meant to be the personification of Jesus (as the Redeemer), who eventually will come to judge the living and the dead. It is therefore more in line with the importance of the time when many will cash in their souls, as one would sell stock that has risen in value, after a period of saving. This redemption will occur as an important result of the times, and take place prior to the return of Jesus, as the Christ.

This means the importance (ampersand) of redemption is introduced, following a separation (comma) from a lower-case "savior." This can include all times since the beginning of Christianity, when individuals used faith in the Savior to be their guide to self-restraint, thus salvation, until now (the present times). That period of saving will be followed by "one to redeem," by ransom or delivery of Jesus. This can then be read as who will become a reflection of Judas (who ransomed Jesus for pieces of silver), with the separate word, "Christ," being a general statement of the whole of Christianity. This, thus, reflects a time when Christians will be failing to spread the message of Jesus, by truly living Christian lives.

On a personal level, where each individual reader sees him or herself as this "redeemer," as those will try to act as "saviors," it becomes an important time (ampersand) for Christians to attempt to redeem messages from Jesus Christ, as his prophets of warning. Nostradamus is thus explaining that he was one to deliverer *The Prophecies* of Jesus to humanity. That was in times past; but others can be the ones in times present and future, to redeem a message that has been hidden for hundreds of years. Such delivery is then stated separately (comma) to portend a birth.

Chapter 2: The Word "*Vierge*" Explained

This then makes the third segment state that the one to whom Christ will be "born," will be the "one to deliver Jesus." This then makes it possible to see another birth "from the unique virgin." Such an implication can be stating that prophecy "born" will come "to, from, of, or with" (multiple possible translations of "*de*") someone or something identified as, "*l'unique*," or "the unique." Prophecies generated by any earthly tool (astrology, Tarot cards, crystal balls, etc.) cannot be termed as solely unique, whereas "the one of a kind" (definition of "unique") source of true Prophecy is God. Thus, the third segment is beginning by stating something will be "born from God," to Christians.

The lower-case spelling of "*vierge*" means that what will be "born from God" will come to one having never prophesied before, as a "virgin." Just as Mary was a "virgin" when she was approached and told she would uniquely become pregnant with the son of God, she was devout and pure in her religion; but at that time her religion was in a state of decay and in need of salvation. The purpose of *The Prophecies* is then being explained as having been born to a virgin prophet, such as Nostradamus, coming at a time when Christianity was still relatively "pure" of outside corruption, but headed towards a future collapse.

This then also states "the pure" ("*l'unique*") in general terms, as a collective of individuals. This could then be seen as a group admiring "the unique" Virgin Mary, who gave birth to the man all believers in Christ would later follow. Those, as believers, would be filled with the Holy Spirit, helping to spread that belief throughout Europe. From those nations of people who would be observed as "pure," chaste as a virgin, France would be led to become Christian voluntarily. That means the true Virgin will be the spirit working with the spirit of Jesus Christ, to save the Christianity from the times into which it is prophesied to fall, through all times, past, present, and future.

This is an important element of the explanation letter to comprehend. These three segments explain (comparatively) how *The Prophecies* were told to Nostradamus to identify the End Times (importantly, due to ampersand, "the times of our savior"). This states when there will be need for believers to save others, along with themselves. It will be a time when the value of Jesus will have been sold for material profit, and those who will work to save others will redeem that value spiritually. It is also the only reference in either of the letters (preface or explanation to the king) telling of "a unique virgin," from which that redemption of Christ will be born. This allows for one to see visions presented by the Blessed Virgin, to young children especially (physical virgins), as a sign of those times of the savior.

The purpose of *The Prophecies* is then to restate how Jesus said the only way to the Father (Heaven) is through following him. This means that recognizing him as the way to Heaven is seeing Jesus as the model demonstrating how one can must act as savior (lower case) for him or herself. It then explains that this message of salvation and redemption, born of Christ, to create Christians, will be continued through other unique encounters some people will have, filled with the Holy Spirit. These can, and will include prophetic instances with the Virgin Mary.

This means that *The Prophecies* of Nostradamus is not unique in the message it tells, as that warning is also stated throughout the Old and New Testaments. It is unique only in its presentation style (a puzzle), and how the stories presented by Nostradamus, once solved, can have more of a modern application to "our times." Those who will believe in the One God, as the Children of Israel (Jews), would then believe Jesus to be their Messiah (Christians). They will then be born as those who will truly follow in ways that honor Christ and the Lord. God will provide protection to all those "born of Christ," as true Christians; and they will find additional confirmation and warning of "our times" from Our Lady.

Chapter 3
He has Spoken through the Prophets

The Marian Apparitions

This makes the historic accounts of Marian apparitions an important category to analyze. The first documented apparition occurred near Mexico City, not long after the Spanish Conquistadors had conquered the Aztecs, in 1531 (known as Our Lady of Guadalupe). That was during Nostradamus' lifetime, but it may be that he knew nothing of this event. The next five Vatican approved visions of the Virgin Mary all occurred in France (between 1664 and 1871).[21] In 1917, a most remarkable apparition occurred in Fatima, Portugal; and others have occurred in Ireland and Belgium (1879 – 1933)[22]

A consistent theme in all of these appearances is that poor people of good faith (Roman Catholic) witnessed the Virgin Mother. Frequently, those seeing her were shepherds, young in age, and with little schooling. On more than a couple of occasions, prior to the appearance of the Blessed Virgin, the word, "penitence," was heard spoken in a loud voice. In several appearances, others accompanied those who saw the apparitions, with none being able to see or hear anything, although the witness(s) were observed kneeling and in fixed stare. On a couple of occasions, the Virgin Mary requested something of the witness(s), such as

---

21   1664-1718 in Saint-Étienne-le-Laus; 1830 in Paris; 1846 in La Salette; 1858 in Lourdes; and 1871 in Pontmain. [per the Wikipedia article entitled "Marian apparition"].

22   Knock, Ireland in 1879; Beauraing, Belgium in 1932-33; and Banneux, Belgium in 1933 [per the book *A Woman Clothed with the Sun*, 1961, Image, New York].

the witness instructed to tell a Roman Catholic bishop to have a church be built in her honor. One witness was shown an image that was to be made into a medallion.

All were told to tell others that the witness(es) had seen her, as she had appeared for the benefit of many, not simply the one or few who could see her. She appeared to benefit believers who had not physically sensed her presence. In most cases, Mary asked the witness(es) either to maintain something she revealed as a secret, never to tell anyone, or only to reveal the secret at a specific later date. Most were told they would have to suffer for having seen her, as others would cast shame on them, as liars, ones deceived by Satan, or as ones simply hallucinating. In all cases, Our Lady, to prove she had appeared, would produce a miracle.

While Nostradamus never made any claims of having seen his namesake (*Nostre Dame*), and he was in his fifties and well educated when he wrote *The Prophecies*, there are some similarities in his claims that his most famous work had a divine source. The biggest similarity is how he was asked not to make his work be known by those who read it when it was first published (1555). When asked by the King of France to explain the meaning of his work, Nostradamus complied, but he did so in a secret manner. Both the quatrains and the letter to Henry II are presented in a scrambled order, making both seem unintelligible. The secret is revealed only after the confusing parts have been correctly realigned into an understandable whole.

The second similarity is how Nostradamus was told to suffer due to his following the instructions given to him. In return, Nostradamus had the bliss of a divine encounter, with the promise of a heavenly reward. This especially compares to the reward promised to the witnesses of the Fatima apparition. Nostradamus understood the themes and stories of his visions, and he explained them in his letters (nebulously), but he had to bear the ridicule of people thinking he had gone mad, because of the way he was instructed to make his prophecy public. The ultimate disgrace would be the widespread ignorance of the divinity of his work.

Those who wanted to benefit from Nostradamus having been shown the future saw astrology and scrying (trances coming from starring at a bowl of water) as the human tools that made him capable of humanly producing visions of the future. On top of that slight by would-be believers, most people would simply write Nostradamus off as a lunatic with a hidden agenda, while the Church of Rome would condemn him for his having been an astrologer. This abuse would continue for centuries, despite a continued interest in his "meaningless" book.

Finally, the divine story revealed to Nostradamus is designed to help others, rather than him. He would never see the fruits of his labors, because "the times of our savior" (of which he wrote, as posted above) was not his times. In his letter of explanation to his king, Nostradamus partially quoted the "minor" prophet Joel, when he wrote, in Latin, "*Effundam spiritum meum super omnem carnem & prophetabunt fili vestri, & filiae vestrae*". That translates to state, "To pour out my spirit on every flesh & your sons will be prophesying, & your daughters". This is in reference to Joel 2:28, which states, "And it shall come to pass afterward, *that* I will pour out my spirit upon all flesh; and your sons and your daughters shall prophesy, your old men shall dream dreams, your young men shall see visions."[23]

Nostradamus then wrote, in French, following that Latin reference to Scripture, "*Mais telle prophetie procedoit de la bouche du sainct esprit.*" This translates to state, "But such prophecy will be proceeding from the mouth of the holy spirit (lower case)." This says all humans who speak for the divine only speak from the divine, with nothing of their own being a source. In other words, no sons or daughters will be making things up, or filling in blanks for the divine, as their prophesying will be totally through divine intervention.

This explanation then explains a nuance that has not been regularly translated in the Book of Joel. As Joel was prior to Jesus, his source was the One God, and primarily masculine. He included "sons and daughters," as representative of a neuter gender, as would be young shepherds. He then places focus on the mature male forms, one old and one young, both of which are to be seen as different from male "sons." With the punctuation and wording used by Nostradamus, and how he was told to separate how men and women will become true prophets, through the systemic use of commas and ampersands, one sees a time when dual deities are present. His words from Christ can then be viewed as an explanation how the Spirit of Jesus will encounter male prophets (as Nostradamus claimed his source was Christ), leaving one to infer that females will likewise prophesy, but with a different Spirit seen as their source. That would be the Virgin Mary.

---
23 King James Version, from the website Biblos.com.

Because of Nostradamus' name, and the divinity of his encounter that made writing *The Prophecies* possible, the miracle that it produces has had to wait until it was capable of being understood. In Paul's first letter to the Corinthians, he wrote in chapter twelve, verses 8-10 (KJV):

> "For to one is given by the Spirit the word of wisdom; to another the word of knowledge by the same Spirit; to another faith by the same Spirit; to another the gifts of healing by the same Spirit; to another the working of miracles; to another prophecy; to another discerning of spirits; to another divers kinds of tongues; to another the interpretation of tongues"

It is beyond question that the "tongue" of Nostradamus' "prophecy" (his style of writing) is foreign, to the point that no one had been able to understand his meaning. This means that someone would be further required to "interpret his tongue," meaning another event of the Spirit speaking through a human being would come when the "times" required understanding. This is then the product of another explanation, one where the systems that make understanding possible (realizing ampersands and commas are only part of this) are necessary. Still, even armed with such a tool, each individual must welcome the Holy Spirit within himself or herself, allowing true "wisdom" and "knowledge" to surface.

As wonderful that experience is, the "working of a miracle" comes from realizing how perfectly *The Prophecies* have prophesied the future. The miracle of "our times" is the tale of the past, which has already come true, perfectly as history has recorded the events of which he told. This is to bring about "faith by the same Spirit" that entered Nostradamus. The assistance *The Prophecies* provides for others is a miracle waiting to be enacted by the faithful, which is to bring about a change of direction. Simply by knowing one is going the wrong way, one has the power to stop going that way, with God's help. The destruction of Sodom and Gomorrah could have been averted, if only there had been five people who had faith and acted upon that faith for the good of others.

The Prophecy of Fatima

Just as *The Prophecies* of Nostradamus does nothing to take away from Biblical prophecies still to be fulfilled, his words confirm and clarify the Biblical, while matching one particular Marian apparition whose secret

Chapter 3: He has Spoken through the Prophets

has been revealed but not acted upon by the faithful. The stories of Nostradamus' future match the secrets revealed by Sister Lucia, a Catholic nun by adulthood, but a shepherd in Fatima, Portugal in 1917.

For that reason, I feel it is especially important to examine the secrets that Sister Lucia revealed from the apparition of the Blessed Virgin she experienced. She was one of three young children who witnessed her appearance, over a seven-month period, with each appearance taking place at noon on the 13th of the month. The other two children died shortly after the last appearance, with Lucia the one who was instructed to send a private message to the pope. She was instructed to wait until a time when the message would make the most sense, and its urgency most felt.

Raised from a peasant child to a life dedicated to the Church, as a nun, she sent letters through the proper church channels, revealing the message from the Virgin Mary to the pope. The pope, and all subsequent popes, read the letters and kept the message secret for some time. Due to public inquiries, they leaders began to release parts of her letters in stages. The Vatican finally made public each of three secrets that Sister Lucia revealed. She wrote one letter revealing two secrets in 1941, and then she revealed the third secret in 1943, with a note that the letter would not be fully understandable until 1960. She withheld those secrets from exposure until coerced by her Bishop, after prayer to the Virgin Mary.

The whole experience is known as the apparition of Our Lady of Fatima. In French, this title is stated as *Notre-Dame de Fatima*. The French title makes the words of Sister Lucia have an importance that relates to the name Nostradamus (meaning "one of Our Lady").

Sister Lucia wrote of two secrets revealed to her and the other two shepherd children, which she was told not to tell until a later date. The Virgin said the secrets would not be understood before a period of time had passed. This is similar to the way *The Prophecies* were published by Nostradamus, in a manner that would not be understable when first published. The reason is his work would require the passing of time, and the history that would later be recognizable established, for any of his words to be remotely understandable.

Sister Lucia revealed two of the secrets in a letter to the Vatican in 1941.

Copies of these can be found posted on the website Crystal Links (www.crystallinks.com/fatima.html). Just as I presented what Nostradamus wrote in his letter to King Henry II, as individual segments of prose made to have a poetic level of singular importance as lines of thought, I will present Sister Lucia's letters likewise. With that distinction, this is what she wrote:

> "Our Lady showed us a great sea of fire which seemed to be under the earth.
>
> Plunged in this fire were demons and souls in human form,
>
> like transparent burning embers,
>
> all blackened or burnished bronze,
>
> floating about in the conflagration,
>
> now raised into the air by the flames that issued from within themselves together with great clouds of smoke,
>
> now falling back on every side like sparks in a huge fire,
>
> without weight or equilibrium,
>
> and amid shrieks and groans of pain and despair,
>
> which horrified us and made us tremble with fear.
>
> The demons could be distinguished by their terrifying and repulsive likeness to frightful and unknown animals,
>
> all black and transparent.
>
> This vision lasted but an instant.
>
> How can we ever be grateful enough to our kind heavenly Mother,
>
> who had already prepared us by promising,
>
> in the first Apparition,
>
> to take us to heaven.
>
> Otherwise,
>
> I think we would have died of fear and terror."

By stating, "This vision lasted but an instant," but the impact made her and her mates feel so strongly, to "think we would have died of fear and terror," is a statement of what awaits should the future proceed without people of faith being filled with the Holy Spirit. She was allowed to experience a vision of what it is like without the blessings of God, which comes when people turn their backs on God and stop praying for penitence.

In the same letter, the second secret is revealed. It explains the first secret as being a vision of Hell, and then goes on to tell how the Blessed Virgin says we (the people of the future) can find "our savior."

> "You have seen hell where the souls of poor sinners go.
>
> To save them,
>
> God wishes to establish in the world devotion to my Immaculate Heart.
>
> If what I say to you is done,
>
> many souls will be saved and there will be peace.
>
> The war is going to end:
>
> but if people do not cease offending God,
>
> a worse one will break out during the Pontificate of Pius XI.
>
> When you see a night illumined by an unknown light,
>
> know that this is the great sign given you by God that he is about to punish the world for its crimes,
>
> by means of war,
>
> famine,
>
> and persecutions of the Church and of the Holy Father.
>
> To prevent this,
>
> I shall come to ask for the consecration of Russia to my Immaculate Heart,
>
> and the Communion of reparation on the First Saturdays.
>
> If my requests are heeded,
>
> Russia will be converted,
>
> and there will be peace;
>
> if not,
>
> she will spread her errors throughout the world,
>
> causing wars and persecutions of the Church.

> The good will be martyred;
>
> the Holy Father will have much to suffer;
>
> various nations will be annihilated.
>
> In the end,
>
> my Immaculate Heart will triumph.
>
> The Holy Father will consecrate Russia to me,
>
> and she shall be converted,
>
> and a period of peace will be granted to the world."

This letter was probably written in 1941, as the young girl, Lucia Santos, was uneducated and unable to write letters in 1917. Still, the verbiage is telling of an end to World War I, with "a worse one to come." That predicts World War II, but the same words could also foretell of any other horrible wars still in the future.

Focus was put on the fall of Czarist Russia, supporter of the Eastern Orthodox Church, to the secular, atheist Soviet Union (which would not officially begin until 1922). This secret puts weight on Russia being saved, because if it were not to be saved, then great punishment would be brought upon the world. Nostradamus wrote metaphorically of the great power of the "North" that would subvert the Christian world, leading to tremendous persecution of that religion.

According to the transcript of the third of the Three Secrets of Fatima, one needs to see the metaphor coming from the imagery and auditory recalled. Recalling her experience as the young Portuguese shepherd, Lœcia [Lucia] Santos wrote in 1943, but placed in an envelope requesting it not be read before 1960, these words (again from the website Crystal Links). The Vatican has acknowledged it immediately opened the letter and read it, then placed it in a vault for a later pope to consider. Pope John Paul II revealed this letter, after he announced that the tragedy foretold had been averted (a lie, if one realizes the stories of *The Prophecies*). Notice that I have placed certain key words in bold type. These highlighted words can be found repeated within the quatrains and letters of *The Prophecies*:

> "After the **two parts** which I have already explained,
>
> at the **left** of **Our Lady** and a little **above**,

we saw an **Angel** with a **flaming sword** in his **left hand**;

flashing,

it gave out **flames** that looked as though they would **set the world** on **fire**;

but they **died out** in contact with the **splendor** that **Our Lady radiated** towards him from her **right hand**:

pointing to the **earth** with his **right hand,**

the **Angel** cried out in a loud voice:

'Penance, Penance, Penance!'

And we saw in an **immense light** that is **God**:

'something similar to how **people** appear in a **mirror** when they **pass in front** of it'

a **Bishop** dressed in **White**

'we had the impression that it was the **Holy Father**'.

Other **Bishops,**

Priests,

men and **women Religious** going up a steep **mountain,**

at the **top** of which there was a **big Cross** of rough-hewn trunks as of a cork-tree with the bark;

before reaching there the **Holy Father passed** through a **big city half** in **ruins** and **half trembling** with halting step,

afflicted with **pain** and **sorrow,**

he **prayed** for the **souls** of the **corpses** he met on his **way;**

having reached the **top** of the **mountain,**

on his knees at the **foot** of the **big Cross** he was **killed** by a **group** of **soldiers** who **fired bullets** and **arrows** at him,

and in the same way there **died** one after another the other **Bishops,**

Priests,

men and **women Religious,**

and various lay people of different **ranks** and positions.

Beneath the **two arms** of the **Cross** there were **two Angels** each with a crystal aspersorium in his hand,

> in which they gathered up the **blood** of the **Martyrs** and with it sprinkled the **souls** that were making their **way** to **God**."

The Prophecy of Malachy

This depiction of a future that has yet to occur is said by many to be a reflection of the prophecy made by Saint Malachy (1139), in which he named the last 112 popes, while in an ecstatic trance. The vision of Sister Lucia is of those final days of the last pope.

The 111th in this line is the present pope, Benedict XVI (Joseph Ratzinger), with only one more name left on Malachy's list. Nostradamus tells a story of the end of the 111th pope's life, and the one who would represent "Peter of Rome," the last pope. In between, Nostradamus tells of a false pope, who will oversee the tremendous persecution of which Sister Lucia wrote, and which many quatrains of Nostradamus detail.

When Saint Malachy came to the last name on his list, Peter of Rome, he wrote this:

> "In the extreme persecution of the Holy Roman Church, there will sit. Peter the Roman, who will pasture his sheep in many tribulations:and when these things are finished, the city of seven hills will be destroyed, and the terrible judge will judge his people. The End."[24]

That makes a perfect summary of what Sister Lucia recalled from the revelation shown to her by the Virgin Mary. It is very clear that another sack of Rome is in the future, in "our times," based on the quatrains and explanations of Nostradamus. While Nostradamus does not name names, and neither did Sister Lucia, the generality of characters paints a picture of a severely punished Church, along with severely punished people surrounding the Church. This story is repeated in many other prophetic works.

It should be known that the prophecy of Malachy is not wholly accepted as a prophecy, by scholars and investigators of the Vatican. It must be understood that Malachy was canonized in 1199, fifty-one years after his death. The document known as his "Prophecy of the Popes" was not dis-

---
24   From the Wikipedia article "Prophecy of the Popes," under the subheading, "Petrus Romanus." (http://en.wikipedia.org/wiki/Prophecy_of_the_Popes)

Chapter 3: He has Spoken through the Prophets

covered until 1590, and not made publically available until 1595. Thus he was a saint by his works and not because of his prophecy.

Due to this late discovery (well after the death of Nostradamus), some disagreement exists about the possibility of a desire to find the work prophetic causing the force fitting of symbolic words he wrote, in Latin, to sicne posthumus popes, then providing self-fulfilling prophecies for the popes who would come later. This preference to doubt is a common response to most yet unfulfilled prophecy. It certainly is the delima the writings of Nostradamus have faced over the centuries; and it the apparitions of the Virgin Mary have consistently brought out doubt before belief, in Church officials who have been made aware of those instances.

I recommend everyone investigate with an open mind and with a heart that is willing to be led to the truth of discovery. Truth exposed false prophets and verifies those bona fide. It has become my belief that the Latin words written by Malachy were precisely like the Latin and French words written by Nostradamus, in the sense that they appear as poor grammar. This can be explained by everyone wanting to read multiple words as one statement, which is what normal syntax leads us to do. When God speaks, however, one word makes multiple statements and multiple words yield paragraphs of meaning.

As such, for example, when Malachy wrote "*De labore solis,*" which has been attached to Pope John Paul II. This is not a statement of the man who would be pope, as most have assumed it to be, well before Pope John Paul II was born. Rather, it is a statement about the times that surrounded that papal reign, which all of the Latin of Malachy should also model.

Those Latin words associated with Pope John Paul II are translated wholly as "the labor of the sun," with this metaphorically stating, "the eclipse of the sun." Those who see a prophecy verified by Malachy through those words say, "the man who would be Pope John Paul II was born on the day of a solar eclipse, and his funeral was on the day of another solar eclipse." This, of course, says nothing about the papacy of Pope John Paul II, and is therefore of little value. This is why the Prophecy of the Popes is seen as trifle by religious scholars.

I now see this Latin moniker not as a name but as a statement about the twenty-five year reign of Pope John Paul II. By that, it says one would become pope who would labor to block the light of Christ, who Nostradamus repeatedly symbolized through use of the word "sun." This means whoever would be the one to take up that position on the list of Malachy, who would assume the title Pope John Paul II, would himself be an eclipse on Christianity. Despite JP2's popularity and beatification by the his pal, Cardinal Ratzinger, and the expectation of a fast-tracked canonization, eventually he will be seen as part of the problems our future brings. He will be proved not to be a saint.

Nostradamus makes that clear in his quatrains, and he explains why. The time of Pope John Paul II will symbolize why Our Lady of Fatima warned the Church of a fall. She warned the Vatican, long before he rose to power, the end would come should it not re-consecrate Russia (challenge Communism). Besides Karol Wojtyla's Nazi and Communist background, there are warning signs that connect Pope John Paul II directly to the prophecy at Fátima.

Two assassination attempts on Pope John Paul II took place on, or the eve of, the May 13, 1917 anniversary date of Our Lady's first appearance to three children. He was shot and critically wounded on May 13, 1981; and then, on May 12, 1982, a Spanish priest tried to kill the pope with a bayonet, causing minor injury. Then, on May 13, 2000, in a homily given in Portugal, the pope announced the prophecy of the Virgin, Our Lady of Fátima, was no longer a worry, due to the collapse of the Soviet Union.

Nostradamus points out the connection Russia will have in our dreadful future, using its weapons technology through surrogate nations (like Iran), against the Christian West. The vison of the Blessed Virgin clearly showed the end of Rome, and thus the end of the papal reigns. That was the outcome should the Holy See not re-consecrated Russia, during the Second World War, when Sister Lucia sent her first letters. Re-consecrating the world in the year 2000, without specifically naming Russia, does nothing to fulfill the demands of Our Lady of , thus it does nothing to eliminate the prophecy shown. The fact that Malachy's list reached the second to the last when Pope John Paul II became the head of the Church is just one more reason to believe the danger still looms ahead.

Chapter 4
The First *Vierge* Quatrain

Quatrain II-17

It is not the point of this work to try to sell the world on belief of Nostradamus. Belief must be in the power and glory of the One God. Through His Holy Spirit comes visions of Christ, the Blessed Virgin, and prophets like Joel, John of Patmos, Malachy, and Nostradamus. The persecution of Christians is a sign that there will are still many true believers who, just like Sister Lucia, Nostradamus, and others who have witnessed divinity, will suffer for their acts based on faith. Still, the point of this work is to attempt to elicit true believers in God and Christ to act prior to the point of ultimatum the prophets foretell.

This work is attempting to make a connection between the name "Nostredame" and the apparitions of the Virgin Mary (Our Lady). For that reason, I believe it is important to present the seven quatrains that state some version of the "virgin" in them, to show them in that light of her appearances. While it is also important to realize that there are many quatrains containing the word "dame," in some version (minimally 24),[25] that word is most often used in the prophetic story that pertains to "Lady" Diana Spencer, who was given that title through marriage to a royal Prince. While that is not the only way to see Nostradamus' use of the word "*dame*," I will leave discernment of that word to those who should be later filled with the Holy Spirit and seek to further examine the verses linked by that word, and others. For now, I will only present the quatrains

---

[25] Per the totals listed for "*dame*" and "*dames*" on the Nostradamus Index D – E, by the website Alphabetical Nostradamus Index. (http://alumnus.caltech.edu/~jamesf/nindex/de_index.html)

that have the word "*vierge*."

The first quatrain (in order of presentation in *The Prophecies*) is found in *Centurie II* (like Chapter 2). It is number 17 in that chapter's one hundred poems. The first two lines of the quatrain, the main and secondary theme lines, can be seen as linking its use of "*vierge*" to the apparition of the "virgin" in Lourdes, France.

Lourdes is recognized for the location of several Marian apparitions in 1858. A young girl named Bernadette Soubirous was 14 years of age when she saw the lady of the Immaculate Conception. Lourdes is located in the *Hautes-Pyrénées* department, in the *Midi-Pyrénées* region of southern France. It is in the central foothills of the Pyrenees Mountains.

Southern France is generally the geographic area associated with *Saintes-Maries-de-la-Mer* being roughly 270 miles east-northeast of Lourdes. The border between France and Spain, at the eastern edge of the Pyrenees Mountains, along the Mediterranean Sea, is only 150 miles south-southwest from the delta of the *Petite Rhone*. Lourdes is about 140 miles to the west of that Mediterranean border point.

Knowing this geography, quatrain II-17 can be seen as stating (in Old French, followed by my English translation):[26]

> *Le camp du temple de la vierge vestale,*
>
> *Non esloigné d'Ethne & monts Pyrénées:*
>
> *Le grand conduict est caché dens la male,*
>
> *North getés fluves & vignes mastinées.*

> The camp of the temple to the virgin pure,
>
> Not far away from Gentiles & mountains Pyrenees:
>
> Him great conduit east hidden destructive power there harmful,
>
> North cast ones streams & vines mated with mastiffs.

---

[26] Each Old French word has multiple alternate translation possibilities, making this translation only one possibility. For example, the word "camp" was shown in Randle Cotgrave's 1611 French-English Dictionary, as possibly usable in a sentence with the context meaning, "A camp; An host, or army lodged; A field." I have selected "camp" in the translation above, but this does not eliminate the possibility of the other uses being substituted.

Chapter 4: Quatrain II-17

This translation is only one of several possibilities, as all of Nostradamus' quatrains have different translation capabilities. When read in this way, one can see the main theme (line one) placing focus on a significant "camp," because the capitalized article beginning that line. "*Le*" preceding any line (any capitalized article) identifies that to follow as "The one of significance," and in this case one finds a significant "camp." That then becomes relative "to the temple" or "of the temple," which can be read as some shrine or basilica, either pagan, Roman, Jewish, or Christian.

This place of worship or holy presence can then be seen as dedicated "to the virgin." The "virgin" is then described as "pure," "virginal," or "chaste," by the word "*vestale*." The word, "*vestale*," by itself, can be seen as how the people of France described the Cathar people. Cathar Country is generally represented in French travel brochures as the Aude Department, especially that land surrounding the city of Carcassonne, which is roughly 120 miles due east of Lourdes.

This main theme statement can also indicate the presence of a convent, as "The camp of the temple," dedicated "to the virgin." As such, a "vestal virgin" (from "*vierge vestale*") can be seen as meaning "nun," while also making one notice an ancient Roman element, as the "vestal virgins." Those were young maidens dedicated to the goddess Vesta, in Rome. In Lourdes, there is a convent of Carmelite nuns, with the Carmelite Order recognized by the Roman Catholic Church as under the special protection of the Blessed Virgin Mary.[27]

A reading of "vestal virgins" ("*vierge vestale*" is singular, not plural) then links line one to the *Oppidum Priscum Râ*, the Roman name for the place later named *Saintes-Maries-de-la-Mer*. That place referred to as *Oppidum-Râ* was known as *Notre-Dame-de Ratis*, where *Râ* became *Radis*, meaning "boat." This place has since become named *Notre-Dame-de-la-Mer* (Our Lady of the Sea).[28] In that location is a church, called an old fortress, with a shrine to Saint Sarah in the crypt. This was a point of interest for the Romani pilgrims, from the east.

Gentiles in the Pyrenees

Line two then confirms this by giving information relative to the location of that "temple," as being "Not far away" from "Gentile people."

---
27 From the Wikipedia article entitled "Carmelites." (http://en.wikipedia.org/wiki/Carmelites)
28 From the Wikipedia article entitled "Saintes-Maries-de-la-Mer." (http://en.wikipedia.org/wiki/Saintes-Maries-de-la-Mer)

The key word of line two is "*d'Ethne*" (actually a combined preposition-noun) which has been translated as "Gentile people." The word "*Ethne*" is similar to the French word "*ethnie*," which comes from the Greek word "*ethnos*" (or "ἔθνος"). In general, the word translates as "ethnic groups," but the capitalization makes it act more as a proper noun, identifying a specific ethnic group. When seen in this light, one can then see the Jewish and Christian use of "*ethnie*," which was specifically applied to Gentile followers of Jesus as Christ.[29]

This precedes the ampersand that leads to "mountains Pyrenees." The ampersand use designates importance of a location near, or "Not far away," which is "Ethnic," rather than Jewish. The ampersand points away from the sea-level site of the place of the "virgin" of the "pure," to the "mountains." The lowercase spelling is then generally showing the significance of "mountains," which acts as an identifier of the "Gentile people near." Once we see the "mountains" identified as named "Pyrenees," the capitalization shows the importance of those specific "mountains" that are the boundary between France and Spain. This is in the proximity of Lourdes.

As a whole statement, line two is focusing on a place that is related to the "church" of the "virgin pure." It does this as a secondary theme building off the main theme stated in line one. In one way, it shines light on where the influence of the "virgin" will be found importantly (from capitalization) "Not" to be as "pure" as expected. As such, that place will be "far removed from" that "temple" of worship. The people there will be further removed from Judaism than are Christians, as they will be "far removed Gentiles," and not part of the "camp" dedicated to the "virgin" (Catholicism). This place and its peoples are then importantly identified (ampersand usage) as being in the "mountains" named "Pyrenees."

In the south of France (southwest, between the Pyrenees and the Atlantic Ocean) is the land that was once Gascony. That region was inhabited by "Basque-related people,"[30] who spoke a language (Gascon) that was similar to the Basque language. The Basque people are recognized as one of the oldest "ethnic groups" in Europe, pre-dating the influence of Indo-European language.[31]

---

29   From the Wiktionary [English] information about the word "ἔθνος," as the 5th of a list of 6 "Noun" uses. (http://en.wiktionary.org/wiki/%E1%BC%94%CE%B8%CE%BD%CE%BF%CF%82)
30   From the Wikipedia article on "Gascony." (http://en.wikipedia.org/wiki/Gascony)
31   From the Wikipedia article on "Basque people." (http://en.wikipedia.org/wiki/Basque_people)

Chapter 4: Quatrain II-17

The significance of this element, as far as a religious (Christian) theme is concerned, is the debate over Christian influence on the Basque people. Some say this influence did not begin until the 13th century (the time of the Cathars); and the pre-Christian Basque religion is believed to focus on a goddess named Mari (possibly from the influence of the "Three Marys"). Further, the apparition of the "Virgin" Mary at Lourdes was to Bernadette Soubirous, who spoke Gascon Occitan,[32] which is a language of the Pyrenees, both in Spain (Catalonia) and France.

While lines one and two can conveying multiple meanings, with all being viable, the two themes clearly address southern France and the border between France and Spain. As a prophecy of the future, that region of the world is projected as important, at a time well beyond the 16th century. Still, being able to see that region's future requires understanding its past.

That past predates the times of Nostradamus, but our past goes back to the times of Nostradamus and the first publication of *The Prophecies*, in which quatrain II-17 is found. Since the apparition of the Virgin Mary at Lourdes did occur in the future of Nostradamus, and because it is relative to a Christian theme, the focus here will be towards that history. However, there certainly is a future aspect of this quatrain that points to a time still to come, when a word translated as "camp" will have military usage. Such a main theme has yet to unfold.

By stating a main theme that is relative to an important "Camp" (due to capitalization of an article preceding a noun, "*Le camp*"), it can then symbolically link "Camp" to the use of "*d'Ethne*," allowing for a translation pointing to a "Sect" of "Gentiles." Those would be of "THE camp" (capitalized article) who are then "of, to, with, and from" peoples (moreso than buildings) reflecting the beliefs of a "temple," as a "church" in its purest sense. Such a Church would particularly be dedicated "to the virgin," making a statement about "purity" ("*vestale*"). This allows the main theme to be recognized as another way of stating "*katharos*." That becomes another connection to the Cathars of southern France; but that connection is relative to the religious history of the region.

When one sees "*temple*" in the main theme line linking to the word "*vierge*," one can come away with a taste of a Jewish theme. After all, the Jews had their "*temple*" in Jerusalem (the root of the word "Jew" comes

---

[32] From the Wikipedia article on "Bernadette Soubirous." (http://en.wikipedia.org/wiki/Bernadette_Soubirous)

from "Judah," the Kingdom containing Jerusalem) and Mary and Jesus were Jewish, descended from the house of David. The evolution of Judaism to Christianity is then the belief that Jesus was the promised Christ, and this is how one can see "*temple*" translate equally as "church." This makes the word become representative of a Christian fellowship, in a house of worship for Jewish and Gentile believers in the Messiah. From the religious theme in the main theme line, one can see "Gentile" (from "*Ethne*") as a religious term (New Testament Greek). "*Ethne*" is a proper name for any non-Jew, and thus it is representative of those who would become Christians, without having ever been Jewish.

The second line ends with a colon, which means the information found in line three will clarify the focus placed on the "Pyrenees." Because line four is where the supporting details are found for the secondary theme (line two), it is important to further understand that "mountain" range. This makes an examination of the whole quatrain important, knowing that everything will support and strengthen the main theme, and its element focusing on "the virgin pure."

Line three begins with another capitalized article, "*Le*," remembering that line one also began with that same word. When words are repeated in any quatrain of *The Prophecies*, each time the word is presented it will take on a different definition, as long as the word repeated has multiple meanings.[33]

For example, the article "*le*" can indicate an individual (as "a, an, or the"), while the repeated use of "*le*" can represent a masculine pronoun, such that the word is read as, "him" or "it." The capitalization indicates, in both of these cases, an introduction of importance.

Since line one stated, "*Le camp*," and because a "camp" is not a specific individual of male gender (regardless of the gender of the word "*camp*"), it better fits a general article translation, as "A camp," or "The camp." Because "*grand*" can act as an adjective, describing a person, that means line three's "*Le grand*" can be better translated to state, "Him great." In that scenario, "Him" is clarifying a male that is associated with the "Pyrenees," also related with "The camp … of the virgin pure."

By understanding this element of direction, as a systemic guide for re-

---

33   Some words only show one translation possibility, such as proper names, such as Italy, Heracles, and Jesus. Still, some lower-case words show as having only one translation word, such that the word "*mon*" only shows it to mean, "my."

peated terms, one can find how this important male ("Him") is one who will have "An army lodged" (translation possibility for "*Le camp*") in the "Pyrenees mountains." That place is where "Gentile people" live, known as the Basque people. They are "not far removed" from the place of the "virgin," while "Not" being Jews scattered to those mountains. The Basque are indigenous to that region, who came "near" to Christ, as Gentiles.

In my book, *The $25-million Answer*, I explain this specific quatrain from a different perspective. I explain how the Pyrenees Mountians is where Osama bin Laden will have found asylum, and where he will be found to have raised an army of Muslims. That "Camp" will be for the purpose of planning an attack on Spain and France. That book focuses on the linking of quatrains containing the one word, "mountains," rather than "virgin," but quatrain II-17 shows an interlinking of two stories (two of many) spun within *The Prophecies* of Nostradamus.

The purpose of attacks will be to bring about retribution on Christians. I see this as the primary focus of this quatrain, which is yet to be realized, meaning it is in the future. However, the underlying link is relative to the main theme's focus on "the virgin pure." This means the apparition of the "virgin," especially at Fatima (Portugal), but also at Lourdes (France) and elsewhere in Western Europe, can be seen as associated with a prophecy of a future plan of retribution.

The Virgin Mary has warned of such devastation coming, should the Church not act against Communism (the re-consecration of Russia), in her prior apparitions to children (themselves virgins). In that underlying scenario, line three can then be seen as presenting an important (capitalization) "Him" that is dedicated to the "virgin," and relative to the religious theme of Christianity (found in lines one and two). That "Him" would be the "Pope," meaning the "Pyrenees mountains" is a Europen location that is "not far removed" from Rome. It is "Not" the normal place for "Him great," but it is "near" to that standard of protection. As such, this could indicate the former palace of the pope, known as the *Palais de Pape*, which would be the one built in Avignon, France, for papal residency. This took place in the 14th century, after a sack of Rome.

Avignon is in southern France, about 130 miles north-northeast of the Pyrenees Mountains. This puts it in the vicinity of *Saintes-Maries-de-la-Mer*, as Avignon is roughly 25 miles north of that site. Still, a reference to a time when Roman Catholic popes reigned in France, which was prior to the birth of Nostradamus, is not prophetic. Therefore, seeing that history in the wording of quatrain II-17 acts as a projection of the past onto the future, comparing one to another.

The history of the Church that reveres the Virgin, being "not far from the Pyrenees," is then relative to a future event of a prophecy by the "virgin." This links her warnings to the prophecy repeated in some of the quatrains of Nostradamus.

That historic link to a series of 14th century French popes can then be seen as coinciding with the time of the final annihilation of the Cathar people in southwestern France. That crusade was begun in 1209, with the genocide of the Cathar people lasted until 1321. The Church of Rome had declared the Albigensian Crusade (1209-1229), so named because the French country surrounding the city Albi was where Cathars were in their largest numbers. That is "not far removed" from the "Pyrenees mountains" (roughly 125 miles due north).

By having been declared heretics, for not being Roman Catholics, the Cathars were "Gentile peoples" (non-Jews) condemned for being Gnostics. It did not matter that they were dedicated Christians. The genocide of the Cathars was the first "crusade" initiated by the Church of Rome on Christians, but it would later see the success of that "purification" as reason to persecute Jews, Muslims, and other non-Catholics. Those would fall under the heading of Inquisitions, rather than a direct declaration of war.

That intense program of "questioning" first took place in France, when Nostradamus' grandfather converted to Catholicism. They then became more radically introduced in Spain. The Spanish Inquisition required more force be involved, due to many Jews and Moors refusing to convert. For those who resisted, like the Cathar people, the military surrogates of Rome used the sword to murder many and drive the rest away.

This history then reflects another "ethnic cleansing" that Nostradamus was shown, which is still to come. As an exact reversal, a plan is in place now, calling for the genocidal persecution of Christians. This will be exercised by Gentiles (non-Jews), working as surrogates for those with axes to grind against the Roman Catholic Church, and "Him" who leads the "great" nations of the Christian West. This is coming in our future, targeting (among others) France and Spain.

The past history of genocide reflects how the Pope(s) ("Him") proceeded to use military force ("The camp") around the "temple of the virgin," a holy site for Cathar ("pure") people. Their ethnic roots were Roma, as from the Eastern Empire regions, believed to be Bulgaria or Romania. Just as nations are to be considered "great," so too are those who hold the power and influence of the Roman Catholic Church.

This means "Him great" is a statement of the power of the Pope, and the word "*conduict*," which follows, states how a "flow" ensued. The word "*conduict*" is the past participle of the verb "*conduire*," meaning, "conducted, led, guided, brought on; trained, governed, swayed," and/or "wholly disposed of." Its use in line three then relects the flow of events that took place, following the actions taken by those "great."

The word following "*conduict*" is then seen simply as a form of the verb "*estre*," (modern "*etre*,") meaning "to be", where "*est*" is read in the third-person present, as "is." While this does work as showing a present sense of being, relative to that "guided" and "conduits" to channel a flow of military personnel and equipment, that is not the only way the word can be read.

The word "*est*" is also a perfectly clean word in French, meaning "east." When read as this translation, "east" then sets up a direction for the "conduit." This can then reflect the context of Osama bin Laden leading an army that is lodged in the Pyrenees, with the caves and tunnels of those mountains filled with men coming from the "east." However, in a way of seeing the Roman Catholic Church using military force ("great" power) "not far removed from the Pyrenees," then their influence will have also come from the "east," from Rome.

Regardless of how one reads an "eastern" direction in line three, as a clarification of the secondary theme (line two ending with a colon) "east" is also relative to the "Pyrenees." This is the region known as Catalonia, where French Catalonia is on the eastern side of the "neck" of southern France, which extends along the Pyrenees, from the Mediterranean Sea to the Atlantic Ocean (Bay of Biscay). The French citizens in that southern part of France strongly feel more related to the Spanish region of the same name that is on the southern side of the Pyrenees Mountains.

In the Albigensian Crusade, France used force to take land along the Pyrenees, which was part of the Kingdom of Aragon, closely connected to Catalonia. The last Cathars were expelled from Carcassonne, which is today France, but was (in 1321) a vassal of the Kingdom of Aragon. The situation that still exists "is" relative to the "Gentile people" of the "Pyrenees," not only the Basque people of the west, but the Catalonians of the "east" as well.

In all places, autonomy is desired, with domination by a "great" nation unwanted. This harbors "hidden" resentment, welcoming all who offer "teeth" to fight for autonomy. Any such elements welcomed "there" (translation of "*la*" as the adverb, "*là*") can be potentially "harmful" (translation of "*male*" as the feminine form of "*mal*").

In line three, the word "*dens*" is commonly read as meaning "teeth." That spelling is not perfect French, despite being an acceptable abbreviation for "*dents*." Instead of seeing an abbreviation, "*dens*" should be seen as perfect Latin, bearing the same meaning as "*dent*" (in the singular – "a tooth"). Besides that most common translation of the Latin, "*dens*" also has abstract meanings, such as, "of anything biting, sharp, or destructive."[34]

The website Wiktionnaire also shows "*dens*" as Catalan (a language of the "Pyrenees"), meaning "dense." Further, that same website shows the word "*dens*" as being Occitan (another language of the "Pyrenees"), where it means, "inside, (or) within," synonymous with the French word "*dans*." Each of these possibilities has merit, due to the surrounding context and a religious (Christian) theme, where Latin is the language of the Roman Church and the language used by Nostradamus to denote a religious context.

In *The Prophecies* of Nostradamus, all uses of Latin have a Christian aspect, as Latin is the language of the Vatican. When the word "*Le*" is translated as "Him" and seen as a focus on a "Pope," then a flow of thought from that focus details a "great conduit" coming "east," from that important figure. This could be the knights who took up the challenge of the "Pope," to rid the "Pyrenees" of heretics and infidels. As such, the "great" would be "guided" by a philosophy or doctrine that "is hidden" and "secret," as Jesus Christ would not promote the genocidal extermination of Christians. The Cathar people were known to be "*bon hommes*," or "good men," with good Christian understood with that moniker.

---

34   From the Notre Dame "Latin Dictionary and Grammar Aid," from a search for "dens." (http://catholic.archives.nd.edu/cgi-bin/lookup.pl?stem=den&ending=)

The word "*caché*," which can translate as, "hidden, concealed, kept secret; in covert, in corners; lurking in some odd nook or another; or conveyed away,"[35] can also relate back to a "Pope," as "Him" who runs a "great" church. To "Him," a nun will have been "guided" (by the "virgin") to write a "great" letter, designed to keep the power of the Church "great." Sister Lucia, the nun, would then use Church "conduits" (or the proper channels) to flow her letters to the papal office. From Portugal, that travel would be to the "east," and once it arrived at the Vatican, the contents would become presently known to the presiding Bishop of Rome (a state of "is"), but then "kept secret," and "hidden away."

The contents of the letter from Sister Lucia certainly are "biting," in the sense that the vision allowed her by the "virgin" depicted a "destructive" end to the papacy, through warfare and persecution. Destruction would be "there" (seeing "*la*" as an adverb), surrounding the pope as he would be climbing one of the hills of Rome. Her letter told of a "Pope" meeting a "hurtful, harmful, unseemly, indecent, and pained" (all viable translations of the feminine version of "*mal*," as "*male*") end.

Because line two ends with a colon, line three is clarifying the secondary theme (the purpose of a colon is to clarify) and its focus on the "Pyrenees," while also directly supporting the main theme's focus on the Catholic Church. This then tells of the "destructive" nature of the popes, hiding and keeping secret the vision shown to young Lucia at Fatima. This destructive nature is reflected in the history of the Church, especially towards others, and that misuse of power will bring an equal measure of revenge back upon it. The clarification points to resentment held by Muslims, Jews, and the indigenous Gentile people in that mountainous region.

The North Wind

This view of line three is then separated from line four by the presence of a comma. That break then leads to an important (capitalization) focus of "North." This separate direction is in contrast to the use of "*est*," ("east") in line three. This spelling is English, and the only time that spelling is used by Nostradamus, anywhere in *The Prophecies*.

"*North*" does appear in Cotgrave's 1611 dictionary, with a reference stat-

---

35   From Randle Cotgrave's 1611 French-English Dictionary, published online by Greg Lindahl. (http://www.pbm.com/~lindahl/cotgrave/search/149l.html)

ing, "see *nord*." That means it may have been an ancient French spelling, perhaps related to historic eras when the English maintained partial continental rule of what is now France, in particular that regions along the Bay of Biscay, in southwest France, which borders the Pyrenees. The word "*nord*" then is shown translatable as "north, or north-wind."

There are no uses of "*nord*" anywhere in *The Prophecies*, but Nostradamus did write "*Septentrion*," "*septentrionaux*," "*Boreas*," "*Aquilon*," and "*Aquilonaire*(s)"in his letter to King Henry II. Those uses explained the the uses in the quatrains, where each was repeated.[36] All of those words bear the meaning of "north-wind." Thus, "*North*," in its uniqueness, needs to be understood as a synonymous match to those others.

When one understands the context of *The Prophecies*, where Nostradamus wrote in the mid-16th century, very little was known about the "New World" then. This means, as far as places that would be importantly identified (capitalization) by the "North-wind," Russia is the northernmost point of Europe. Scandinavia can be viewed as a separate land mass, and although it is actually northern Europe, it is commonly called the Nordic countries. Even with Scandinavia included, the northernmost, Asian part of Russia, Siberia, is closer to the Arctic Circle. The Taymyr Peninsula, in northernmost Siberia (77-degrees latitude), has an average high temperature above freezing only three months a year, with the historically warmest months averaging only 41 degrees (July) and 39 degrees (August) Farenheit.[37] Certainly, this place can be termed a land of the "North-wind."

In addition to that association of Russia to the "North Wind," Boreas was a god-like figure from Greek mythology who controlled the cold winds from the "North." The website All Voices posted an article that stated a top secret Russian military project was named "Northwind."[38] The article reports that a significant advancement to the Russian Strategic Nuclear forces has been developed, resulting in a new Bulava ICBM. These were expected to be "on line" in Russian submarines in mid-2011. Initial projections had this technology readied by the year 2040. However, the report said the project was "fast-tracked," cutting 29 years off that expectation.

---

36   A variation, "*septentrionale*," appears in one quatrain, replacing the use of "*septentrionaux*" in the letter to Henry.
37   From the Wikipedia article entitled, "Taymyr Peninsula." (http://en.wikipedia.org/wiki/Taymyr_Peninsula)
38   Article posted on the website All Voices, entitled, "Top Secret Russian Military Project Codename "Northwind" is a go!" (http://www.allvoices.com/contributed-news/6994319-top-secret-russian-military-project-codename-northwind-is-a-go)

Russia also has a nuclear-powered ballistic missile submarine, in what they term the Borei class, first launched in 2008. That name (Borei) is said to be derived from the word Boreas, the Greek god known as the "North wind."[39] In the only quatrain where Nostradamus wrote the name "*Boreas*" (II-99), he began line four with that word and then followed it with the word "*classe*." By Russia giving its own military projects the name "Northwind," and Nostradamus using a defining word that can be read as the name of a "fleet" (the word "*classe*" is rooted in the Latin word "*classis*," meaning "fleet," when referring to armed forces) this solidifies how a reference by Nostradamus to "North" should be seen as a focus on Russia and their military-industrial complex.

When "North" is associated with Russia, and when one is looking at quatrain II-17 from a religions perspective, where "virgin" hints at a divine revelation, there is a perfect fit. One can see how "Russia" (in particular Communist militarism) was named in the warning given to "Him," the "Pope," by Sister Lucia, from the Virgin Mary. When the second word of line four is seen as the past participle, plural number, of the verb "*jeter*" (Old French: "*iecter*" and "*getter*"), where the spelling "*getes*" requires the addition of an accent mark (as "*geté-s*), we see the action of "cast ones."

Certainly, this fits the scenario of ICBMs being "hurled," "darted," or "violently sent forth," but this is the same position the Vatican found itself "cast" or "pushed" into, by being told it needed to confront Russia (to re-consecrate it), after Russia had "cast out" all influence of religion. It is this atheistic position that was the danger, which would require the "virgin" to warn children in Fatima, Portugal. Sister Lucia would then be "guided" (translation possibility for "*conduict*") to tell the Vatican her "secret" (translation possibility of "*caché*"). This revelation would be because, without Russia's instilled moral fiber being renewed, that land of the "North" would be "led" (translation possibility for "*conduict*") to plot "concealed" (translation possibility of "*caché*") weapons transactions, selling missiles that were foreseen to be "launched" (variation of the meaning for "*getés*") by the "east" (translation possibility for "*est*") against the West.

The action that will "cast out" missiles and military attacks can then be expected to be focused on the "Northern" Hemisphere, where other "great" nations of the "North" reside. This would include the English,

---

39   From the Wikipedia article entitled, "Borei class submarine." (http://en.wikipedia.org/wiki/Borei_class_submarine)

and the British Islands, as well as Canada and America, since both are in "North" America," with Alaska an American purchase from the Russians.

That breadth of conflict is then explained by the word "*fleuves*," which is French for "flows of water, rivers, and streams." In Old French, "*fleuve*" was synonymous with "flood." That means line four explains a tremendous "flood" of "darts" (translation possibility for "*getés*") being "projected" (variation on "*getés*") upon the "North." However, a religious link can be made to the word "*fleuves*."

When one does an general Internet search for the word "*fleuves*," with the word "mythology" attached, one sees links to French sites explaining "*fleuves des Enfers*," or simply "*Enfers grec*." Those titles translate as, "rivers of Hell," or the "Greek underworld," which included the "five rivers of Hades": Styx – river of Hate; Acheron – river of sorrow; Phlegethon – river of fire; Lethe – river of forgetfulness; and Cocytus – river of lamentations. By seeing "*getés fleuves*" as the fire and brimstone warning of Biblical prophecy, the words of Nostradamus (in quatrain II-17) can be seen to state, "cast into the depths of Hell and its rivers of fire."

This is precisely what Sister Lucia wrote in her first letter ("secret"), which was a "vision of Hell." The first line of that letter stated: "Our Lady showed us a great sea of fire which seemed to be under the earth." She further explained this scene as:

> "Plunged in this fire were demons and souls in human form, like transparent burning embers, all blackened or burnished bronze, floating about in the conflagration, now raised into the air by the flames that issued from within themselves together with great clouds of smoke, now falling back on every side like sparks in a huge fire, without weight or equilibrium, and amid shrieks and groans of pain and despair, which horrified us and made us tremble with fear."

This vision of a "great sea of fire" would later be revealed to be associated with Russia having fallen from the fold. It would be up to the Good Shepherd ("Him," as "Pope") to bring Russia back, safely consecrated again. Otherwise, this vision of Hell would "flow" consciously, in reality, rather than as a metaphorical glimpse.

As just a brief look, Sister Lucia wrote, "This vision lasted but an instant,"

Chapter 4: Quatrain II-17

but it seemed longer. If not for the prior comfort of the "Virgin" Mother telling them heaven was to be their reward, Lucia said, "I think we would have died of fear and terror." Many people would feel the same, if confronted with ICBM missiles named "Northwind" being "cast" down upon them, creating "rivers" of fire.

At this point in line four, Nostradamus placed an ampersand, which separates the first portion of the line from the second. The ampersand introduces the second segment of words as important. The first word, following the ampersand, is the most important to understand; and that word is "*vignes.*"

The word "*vignes*" has the meaning of "vines" (plural number). This word has Christian connotations, because Jesus declared himself "the true vine," while alluding to his followers as the "branches" (John 15:1-6). Jesus told his followers that those who remain living "vines" (as branches) would be measured as to whether or not they "bear fruit." Those who remain productive will be left with the true vine, as "No branch can bear fruit by itself; it must remain in the vine." (John 15:4b). However, those branches that no longer bear fruit "are like a branch that is thrown away and withers; such branches are picked up, thrown into the fire and burned."

This reading links back, to the word "*fleuves,*" before the ampersand, which were found possibly to read as the "rivers" of fire in Hades. The importance is then seen relative to Russia as the "North," which had become a withered branch due to Communism and the rejection of Christianity. Thus, the warning sent by the "virgin," through a child, was to make the "vines" so they can "be even more fruitful." Otherwise, that branch must be pruned.

On a symbolic level, the use of "vines" represents (according to a dream interpretation website), "Using external resources to one's advantage. Insidious, creeping, insinuating one's way into everything. Taking over. Covering up or distorting."[40] This is the danger that the Church faces as the spread of Socialism slowly creeps into the lives of everyone, when no one takes on the symbolic responsibility to be the "gardener."

By 1943, when the "secrets" of the "virgin" were first revealed to "Him" (the "Pope"), the fear of World War II and Bonito Mussolini's fascist con-

---

40 Definition found on the website Dream Visions, under the heading, "vine dream symbol," from a search for the term "vine." (http://www.mydreamvisions.com/dreamdictionary/symbol/1647/)

trol of Italy certainly caused the Church to hesitate from responding to Sister Lucia's letters. In 1943, the Nazi hatred of Communism had led Adolph Hitler to order an invasion of Russia, which had advanced to a brutal siege of Stalingrad. Because hopes were for the defeat of the Soviet Union, albeit through German orders (rather than Rome's), the Church's fight seemed to be ongoing. This left Pop Pius XII with enough reason to do little else towards that end.

Between 1944 and 1945, the war had turned. The Germans were in a defensive retreat, with the Soviets emboldened by their ability to survive. With Russia becoming more powerful, the Church cowered to that power. They had likewise cowered to Hitler's strength, while knowing he was ordering the genocide of European Jews (and other "undesirable" minorities). The positive actions of Pope Pius XII were miniscule and mostly silent, only exposed after blame for their failures to speak out against the evils of war were made loudly public.

The Church had failed to respond to the warnings of the Virgin Mary, as exposed to a "virgin" peasant girl, in 1917. The "Pope" chose to hide the fact that letters had warned "Him" to act, causing the Vatican to deny and evade questioning along those lines. In that "insidious" way the Vatican began "covering up" its waywardness, having "hidden" the severity of the "secret" warnings. It would later do greater "secret" deeds that would need to be "concealed," such as murdering "Him" who would finally take the warning from the letters to heart (Pope John Paul I). Thus, the "vines" are the tendrils of Satan, slowly entrapping those who tread among dead "vines," not trying to prune them and clear the path.

Line four then ends with the word "*mastinées*," which is the past participle plural number form of the verb "*mastiner*." That is a word that indicates dog breeding and in particular the mating of a "bitch with a mastiff or great cur."[41] This is a lineage distinction for dogs, which represents quite large and strong dogs, without true pedigree. The "mastiffs" bred were mongrels. As such, the word "mastiff" is believed (by some) to be derived from the Old French word, "*mestif*," which translated as "mongrel."[42] The plural number then indicates a multiple of "dogs," but when the "-s" is separated from the root word, it acts to indicate the

---

41   From Randle Cotgrave's 1611 French-English Dictionary, published online by Greg Lindahl. (http://www.pbm.com/~lindahl/cotgrave/search/615l.html)
42   From the etymology of the word "mastiff," stated on the Free Dictionary by Farlex, referencing The American Heritage Dictionary of the English Language (2000) as the source. (http://www.thefreedictionary.com/mastiff)

"ones" breeding bitches with large curs. A "cur" is then defined as, "A dog considered to be inferior or undesirable; a mongrel."⁴³ As "mongrel dog breeding ones," the last word of this quatrain symbolically indicates those who would act to create dangerous, fighting canines.

When one sees the religious theme of quatrain II-17, and understands Nostradamus to have quoted (in Latin) Matthew 7:6 in his preface ("Give not that which is holy unto dogs"), one can then better see the religious aspect of "vines" being linked to "large, strong dogs." Those are then representative of the elements in the Church who act like dogs, guarding over branches that are no longer bearing fruit. The "vines" are only giving the impression of still be connected to the true vine, when that which was holy will have been given over to unholy "dog handlers," making *"mastinées"* represent the swine given the pearls of Christianity.

A dog's "destructive" (from line three's *"male"*) power comes from its "teeth" and strong "bite" (both from line three's *"dens"*). This relates to those who should have been "pure" (from line one's *"vestale"*) for the "virgin" (from line one's *"vierge"*). As a Church given over to "mastiffs," it will "Not" (from line one's *"Non"* linking to line one's *"vestale"*) be as intended (a living, producing "vine"). Instead, it will be "far removed from" that original plan (from the meaning of line two's *"esloigné"*). It will have been turned over "to Gentile people," where "Gentile" is defined as, "a pagan or heathen,"⁴⁴ but who will also be so-called Christians, those are in reality only giving lip-service to religion.

This is the state prophesied by Sister Lucia, through her "secret" revealed to the "Pope." The is the state prophesied by Nostradamus, where he confirms that prophecy well in advance of it occurring, while repeating the vision shown to three children at Fatima, Portugal in a series of quatrains. The words of Nostradamus mirror are those of the *Holy Bible*, in ways that cannot be explained as being from conscious attempts at mimicking biblical prophecy, which itself is not clearly known, not well enough to model. Thus, quatrain II-17 can be seen as showing the importance of the word "virgin" as that of the "unique virgin," the mother of our "true Savior, Jesus Christ." This means the rest of the "virgin" series should likewise follow this line of thought.

---

43 From the Free Dictionary by Farlex, referencing The American Heritage Dictionary of the English Language (2000) as the source. (http://www.thefreedictionary.com/cur)
44 The "archaic" definition for "gentile," found in The Free Dictionary by Farlex, referencing The American Heritage Dictionary of the English Language (2000) as the source. (http://www.thefreedictionary.com/gentile)

Chapter 5
The Second "*Vierge*" Quatrain

Quatrain III-44

The second quatrain stating the word "*vierge*," in order of presentation in *The Prophecies*, is found as the 44th listed in Centurie III. One finds "virgin" written in line three of that quatrain. Because line three is where the supporting details are found for the main theme statement (line one), the whole quatrain needs to be examined. This avoids "cherry picking," or taking words out of context.

That quatrain is presented below, first in the Old French of Nostradamus, then followed by my English translation.

>*Quand l'animal à l'homme domestique,*
>
>*Apres grans peines & saults viendra parler,*
>
>*Le foudre à vierge sera si malefique,*
>
>*De terre prinse & suspendue en l'air.*

>When an animal with the man domestic,
>
>After great ones forfeitures & leaps will come to tell,
>
>Him thunderbolt with virgin will be as evil doing,
>
>From country taken, & removed any the breath.

Chapter 5: Quatrain III-44

To look at line three first, one finds the only capitalized word in this line is "*Le*," which appears to be an article, attaching to the following noun, "*foudre*." The word "*foudre*" (more as "*fouldre*," in Old French) means "thunderbolt," or more commonly, "lightning." As an article, "*Le*" takes on a role of introducing line three to a most important "one" that follows, one which is of such singular importance it requires a capitalized article (A, An, or The). In this case, it introduces one to "THE lightning," or "A" significant "thunder bolt," "one" that can be easily identified, and not confused with others.

This capitalized article, followed by the distinction of "The thunderbolt," begins this supporting statement (line three directly supports line one and its main theme), which then leads to the preposition-noun combination, "*à vierge*." The preposition "*à*" can translate as "at, in, to, with, or from," making the combination yield the various possibilities of direction, all associated with the word "virgin." This results is "The lightning" that is either "in virgin," "to virgin," "with virgin," "at virgin," or "from virgin."

Without knowing anything else about quatrain III-44, by simply seeing line three in a vacuum, without any contextual direction to rely on, thoughts come to me of Saint Teresa of Avila (Spain). She was a Carmelite nun (a "*vierge*"), the same order that built a convent at Lourdes, France, because the order is believed (by the Roman Catholic Church) to be under the protection of the Blessed Virgin Mary.[1] Saint Teresa is known to have told of an encounter with an angel (a Seraph), who pierced her heart with a fiery pointed golden spear. A spear or lance can be seen as something designed to strike suddenly (when thrown or jabbed), becoming a symbolic "thunderbolt." The imagery of Saint Teresa is that of "The lightning in nun."

The famous Italian sculptor, Bernini, depicted this encounter in his work entitled "The Ecstasy of Saint Teresa." That piece is displayed in *Santa Maria della Vittoria*, in Rome, a basilica whose name means, "Saint Mary of Victory," or, more commonly, "Our Lady of Victory." According to Teresa (a "virgin"), the experience was quite painful, but she "could not wish to be rid of it."[2] As such, line three in this quatrain continues on to state, "*sera si malefique*," which translates as, "will be so hurtful." This means line three could be alluding to this event, which was contempo-

---

[1] From the Wikipedia article entitled "Carmelites." (http://en.Wikipedia.org/wiki/Carmelites)
[2] From the Wikipedia article entitled "Teresa of Avila." (http://en.Wikipedia.org/wiki/Teresa_of_%C3%81vila)

rary to Nostradamus' life (1556), taking place soon after *The Prophecies* was first published (1555).

Still, the focus of *The Prophecies* is primarily on a time that is still future to us. This means that any reading appearing to depict the rapture of Saint Teresa is comparative. This needs to be related to the overall context of this quatrain's main theme, while also fitting the overall themes of the whole work Nostradamus produced. Before one goes to line one, where the main theme is stated, to see how "lightning" associates "with" the word "virgin" it is important to look at some of the verbiage just reviewed in quatrain II-17, which was the first quatrain of the "virgin" series presented.

In that quatrain we found the word "*male*" in line three, which was read as the root for the word "*malefique*," the word now found used here, in quatrain III-44. Both words are in the third line, and line three in quatrain II-17 stated, "Him great conduit east hidden teeth there hurtful" ("*Le grand conduict est caché dens la male*"). From reviewing that line, one also sees how the capitalized word "*Le*" begins that line, just as "*Le*" begins line three, in quatrain III-44. This allows one to see how "*Le foudre*" can then also state "Him," with "thunderbolt" then being a separate element of someone.

Without trying to go further with an interpretation of line three now, seeing a word linking to the one other quatrain discussed so far is enough at this point. It is best to return to line one and work down, in order to understand the meaning of line three best, from a contextual standpoint. As such, the main theme of quatrain III-44 must be examined, in order to see how "lightning" and "virgin" support that theme.

The Animal in Man

The main theme statement says, "*Quand l'animal à l'homme domestique*." The words, "*l'animal à l'homme*" can state, "the animal in the man." This can easily be telling of the reality, that "man" is just one species of "animal," but it also supports a metaphoric comparison of "man" to "swine" and "dogs."

In the last quatrain (II-17), one was exposed to the aspect of "vines" that were fruitless, due to "*mastinées*," or "animals" (dogs). We learned that mastiffs are large dogs, bred to protect through the force of strong

Chapter 5: Quatrain III-44

"bites." Thus, the main theme here in quatrain III-44 is telling of an important (capitalization) time, "When" one will be able to see "the animal" will be present "in the man."

Since quatrain II-17 told of "Him," as a "Pope," linked to the "virgin pure," quatrain III-44 can be seen as alluding to "When" an important (capitalization) male ("*Le*" as the pronoun "Him") will be a "great conduit." This fits the pope's role as the foremost Apostle to Christ and God. "When" this "Pope" will be in possession of "concealed" (from "*caché*") "teeth" (from "*dens*"), which will be "harmful" (from "*male*") for the Church, a time of danger is being identified. This is confirming a future state, "When the [hidden] animal [will be one] with the man" believed to be "great."

The last word in line one is "*domestique*," which translates to mean, "domestic, of a household; also tame, familiar, and privy."[3] When one is seeing a main theme be developed that speaks of "animal" and "man," one needs to realize how "*domestique*" is a word used to describe an "animal" that "man" has tamed, so it is no longer wild or savage. This includes "household" pets, like smaller breeds of "dogs" and cats. Still, the word "domestic" also has implications relative to trained human beings, who are hired to maintain a "household."

Homes in which a "domestic" will be found working are most often those of the upper financial classes. To associate that class with those ranking highest in a particular social order, "domestic" can imply the ordinary citizens who recognize and support those ranking higher than themselves. Rather than living "in the wild," or in a normal "household" relative to their class of people, many professional "domestics" will have a small room provided within a mansion of their wealthy employer. In fact, the English word "domestic" is rooted in the Latin word "*domus*," meaning "house." In French, the word for "house" is "*mansion*," coming from an original meaning, "abode, dwelling," and "manner." The English word "mansion" evolved into meaning, a "large house or building."[4]

The main theme of quatrain III-44 is stating the importance (capitalization) of a time, "When" a significant occurrence will follow. "At that time" (alternate translation possibility for "*Quand*") there will be "an animal," meaning "one animal" who will be "in" place (translation possibility for

---

3   From Randal Cotgrave's 1611 French-English Dictionary, published online by Greg Lindahl. (http://www.pbm.com/~lindahl/cotgrave/search/32or.html)
4   From the website Wiktionary, and a search for the word "mansion." (http://en.wiktionary.org/wiki/mansion)

the preposition "*à*"). That place is "in a man," "in one man," who is "the man" of a "household." That "one man" is known to be a servant to all "mankind," but "At that time" he will be just a hired hand, as "an animal" posing as "the man."

It is important to understand the full scope that the word "*homme*" bears. In the Old French of Randal Cotgrave the word also meant "vassal," as well as a "tenant, liegeman, and subject."[5] Still, the word is synonymous with being "human" and "humane." It was used to denote a military soldier; a male of adult age; and a level of wisdom accrued from having lived. To a wife, the word "*homme*" it is synonymous with "husband;" and alone the word is a statement about a male's "virility" and "courage." Figuratively, the word "*homme*" means being prone to err, and full of weakness, thus always in need of help. When all of these meanings are assessed, one can see how the main theme of quatrain III-44 is focusing on a "domesticated" (translation when an accent mark is placed over the last letter, "*domestiqué*") "man," turning him into a "subject" without courage.

This becomes significant of an important time, "When" there will be a taming of one who is expected to run a "household" with "courage." In religious terms, this can be seen as turning a ram (a natural leader of a flock) into just another sheep; and it can be seen as dressing up a "dog" ("an animal") to look like "the man" (the leader) of a holy "household."

To understand more about the meaning of "the animal in the man domestic," one must continue into the quatrain. Since line one ends with a comma, one knows there is a separation between the main theme statement and the secondary theme, found in line two. This is important to recognize because the main theme tells of a time "When" something will be in effect, and line two importantly (capitalization) begins by stating, "After." Thus, the main theme is making a statement about a beginning time, with the secondary theme then being relative to that beginning, but later.

Line two is divided into two parts, due to the placement of a mid-line ampersand. By recognizing that break point, the secondary theme's first focus is on "*Apres grans peines*," which can translate as "After great ones forfeitures." This translation is based on seeing "*grans*" read as

---

[5] From Randal Cotgrave's 1611 French-English Dictionary, published online by Greg Lindahl. (http://www.pbm.com/~lindahl/cotgrave/search/528r.html)

the plural of "*gran,*" an abbreviated form of "*grand.*"⁶ The French word "*grand*" means "great; big, large; huge, mighty; substantial; also high, lofty, stately."⁷ As is always the case in *The Prophecies*, the use of "great" should be seen as a noun, such that "great ones" is the translation when "*grand*" is used in the plural number.

Because the first word of line two, "*Apres,*" is directly linked to the last word in the main theme statement, "household," the secondary theme is then referencing that "house" as being one importantly (capitalization) "After," "Following," or "Next" in line to "great ones." However, those who will be called "great ones" in that "household" will be "Following" the one of the main theme, "the animal-man."

The word "*peines*" bears the meaning, "a pain, penalty, forfeiture, punishment; also pains, labor, toil, swink [drudgery], travail; endeavor; also pain, trouble, restlessness, affliction, anguish, cark [burdened with worry], and vexation of thought." In these applications of meaning, one has to see that "great ones," while still relative to the "household" or "domestic," is more connected to an "After" time, when "pain" and "punishment" is at hand. In this scenario, "*grans*" can better translate as those of "large" numbers, who are so "great" their leader is a "great one." In terms of the Pope, all Christendom (mainly the Western world) must be considered, more than simply the place named Vatican City.

Despite instances where the "Following great ones" may experience some "pains, travails, and anguished thoughts," it will be best to read the separate secondary theme as "pains, forfeitures, penalties, afflictions, and troubles" set upon the ones "Following" the "great ones." When looking for a religious-Christian lean to the words, this first half of the secondary theme is prophesying all of the ordeals that have befallen the Roman Catholic Church. "After" the "virgin" had Sister Lucia send letters to "Popes," who then became "dogs" in "men's" clothing, quite "tamed" and afraid to act as instructed. Therefore, the "punishment" of having not acted on that warning will be the focus.

From that first half statement made in the secondary theme, the ampersand announces that what is to follow is important. The second half of

---

6 The word "*gran*" is good Catalan and Spanish for "great," and that could indicate the southern region of France, along the Pyrenees into Spain, if that use is found to be relative to the focus of other elements in this quatrain. However, "*grans*" is found written nine times in the quatrains and should be seen as a common abbreviation of "*grands.*"

7 From Randal Cotgrave's 1611 French-English Dictionary, published online by Greg Lindahl. (http://www.pbm.com/~lindahl/cotgrave/search/500r.html)

line two then states, "*saults viendra parler*," which can translate to say, "leaps will come to tell." This must be seen as important (ampersand introduction) "leaps" that "will tell" how the "pains" suffered by the "great ones," at the hands of "those great," will be a "telling" sign. This is a revelation of that hidden, which relates to the theme that "the animal in the man" has taken over the "household." This requires better understanding the meaning of "leaps."

In French, the word "*sault*" is used most frequently in the names of "waterfalls," or the "rapids" leading to them. It is a word that is derived from the Latin word "*saltus*," meaning, "a leap," with that rooted in the verb "*salīre*," meaning, "to leap/jump."[8] Randal Cotgrave listed the word "*sault*," and in addition to showing it to mean "a leap, etc.," he referenced the word "*saut*." Under that spelling, he wrote the meaning to be, "a leap, bound, sault [as summersault], skip, jump; (at bowling) a rub; also an ill-polished part of a precious stone, which in a curious eye disgraces all the rest."[9] In the French Wikipedia article entitled "*Saut*," the word is explained to be relative to "animal" characteristics, especially in horses trained to "leap" rails [equestrian events] and dogs that are trained in agility exercises performed at dog show competitions.

When all of those possibilities are realized, the ampersand introduces an important time when the "pains" brought upon the "great ones" will come fast, like "rapids," signaling a terrible fall approaching. The symbolic reference to water can then be seen as an emotional "rush" that accompanies (use of an ampersand as a joiner between two opposites or two similarities) "Troublesome thoughts ["*peines*"] AND ["&"] emotional upheavals ["*saults*"]." The use of "saults" also signals quick changes that are subsequent to the "endeavors" causing the "worries."

When these are seen as levels of "agility" displayed by "the animal" trained to avoid obstacles, it importantly shows how that which is holy, having been given unto "dogs," will have a trained abilitiy to "skip" a direct confrontation about scandals and improprieties. When the "household" is seen as a shining example of worth, such as a gem, in particular a diamond, one is seeing the "pains" as an important reflection on the "flaws" and "imperfections" that greatly diminish that value once held.

From "*saults*," the second half of line two leads to the future tense form

---

8   From the Wikipedia page entitled "Sault." (http://en.wikipedia.org/wiki/Sault)
9   From Randal Cotgrave's 1611 French-English Dictionary, published online by Greg Lindahl. (http://www.pbm.com/~lindahl/cotgrave/search/852r.html)

of the verb "*venir*" (as "*viendra*"). That word states what "will come; will arrive, approach, draw near unto; will proceed from, be issued from, be derived from; will spring, prove, grow; and also will happen, chance, or fall out."[10] This is stating what "will grow" from the "After pains," which will be the result of "When the animal" will be "the man" of the "household" of the "great ones."

Adding to what "will come," the verb "*parler*" makes a statement that the "leaps" of faith taken in denial of the "worries" and "troubles," due to the "rubs" and "skips" of an "agile" dog, will be fodder for gossip and rumor. That painful series of dog tricks "will come to tell" the truth about the leader of "a great" group of people. The word "*parler*" is defined (as a noun) as, "speech, language, talk, utterance, words," and (as a verb) as, "to speak, talk, declare, say, tell, utter the mind; to commune, parlay, reason, confer, discourse, converse." As such, actions (from the verb "*viendra*") "will grow to reason," which will arise, not so much as admitted fact, but as theory, conjecture, and deduction, based on facts unexplained.

This means the primary and secondary themes of quatrain III-44 are telling of a state of decline in a "house," whose leader ("the man") will then lead "many" to a state of "worry." Those "troubles" "coming" "rapidly" will be the "talk" going around. Thus, a declined state brought about by poor leadership will lead to a more advanced state of decline.

While these themes can apply across the board to any failed system, it certainly fits the model the Roman Catholic Church has been known for since the 1960s. While very few of the scandals and innuendos have been honestly addressed by the Vatican, all sorts of accusations have abounded. Because nothing of value has been done to right that ship (the holy bark), the Church has experienced a seemingly endless stream of exposé press, with less Catholics practicing their religion faithfully. Therefore, these themes reflect a Church that has led an erosion of Christian values.

Coming to that conclusion of themes, the third line of quatrain III-44 follows the comma at the end of line two. This means there is another point of separation, such that the supporting details to the main theme (always found in line three) are subsequent details to the timing of the secondary theme (due to line three immediately following line two). This is

---

10   From Randal Cotgrave's 1611 French-English Dictionary, published online by Greg Lindahl. (http://www.pbm.com/~lindahl/cotgrave/search/944r.html and continued onto http://www.pbm.com/~lindahl/cotgrave/search/945l.html)

where Nostradamus wrote, "*Le foudre à vierge sera si malefique,*" where the word "*vierge*" is found. Again, line three can translate to state, "Him thunderbolt with virgin will be so evil doing."

When it is understood how the systems of Nostradamus view line three as having a direct relationship with the main theme statement, where the rhyme scheme links line one to line three, it becomes easier to see how the capitalized first word of line three, "*Le,*" should be translated as "Him," rather than "The." This is because "the man" ("*l'homme*") establishes the presence of a masculine human being in the main theme, who can then be expected to be referenced in the supporting details of line three. Thus, one knows that line three is importantly (capitalization) identifying a male who is "the head" of a "household." With that connection made, one can then see how "Him" is the one about whom "great ones will come to talk."

The Lightning of Evil Doing

According to the Randal Cotgrave 1611 dictionary, the spelling "*foudre*" finds one referred to look up the Old French spelling, "*fouldre*." That is simply shown to mean, "thunderbolt." Because "*foudre*" is how the French today spell the word meaning "lightning," this spelling in quatrain III-44 is an indication that some Old French words were being changed, in particular many of those containing a "silent *l*" in the spelling. In fact, there is evidence that Nostradamus wrote both "*foudre*" and "*fouldre*" in the quatrains (as well as "*foudres*"),[11] with the meaning always being the same. This is where the various uses of "lightning" come into play, especially since "lightning" connects "Him" to the word "virgin."

On the website Wiktionnaire, in the French language version of Wiktionary, the word "*foudre*" is shown to mean the meteorological occurrence of "lightning," while also shown to have the hyperbolic meaning of "quick, rapid, and destructive." The site also lists a religious meaning, most often presented in the plural number, being a religious reprobation or condemnation aspect associated with "*foudre.*" Also when written in the plural number, "*foudres*" is associated with anger, where the "strikes out" are uncontrolled bolts of rage. Finally, the word "lightning" is explained as an expression of military capabilities, again where one

---

11   Based on the information posted by the website Alphabetical Nostradamus Index, created by J. Flanagan, on the page entitled "F-H Nostradamus Index." (http://alumnus.caltech.edu/~jamesf/nindex/fh_index.html)

strikes out quickly against an enemy, usually with weapons of artillery. The expressions, "*fougres de l'excommunication*" and "*fougres de l'église*" are read as "the reprobation of excommunication" and "condemnation of the church," with both idioms being used in religious context.[12]

When "*foudre*" is seen to have religious uses, and when the capitalization of "*Le*" is an indication of an important "Him," the link to "*à vierge*" must be viewed within that context. When read separately, "*foudre*" is a statement of "quickness," which can be seen as a "flash" of insight or thought that comes so suddenly it is beyond deep thought. It can then be seen as a knee-jerk reaction, a sudden act of anger, or a divine inspiration from the Holy Spirit. All of these can be linked to "Him," which would reflect "the rapids" [or "falls"] that "will have come up," leading many "to talk" and "to converse."

When read in that light, the lightning-like reactions of a "Pope" can be seen. This quickness will then be directions, "to, from, with, at," and/or "in" (all translations of the preposition "*à*"), based on the "thunderbolt" linked to "Him." This, of course works both way, such as the principle of "what goes up must come down," meaning "lightning" actions "from Him" become "lightning" actions "to Him."

When the direction reaches the "virgin," who in Roman Catholic terms is the Blessed "Virgin," Mother of Christ, the one woman deified by the Church of Rome, it is quite possible to see a "Pope" making a "quick" decision about following through on a letter sent by Sister Lucia. The talk that is generated quickly is that responding to the instructions found in the letters coming "from" the "virgin." The topic of discussion quickly turns towards Sister Lucia and he letters requiring the Church act to stop Communism.

That becomes the supporting details for a main theme, which places focus on a religious main theme. The support coming from the details of line three make the main theme state, "When an animal" [a dog] is given something holy [such as a letter stating the will of Saint Mary, representing the Holy Spirit], only to set it aside for "the man" who will come next upon the "house," this had been the Vatican's known response to that warning. Line three's supporting details adds that "After great ones pain" (the Iron Curtain smothering the Eastern Church), "AND falls [that] will come to tell" (the indoctrination of three generations to the anti-reli-

---

12   From the website <u>Wiktionnaire</u>, under a search for the term "*foudre*." (http://fr.wiktionary.org/wiki/foudre)

gious politics of Communism), to then have "Him" respond "quickly to [a warning] from [a] nun," this act "will be so hurtful."

The one "Pope" who did act with "lightning" speed, immediately responding "to" the plea "from" the "virgin," was Pope John Paul I. As a Cardinal, he was one who heard the "talk" and knew the "discourse" about the improprieties of the Vatican Bank. He knew the "pains" and "troubles" that Catholics were facing in the modern era, which were beginning to drive them away from the Church. Thus, he took "prompt" actions to have the bank audited, and was preparing to make "swift" changes that would right the ship.

Pope John Paul I, within one month, strongly stated what "will be" ("*sera*") under his reign; and despite his not giving credit for his actions to the "virgin," he responded to what the "virgin" said "will be," if no action is taken. His first step was to clean his own "house," knowing that before he could go out accusing others of heresy, with "condemnation," the Vatican must be in order first.

Before Pope John Paul I's time was up (his rule lasted but 33 days), he found his Church was "so" filled with "evil doing" (translation of "*malifique*"). He realized the Church's bank had been infiltrated "so" strongly, by those "having a malignant influence" (definition of the English, "malefic") on the Church, swift changes must be made. He sent "lightning bolts" out in "anger," just as Jesus did on the steps of the Temple of Jerusalem, when his Father's "house" of prayer had become a den of thieves.

This interpretation of line three supports line one's statement about "the man" of the "household." However, it also acts as supporting details to a main theme that tells of "the animal in the man," who is "domesticated."

In this second scenario, "Him" is "the animal" [the "dog"] who will act with "lightning" speed to remove the one who has come to put things right. In that case, the "lightning" must be seen as the "sudden strike" that killed Pope John Paul I. That then makes "Him" the beneficiary of that "thunderbolt," who would be Pope John Paul II. It would be that "man" who would have "lightning" twice come to "Him," where others would attempt to take his life.

The first attempt was on the anniversary of the apparition in Fatima (May 13, 1981), with the second "strike" occurring at the sight of the apparition (Fatima, Portugal) a year later (May 12, 1982). The second attempt was on the eve of a recognition scheduled to commemorate the anniversary of the apparition of the "virgin."[13] He would later issue a statement that the letters "from" the spirit of the "virgin" were no longer a threat to the Church or the world. He made that statement after the "fall" of the Soviet Union. This "man" is representative of "the animal" in the "household," and there will still be "leaps" to "come" from what Pope John Paul II would "tell," such that the prophecy of Saint Malachy still projects the end of the papacy, just not by listing all popes leading up to that end.

Rome and the Dilemma of Israel

This information cannot be limited to explaining only those past "troubles" facing the "great ones" of Catholicism. When the aspect of "thunderbolt" is seen to have military applications, this quatrain can "leap" forward into our future. In that case, this quatrain fits in with several that tell of attacks on Rome, targeting the Vatican and the pope, at the onset of a future war (commonly called Armageddon). This, again, relates to the vision shown to Sister Lucia and her cousins in 1917, where they were filled with fear at the sight of Rome being on fire from attacks.

Obviously, this devastation fits the use of "*foudre*" as representing artillery bombardments, in modern applications of "lightning" quick missiles. Still, that future must be seen as being connected to important (capitalization) times, "When" that which was holy will have been handed over to dogs. It will also be "After" the "great ones" will have administered "penalties" upon others; "AND" it will be at that time when "jumps" will have led into places where foreign nations will have long known (past history) how "the great will come," causing many "to speak."

Line three ends with a comma, meaning line four is another series of words representing a subsequent set of information. Due to the systems of Nostradamus, line four is where one always finds the supporting details for line two (the secondary theme). The symmetrical aspect of this quatrain shows the two-part secondary theme statement (line two divided by an ampersand) being mirrored by a two-part line four. This makes two halves of line four's supporting details respectively reflect each half of the secondary theme. As such, "*De terre prinse*" adds details to "*Apres

---

[13] The first assassination attempt was on May 13, 1981, when a Turkish gunman in Saint Peter's Square shot him. The second attempt was a failed stabbing (by an ex-priest) in Fatima, on May 12, 1982, on the eve of his first attack, as he prepared to recognize the apparition anniversary (first occurring on May 13, 1917) – per the Wikipedia article entitled, "Pope John Paul II," under the subheading "Assassination attempts." (http://en.wikipedia.org/wiki/Pope_John_Paul_II#Assassination_attempts)

grans peines," and *"suspendue en l'air"* does the same for *"saults viendra parler."*

At first glance, *"Du terre prinse"* can seem to state, "To the land taken," but one must keep focus on the only capitalized word of this group, which is the preposition-article *"Du."* That combination word is importantly linking to the last words of line three, which are "will come" and "to talk, discourse, converse, speak, etc." This is then marking the important (capitalization) direction that discussion and conversation will take (To the, From the, With the," and/or "Of the"), about the next word, which is *"terre."* This means the "talk" of line three will be importantly (capitalization) going "To the land," "From the country," With a nation," and/or "Of the earth" (all interchangeable translation groupings).

In a religious context, where one reads "the man" of the main theme and "Him" of the secondary theme as the Pope, one way to read line four can be then relative to Italy, "the land" of Rome. However, an often repeated theme in *The Prophecies* is at the core issue for why the "virgin" (Sister Lucia and the Blessed Virgin Mary) came to warn of the Church's need to act against evil. This involves Israel, and places focus on how that "nation" is most often "discussed" by Arabs, as their "land seized."

When that realization dawns, that line four is bringing up the issue over the State of Israel, it relates to the main theme and the Vatican's actions relative (for or against) to that "taking of land." This is adding supporting details to what would come, "After" weak "animals" will have led the holy "house" in Rome and all the "pains" and "worries" that the "great ones" (as those nations winning "great" wars) will have brought.

In this regard, line three can be read as saying, "The thunderbolt to virgin will be as malefic." "The thunderbolt" can be seen as the power of Zeus or Poseidon (gods of Roman-Greek myth), where such a "strike" from the Church could have played a significant role. This means the Church of Rome could have influenced whether or not Palestine would have been allowed to become Israel, without "condemnation."

The word "malefic" is an astrological term, such that two planets in our solar system are described as symbolizing characteristics in humans that are "malefic ones." Those two are Saturn (the Greater Malefic) and Mars (the Lesser Malefic). The movements of those planets are said to reflect the times as harbingers of "pain" and "punishment." Most commonly,

Chapter 5: Quatrain III-44

they are felt through the ravages of "time" (Saturn) and the "lightning" fast "troubles" of war and fighting (Mars).

While both planets play vital and important roles in reflecting everyone's life, symbolically they are most demanding of excellence. Anything short of a dedication to perfection (where most people always seem to fall) is where Saturn and Mars pass out their negative rewards: the lessons of patience and hardship (Saturn), and the agony of defeat and loss (Mars). This must then be seen, in the context of quatrain III-44, as meaning the painful lessons the Vatican experienced from the 1948 creation of the State of Israel.

According to the Wikipedia article, entitled "Holy See – Israel relations," every pope from 1904 (Pope Pius X) to 1993 (Pope John Paul II) had denied the State of Israel a diplomatic relationship with the Vatican. The article states this reasoning to be:

> "Zionism had traditionally been associated with atheist Soviet Communism. *L'Osservatore Romano* commented on the establishment of Israel on 12 June 1948: "The birth of Israel gives Moscow a basis in the Near East through which the microbes can grow and being disseminated." ... Any rapprochement toward the Jewish state was curtailed because of the conviction that, in order to safeguard the wellbeing of Christians under Muslim-Arab rule, the Vatican would have to pay the political price of supporting Arab claims against Israel. The Vatican view of the Near East was dominated by a Cold War perception that Arab Muslims are conservative but religious, whereas Israeli Zionists are modernist but atheists."[14]

Under the leadership of Pope John Paul II, the Vatican began diplomatic relations with Israel (1994), which led to a "Fundamental Agreement" between the two nation states (1997). This recognition was culminated when Pope John Paul II made a pilgrimage to Israel, blessing that nation on March 23, 2000.[15] When this series of events is seen as "After great ones pains," the Vatican would give in and go "To the land taken." This decision will go against the warning of the "virgin," and it has added to

---

14   From the Wikipedia article entitled, "Holy See – Israel relations," under the subheading, "Zionism, Israel and the Holy See before and after 1993," under the list "Pius XII." (http://en.wikipedia.org/wiki/Holy_See_%E2%80%93_Israel_relations)

15   From the website Jewish Virtual History, on the page entitled "Pope John Paul II's Pilgrimage to Israel." (http://www.jewishvirtuallibrary.org/jsource/anti-semitism/jp.html)

the strained relations between Muslims and Christians. That strain is then reflected in quatrain III-44, when read as a future event that "will come" with "lightning" to Rome.

At the midpoint of line four, one finds another ampersand. Again, this is a signal to see what follows as bearing importance, just as capitalization does. This importance is mostly shone upon the immediate word that follows, which in this case is "*suspendue*." That word is the feminine gender form of the past participle for the verb "*suspender*," meaning, "suspended; deposed, removed or discharged for a time; also deferred, put off, delayed, or held in suspense." It can also bear the meaning, "kept in doubt" and "held off with uncertain terms."[16] With all of this meaning considered, and following a statement about a direction relative to a "land seized," the aspect of "suspension" is confirming the "putting off" period the Catholic-Christian-Arab-Isareli "world" went through, between 1948 and 2000. When the "virgin" sought a "lightning" response from the Church, she instead found it "deferred."

When one sees the second half of line four stating, "*suspendue en l'air*," the noun becomes the important word to grasp fully. The article-noun spelling, "*l'air*," simply states "the air," with many nouns applying the abbreviated "*le*" only to drop it in translation. As such, "*l'air*" can translate as "air," but this is more than just an atmosphere of carbon dioxide.

Randal Cotgrave shows "air" as translating to mean, "the air, breath, wind we suck up; also the element ayre [an astrological allusion to "air"]." He then went on to define "*air*" to be, "also a small blast, puff, or breath of wind; air; also a tune, sound, or ayre in music; also the form of species of a thing." He continued, "also the favor, grace, good opinion of men; also the aspect, presence, or appearance of a man; also a good grace, handsomeness, or becoming of what one does."[17] This was further explained to have a horsemanship meaning, where "air" was a state when a horse would raise up with a rider.

When all of this is considered, it certainly can be seen to explain the blessing (a "grace") given by Pope John Paul II, to the State of Israel. Such "air" was like a reward of patience (the Greater Malefic – Saturn), which had been "suspended." "After" 52 years, the Church of Rome would bless

---

16   From Randal Cotgrave's 1611 French-English Dictionary, published online by Greg Lindahl. (http://www.pbm.com/~lindahl/cotgrave/search/891bl.html)
17   From Randal Cotgrave's 1611 French-English Dictionary, published online by Greg Lindahl. (http://www.pbm.com/~lindahl/cotgrave/search/037l.html)

Israel, an honor bestowed "upon" (a translation of "*en*") "the land taken" from the Palestinians.

At the same time, all of the acts of a series of dogs, who had been too afraid to follow a holy command to stop the spread of atheism, will have allowed recognition to a State that used the force of "lightning" to "steal away" the "land" of another. This is a Cardinal Sin (Thou shalt not steal) that was blessed by a pope who was the leader over an atheist flock, in Soviet-controlled Poland. He was the one who officially denied any need to act on the "virgin's" recommendation, such that by the time he blessed stolen "soil" (the Holy Land), he would forever "suspend the breath" of God "To the land seized" by pretenders.

All of this acts to support the second half of the secondary theme, which stated, "jumps will issue from to declare." To see that further explained as the letter sent by Sister Lucia as the result of that warning having been "held off with uncertain terms," in order to enter "into" a "nation" conceived illegitimately and bestow "the air" of benevolence, is to see how wounds in Arabs will be reopened and salt rubbed in.

The visit by the pope to Jerusalem, being the first pope to pray at the Western Wall, and his call for Arabs, Christians, and Jews to live together in peace was well received by Westerners; but this did not ease al-Qaeda's hatred for Christians. The Vatican is still seen by Muslims as having been the source of hatred and persecution towards Arabs, such that a plan for retribution (the vision shown to little Lucia and cousins) will include "lightning" strikes that could create fires that will "suspend the air," replacing it with super heated gasses.

Chapter 6
The Third "*Vierge*" Quatrain

Quatrain III-84

The third quatrain of *The Prophecies* that states the word "*vierge*" is found published as the 84th in Centurie III. The word is found in line three, just as it was in quatrain III-44. Here is the Old French of Nostradamus, followed by my literal English translation.

> *La grand cité sera bien desoleé,*
>
> *Des habitans un seul ny demoura:*
>
> *Mur sexe, temple, & vierge violee,*
>
> *Par fer, feu, peste, canon peuple mourra.*
>
> ---
>
> There great city will be quite desolated,
>
> Of the inhabitants one alone not will stay:
>
> Wall sex, temple [or church], & virgin violated,
>
> By weapon, fire, plague, law people will die.

This quatrain appears fairly clear about what is prophesies, fitting the common theme of Nostradamus' poems - doom and gloom. A series of apocalyptic tragedies are found in line four, ending with death.

The overall vision is very close to that shown to the three children at Fatima, in 1917. Additionally, it parallels the vision shown to Saint Malachy; and it allows one to see how the "lightning" in line three of quatrain III-44 can be read as an attack on the place that reveres the "virgin." All of this, when pulled together, makes it possible for one to see the "city" in the main theme of quatrain III-84 as focusing on Rome.

A Big City Half in Ruins

Support for a conclusion that Rome is the "great city" comes when one sees "*temple*" and "*vierge*" together in line three. Both words add supporting details (the function of line three in all quatrains) to a main theme (line one) that identifies "The great city." Thus, it is a city known to have connections to religion, in particular a "church" (alternative translation of "*temple*") that venerates the "virgin," while having "nuns" (alternative translation of "*vierge*," in the plural).

The use of the word "great" (which always indicates a noun intention first, before acting as an adjective or adverb) identifies the Western world. The West is self-described and seen by the rest of the world as "great," due to its overall power, wealth, and scope of influence. This is also where the world's most concentrated populations of Christians are found, and Western Christianity is attributed to a spread overseen by Rome. However, there is another way to find Rome supported, which is through an indirect translation and interpretation.

This comes when one realizes the French word "*cité*" is translatable as more than "city." While "*cité*" is most commonly used to indicate "a city; a walled and incorporate town, being the seat and see of a bishop, and having a cathedral within it,"[62] there is another use that also acts in support of Rome, the "city." This translation is found coming from the past participle form of the verb "*citer*," which is also "*cité*." As such, the same spelling brings forth the meaning of the past-tense action, being "cited, summoned, warned to appear; also alleged or cited (as a text)."[63] As an indicator of the "great" having been given a citation, "*cité*" means those "great" who will have been "served with a writ," a notification that they must appear before a court for judgment. "The great" who have been "warned."

When this translation is seen connected to "*La grand*," one sees the im-

---

62 From Randal Cotgrave's 1611 French-English Dictionary, published online by Greg Lindahl. (http://www.pbm.com/~lindahl/cotgrave/search/204l.html)
63 Ibid.

portance (capitalization) of the typically feminine article ("*La*") having less to do with a significant one (as "THE") and more to do with the element of place. When the adverb form is derived by the addition of an accent mark, as "*Là*," one then sees the importance of "There" or "Here" indicated, as well as a timing factor, "Then." To see "There" and "great" linked together, one sees an important statement forming, relative to a main theme, which identifies an important place ("There") that is known as a center for those with reputations as the "great" of the world.

This place is then identified as a "city," which is not only a "great city," but "The great city," as the source of all who claim greatness that stem from "There." When this place of the "great" is then seen as "cited to appear for judgment," this is the citation issued by Saint Malachy and Sister Lucia. Other interpretations of Biblical prophecy also identify "There" as Rome, such that scholars have "cited" Rome as the target of God's wrath.

All of this makes it possible to identify Rome as the specific "city" in the main theme line of quatrain III-84. When the main theme statement is translated as, "There great city will be thoroughly desolated," one cannot help but be reminded of the vision written of by Sister Lucia, when she wrote that the three children saw "Our Father" [the pope] in "a big city half in ruins."

The French word "*desoleé*"[64] is the feminine spelling of the word "*desolé*," meaning, "desolate, desert; made solitary; abandoned of all comfort or company." When the definition of "desolate" is seen as a transitive verb (in English) it means, "to lay waste; devastate."[65] This definition relates to the past participle use of "*desolé*" (from "*desoler*"), which bears the meaning "utter ruin."

While Sister Lucia's words clearly state that she saw a "big city," one must remember she was shown this revelation as an eight-year old child. Undoubtedly, at that young age, she had not seen any place larger than the towns surrounding her rural village, and it may be that she had not even seen pictures of cities, having not been educated.

<u>Nostradamus</u> wrote the word "*grand*" (in variations: masculine, femi-

---

[64] The accent mark is on the last letter, which means the word appears to be misspelled. This is not the correct assumption, as "*desoleé*" has to be seen as a "simple anagram," where the last two letters are reversed, making the word be properly spelled, as "*desolée*" of "*désolée*." This is the system of anagrams in play, where simple swapping of letters is most often the answer to a word's meaning, and due to the rule that forbids the removal of an accent mark, although the addition of one is allowed.

[65] From the Free Dictionary by Farlex, referencing <u>The American Heritage® Dictionary of the English Language</u>, Fourth Edition. (http://www.thefreedictionary.com/desolate)

nine, singular, plural) 567 times in the quatrains of *The Prophecies*.⁶⁶ This is, by far, the most used word in all of the quatrains that is not an article or preposition. While this can be seen as matching the description of "big" (because it does), Nostradamus used the word "*grand*" to indicate those places (nations) that were ruled by "great" leaders, as nations with significant worldwide influence.

As such, "There great city will be thoroughly desolate" means, "There in the land of a great power a city will be thoroughly in ruin." Sister Lucia can likewise be seen to be pointing to "a city of a big [great] nation [that] will be half in desolation." As she assumed the Bishop she witnessed, dressed in white (Bishops typically dress in red), was the Bishop of Rome, i.e.: the Pope, who traditionally dresses in white, the "big city" she was shown was Rome. Rome is one of the world's "great" cities. Thus, both Sister Lucia and Nostradamus can be seen as telling of the same vision, at slightly different times. Lucia seeing a place "half in ruin" describes the state that will exist before Nostradamus described the same place becoming "thoroughly desolated."

With the main theme seen as telling of "Then," when the "great" will be "desolate," it matches the terminology of quatrain III-44, when the words "*Quand*" ("When"), "*Apres*" ("After"), and "*Le foudre*" ("The lightning") are translated and interpreted as representing events of a time still in our future. That shows how "lightning" will come "After" the "great" will be "penalized" (a variation on "*peines*") for the time "When the domesticated animal" (a dog) will have become "the man." This connection makes it easier to see the main theme of quatrain III-84 being "When" Rome will be suffering from a state of self-inflicted "desolation."

What can be overlooked is the combination of words in the main theme that state, "*cité sera bien*." This tells about what the "city will be," where "*sera*" is the future tense of the verb "*etre*" (Old French "*estre*"), meaning, "to be," but also "to subsist; to remain, abide, stand, rest." As such, the statement makes a statement about the "city," that "will stand, will abide, will subsist, and will be" as long as it is "good," the basic translation of the next word written, "*bien*."

The word "*bien*" can be read as a noun, such that it means, "wealth, substance, riches, possessions, goods, and a patrimony [an inheritance or

---

66   Per the totals listed for "grand, grande, grands, grandes, grandez," and "grans" on the Nostradamus Index F – H, by the website Alphabetical Nostradamus Index. (http://alumnus.caltech.edu/~jamesf/nindex/fh_index.html)

legacy]; also a benefit, pleasure, favor, good office, or good turn; also goodness, honesty, virtue, sincerity; and also a good thing."[67] These are the qualities of Rome, or the Vatican, which is why that "city" has retained recognition as one of the "great" places on earth, for so long. However, the word "*bien*" also has adverbial uses, where the meaning becomes, "well, good, right, content; fitly, aptly, commodiously; fully, thoroughly; in good case, with good reason, and as it should be."[68] Modern usage includes "quite," as well as it being a word that indicates a result or consequence, and as having moral usage as "right."[69]

When these other uses are considered, it becomes easy to see how a "city will be" strong and "great" only as long as it is morally led to act for "right." Anything less than that "will be aptly" judged, with the result being "quite desolate." This future has been stated prophetically, metaphorically by Biblical prophets, making this judgment a known warning (as "cited").

The consequence is then foretold: one "will be good," or one "will be fitly abandoned of all comfort and company." In the later case, Rome has been "great" because of its link to Christ, God, and the holy "virgin," but the main theme statement can be read as Rome having abandoned that relationship, making itself incapable of receiving the graces it once enjoyed.

With line one ending with a comma, one can see how the "desolation" of the main theme is separated from the focus of the secondary theme. Although the secondary theme is known to directly relate to the main theme of Rome ("The great city"), it is free to represent a factor following that "desolation." In this case, the secondary theme focuses on the aspect of that ruin on the people, of Rome and of Christianity.

Line two then begins with the capitalized word "*Des*," which is a combination preposition-article word, as "*De + les*," where the plural number is expressed. The preposition importantly explains what comes "To them," what goes "From them," who is "With them," and what is "Of them." Based on the main theme being those of "A great city," the secondary theme is importantly (capitalization) placing focus on those ("*les*" as a plural pronoun) making Rome "desolate."

67 From Randal Cotgrave's 1611 French-English Dictionary, published online by Greg Lindahl. (http://www.pbm.com/~lindahl/cotgrave/search/112l.html)
68 From Randal Cotgrave's 1611 French-English Dictionary, published online by Greg Lindahl. (http://www.pbm.com/~lindahl/cotgrave/search/112r.html)
69 Harper Collins French Concise Dictionary, Third Edition, 2004.

This then leads "*Des*" to connect to "*habitans*," which defines "them" as "inhabitants, dwellers, or abiders." The presence of the preposition in the combination word, "*Des*," means the capitalization placed on the word "*De*," which is then made plural in number (-*s*). This allows for the initial importance of the secondary theme to be placed on a multi-directional scope. The events bringing about ruin are the result coming "From ones," sent "To ones," which effected all who stood "With ones," on both sides. Thus, this secondary theme begins by stating, importantly, how "utter ruin" is not created in a vacuum, as there must be some cause and effect yielding that state. In other words, it takes two to tango.

This is then reflected in the plural word "*habitans*," which is seen here as an abbreviated form of "*habitants*," meaning those who live and dwell in a place. Line one set a theme of "The great," which is a statement about a plural number or people acting in a singular capacity: as a government over people; as a nation of people; as one society of people; or, as one philosophy guiding people. Those leaders can now be seen in relationship "To them abiders" (variation of "*Des habitans*"), who are the commoners, citizens, and/or tolerators of "The great." This lets one see a duality in the themes, which not only focuses on Rome's leaders and Rome's inhabitants, but Rome's enemies and those abiding by Rome's rule over them.

On another level of thought, based on the spelling of "*habitans*," where an abbreviation does not precisely spell the word translated, as "inhabitants." This means one's search goes to Latin, which is the root language for the French word.

The base word in Latin is "*habitus*," with the "-*ant*" ending being similar to the French present participle ending, acting like English's "-ing." The word "*habitus*" is translated to mean, "a condition, habit, bearing," with it also representing a "style" of dress. When relative to places, it can mean the "lie of the land," and abstractly it can be used to indicate, "nature, character, disposition, and attitude." All of this meaning can play a role in the deeper meaning of line two and quatrain III-84. However, it is important to realize two things.

First, the use of Latin in *The Prophecies* is always a symbolic indication of religious meaning (Christian, Roman Catholic) being the primary intent. By seeing "*habitans*" as Latin, that language then acts to support the identification of "The city" as Rome. Second, when "*vierge*" is known to be in line three, and that word is known to translate as "nun," one must recognize their style of dress as "habits." Additionally, Vatican City is also known for "vestments," in all its clerics, and the French words "*habit*" and "*habitus*," both directly rooted in Latin, allow for that translation. Thus, "*habitans*" can be seen as inferring "those wearing habits and vestments," who are the main "inhabitants" of the Vatican.

Following the first two words of the secondary theme, which indicate the plural number, the line continues with the use of "*un*," meaning "one." This is an indication of an individual that is "Of them," "With them," "To them," or "From the people" who "inhabit" Rome. In one way, this individual is linked to the "desolation," inferring that this individual is then stated to be the "sole" cause (from "*seul*"), the "one" who "made solitary" (translation possibility of "*desolée*") the "great city." This would also mean he would be "one alone" ("*un seul*"), set apart from the many "dwellers There."

This means the next word, "*ny*," meaning "not," is making a statement about what negative result the "one" will be associated. As the "only one" to be held accountable for the "utter ruin" of a "city's inhabitants," as the "only one not" living up to the status of "great," this states a subsequent failure of "one not" truly "great." While the combination of words state, "alone not," indicating that more than "one" can be held some responsibile, from their support and dedication given to "one solely," this focuses on the relationship of "the great" to "the abiders." It says, "one alone not" will remain to lead. That indication says how "only one" of the "inhabitants will not remain" in Rome, the "one" who is most expected "not" to leave.

The word "*demoura*" is the third person singular, past simple form of the verb "*demourer*," which is a word that has lost its place in modern French. Even in Randal Cotgrave's 1611 dictionary, the presentation of "*demourer*" offered the spelling that remains in use today, "*demeurer*." Both words mean, "to abide, stay, tarry,"[70] as well as "to linger, remain," and in particular to inhabiting a place, "to dwell, live, reside."[71]

Thus, the secondary theme statement is ending with the projection that "one" most important (capitalization) "Of the inhabitants" of Rome,

---

[70] From Randal Cotgrave's 1611 French-English Dictionary, published online by Greg Lindahl. (http://www.pbm.com/~lindahl/cotgrave/search/282r.html)
[71] From the Wiktionnaire website, in a search for the word "*demeurer*." (http://fr.wiktionary.org/wiki/demeurer)

"he[72] will reside" and be the most important representative (capitalization) "There." However, once a state of "desolation" presents it ugly head, "only" that "one" "not will remain," "nor will linger." This becomes an important statement of desertion at a time of need, relative to a main theme when the "great will be goodness desolate."

At the end of the secondary theme line is a colon. This is a sign that the two theme statements, particularly the secondary theme, will be clarified in the remainder of the quatrain. The presence of a colon also acts as a signal to expect to find examples of who and what "will remain." The colon leads to the line that contains the word "virgin," but the immediate clarification-example found is an important (capitalization) "Wall."

A Wall and a Plumb Line

The French word "*Mur*" is said to translate simply as, "a wall, or rampier [rampart]."[73] There is, however, a figurative use to consider. That makes "Wall" represent a barrier that impedes one's progress, like running into a "brick or stone wall."[74] Such intent would act as a metaphor for difficulty encountered, usually unexpected, forcing one to alter an approach or direction from that originally planned. The implication is an insurmountable blockage. Still, there is another way to see "*Mur*," which can easily be overlooked.

As the first word in line three, and knowing the systems of Nostradamus has one look for supporting details to the main theme statement (line one), which are found in line three, the use of "Wall" supports the Cotgrave definition of a "city" being a "Walled" town. In the 16th century, having a "Wall" around a place was a "great" defensive and protective asset.

In respect to the city of Rome, the Aurelian "Walls" were built between 271 AD and 275 AD and they still surround the seven hills of Rome. They served as a military defense of the "city" until 1870, when the walls were breached and the commander of the Kingdom of Italy captured Rome. To this day, the Aurelian "Walls" are very well preserved, but today those "Walls" act more as tourist attractions than as a defensive structure or as a boundary marker.

---

72   The third person singular implies "he, she, or it" as the one that "will reside."
73   From Randal Cotgrave's 1611 French-English Dictionary, published online by Greg Lindahl. (http://www.pbm.com/~lindahl/cotgrave/search/651l.html)
74   Harper Collins French Concise Dictionary, Third Edition, 2004.

When the "city" is seen as Vatican "City," it too has a "Wall" surrounding it, as a "Walled" conclave. While outside the Aurelian "Walls," Vatican "City" is within the boundaries of the "City" of Rome. However, the defense of the Vatican, an independent "city"-state since 1929, with a population of only 800, cannot be seen as provided by a "Wall," no matter how high. The true defense of that "city" would have to be its declared neutrality, along with the protection of Heavenly guardians.

In the Book of Amos, a prophet of Israel before its total collapse, God appeared before a "Wall," holding a plumb line. The symbolism does not only apply to that ancient Northern Kingdom, but to all kingdoms whose protection is based on a covenant with God for protection. In those cases, the "Wall" represents the basic Laws, to which all must adhere. The plumb line shows if there is a lean away from true vertical, because the weight at the end of the line points to the power of gravity. A lean will result in a collapse.

When the aspect of "Wall" is seen in this light, and following a statement that "one alone not will stay," it becomes easy to see how a pope becomes the most important "Wall" of defense to the "inhabitants" surrounding Vatican "City." For that figurative "Wall" of strength to be found leaving, not truly aligned with God, the symbolic statement, as a clarification of a statement of desertion, is a "Wall" crumbling, or a "Wall" breached. For the pope to feel the need to escape his sanctuary, this is a sign of his having run into a "Wall" of danger that is insurmountable. For such a holy-man to have such doubts and fears, this represents a "Wall" built up between the Church and Christ, where an absence of God leaves one trembling.

As explained in the analysis of the word "*desoleé*," at the end of line one, the accent mark is on the incorrect letter. It should be spelled "*desolée*." Since one cannot change anything written by Nostradamus (as published), the answer to making the letters spell a known word is through a simple anagram solution, flip-flopping the two e's (from "eé" to "ée").

The systems of Nostradamus show that if an accent mark is present in the original publication (I consider the 1568 Lyon edition the official publication to use), then that accent mark cannot be removed. However, if there is no accent mark and the only known spelling requires one (accent marks are relatively modern additions to French), then one has the right to add the necessary pronunciation emphasis (the purpose of accent marks).

In the case of "*Mur*," despite it being a correctly spelled word as such, it can also be seen as "*Mûr*," which means, "ripe, mature, or matured."[75] When one reads the letters "*M-u-r*" as the accented word "*Mûr*," the significance becomes an important (capitalization) "Ripening," which can be seen as alluding to fruit. When one sees the use of "*vignes*" ("vines"), in quatrain II-17, as the bearers of fruit, with the non-production of fruit meaning a dead branch from the true "vine."

This connection makes it possible to see what "not will live" or "will not remain" as being the "Ripening" of any fruit, associated with "inhabitants." This can be furthered as a statement that there will be "one solely not" having been "Matured" by the Holy Spirit, because the "vines" will have become "desolate." From a papacy that will have found "wealth" and "riches" (from "*bien*") on the earthly plane more important that the promise of heavenly rewards, no fruit will inhabit Rome, as none will have been produced that could "Mature."

The word "*Mur*" then connects to the word "*sexe*," which has several uses. As a noun, the word can mean, "sex, kind or gender." As an adjective, it represents elements of "sexuality;" and as a verb, "*sexe*" means the act of procreation and sexual play, "sex." From a "Wall" that "will remain" at the time of desertion, the indication could be the barrier strongly held by the Roman Catholic Church against women priests, denying them any such recognition. This is a gender barrier, one that can be seen as a "Wall of gender." However, in our modern age of military staffing, the personnel found acting as a defensive and protective "Wall" for a "city," that protection can now be understood as consisting of soldiers of both "sexes," male and female.

Still, when one is looking for a reason why the Vatican would have erected a "Wall" between itself and Christ and God, the clarification then focuses on the "sexual" scandals that have faced the Church. The Church is not plumb. The symbolic use of "*Mûr*," as a level of "Wisdom" and spiritual "Maturity,"[76] will have be left "desolate," when "none will remain" able to stay behind the "Wall" celibacy.

Catholic priests make vows to deny their "sexual" appetites, where "*sexe*"

---

75   Harper Collins French Concise Dictionary, Third Edition, 2004.
76   From the website *Wiktionnaire*, under a search for the word "*mûr*." (http://en.wiktionary.org/wiki/m%C3%BBr)

represents the temptations of carnal delights in the physical realm. Sexual drives come from the most base and instinctive drives of man the animal, from which the priesthood seeks to ascend beyond. This element of natural drive connects this quatrain to the main theme of quatrain III-44, where one finds focus placed on "the animal the man domestic."

By seeing this view of "*Mur sexe*," such that it stands alone as a singular statement, separated for the word "*temple*" by a comma, it takes the important position of identifying "Mature sex." As such, the importance (capitalization of "Mature") takes on the time when children reach the age of "Puberty" and the innate urges and drives for "sexual" experiences take control. When this view is then coupled with the aspect of "Wise" about "sex" being read into "*Mur sexe*," one who knows of "sex" from experience is visible.

Adults are so experienced, and some adults will also know about the vulnerabilities of immature boys and girls, seeking to capitalize on that intelelctual advantage. That is then a statement that shows how sexually self-deprived men can take advantage of young fruit, not yet "Ripe." This may allow one to coax favors from children, but the reality becomes the abuse of forced "sex," as rape. This short segment of line three, "*Mur sexe*," then adds supporting details to a main theme of "an animal" running the "household." It explains why "one alone not will remain" on the vine until "Matured" by the Holy Spirit.

Following the comma's point of separation,[77] the use of "*temple*" acts to connect quatrain III-84 to quatrain II-17, where that main theme statement reads, "Him camp to the temple of the virgin pure." In quatrain III-84, "temple" is found in line three, supporting a "great city" stated in the main theme line. The use of "temple" can then act to show the pagan roots of Rome.

During those times, the "vestal virgins" were found serving in the "temple" dedicated to the goddess Vesta. Those priestesses were young girls at first, later to "Mature," devoted to remain "sexually undefiled" (from "*sexe vestale*"), as "virginal." When the use of "temple" is seen to morph

---

[77] The 1555 editions, the 1557 editions, and the 1566 edition shows a comma between "*Mur*" and "*sexe*." However, the 1568 Lyon edition does not show this punctuation being present. It is my opinion that the 1568 Lyon edition represents the corrected version of The Prophecies, perfected by the supervision of Nostradamus' secretary, Jean de Chavigny, who is known to have posthumously edited some of Nostradamus' works. There is no reason for a 1568 edition, other than to correct errors found in the 1566 edition and earlier ones. For all who prefer to interpret line three with a comma after "*Mur*," I do not believe it will change the interpretation I have presented.

into a Christian "church," again in Rome, the same application of "virgins" can be found in altar servers, of both "sexes."

The stand-alone meaning of the word "temple" should then lead one to look into its Latin root word, "*templum*." That root means a place of "consecrated ground, especially a place dedicated to a deity, as a shrine." This solitary aspect, as a one-word statement, becomes the request (warning) of the Blessed "Virgin" at Fatima, such that the Church was challenged to "consecrate Russia as a temple to Jesus Christ." Following the statement of a "Fortified defense" (a major "Wall"), built from the prayers of priests and nuns (cloistered by "sex"), that support of a pope's calls for consecration would allow a believer to expect miracles. Faith that the support of God, Christ, and the Blessed Virgin would enable Russia to return to the sheepfold, as a living "church," would have led Pope Pius XII to immediately act on Sister Lucia's first letter.

When the use of "temple" is seen as a reference to Biblical terminology, it becomes a statement about Jerusalem. The Western "Wall" (or Wailing "Wall") is along one side of the "Temple" Mount. That location is where the "Temple" of Solomon was built, then later rebuilt as the "Temple" of Jerusalem. Those temples were destroyed by the Babylonians and by the Romans, respectively, such that the Islamic Dome of the Rock now stands on that mount, built by Muslims.

End Times prophecy is said to commence at a time when the "temple" will be built a third time. This consecrated ground, recognized by three religions, is where Pope John Paul II became the first leader of the Vatican to bless the State of Israel. At that time, the Vatican made its first official declaration recognizing the taking of Palestinian land. The pope supported the awarding of Palestine to Zionists, as a gesture of "goodness." This makes "temple" reflect an issue that could very well come back to haunt Rome, as the Roman Catholic Church has sided with the Jews, over the Arabs, in a legal dispute over earthly "possessions" (a translation of "*bien*").

Commas surround the word "temple," but before one reaches the word "virgin," an ampersand appears. The presence of a comma, followed by an ampersand, which is redundant punctuation in standard language (thus unnecessary), is a sign that the final phrase of line three is not to be directly joined to the word "temple." In this way, one does not need to have the word "*vierge*" relate directly to a "temple," in Rome, or Jerusalem.

An Important Virgin

The comma acts as a point of separation from "temple," and the ampersand acts to introduce an important series of words, beginning with a most important word, "virgin." This has an effect on that word, making it become "Virgin." The placement of an ampersand before the word "*vierge*" has the impact of giving the word the importance of capitalization. By seeing the word as "Virgin," this elevates the meaning to the level of importance shown in the capitalization of "Blessed Virgin," where proper name status comes from descriptive terms.

This means that line three is importantly emphasizing the role the "Virgin" Mary plays in the "wellbeing" (possible translation of "*bien*") of the Church of Rome. This is because Mary is seen as a "protector from dangers and most powerful intercessor with her Son, Jesus, who is God."[78] An article on the "Virgin" (Wikipedia) states that the Marian influence has been more of a "bottom-up" process, coming from the rank and file of the Roman Catholic faithful, more than a "top-down" edict for this veneration. Much of this grassroots love and devotion has come from apparitions of the "Blessed Virgin," and the miracles that have been reported and verified.

In several of the apparitions, those which have been verified by all Roman Catholic Church standards, the "Virgin" told those she appeared before to have a small church built and dedicated to her. This instruction was so she could help the people. Such a request, and such a response by the Church, has led to many buildings being erected in honor of the Blessed Mother of Christ.[79] These places have become focal points for the faithful, and pilgrimages are said to keep the places of Marian apparitions regularly visited by multitudes of people, many seeking miracle

---

[78]   From the Wikipedia article entitled "Blessed Virgin Mary (Roman Catholic)," under the subheading, "Mary's protection and intercession." (http://en.wikipedia.org/wiki/Blessed_Virgin_Mary_(Roman_Catholic))

[79]   In the book A Woman clothed with the Sun (Image Books, 1960), the lady reportedly requested a "*teocali*" (Aztec language), meaning "church or temple" (1531). A "*basilica*" (church) was built in La Salette, France in 1879, after an apparition there in 1846. The "virgin" told a child, Bernadette, to "tell the clergy to build a chapel (a small church or part of a church) on the site of the grotto," at Lourdes, France (1858). In December 1932, the "Virgin" asked several children who witnessed her presence for a chapel to be built at Beauraing, Belgium. Two small, open chapels were built in Banneux, Belgium, beginning in 1933, where the "Virgin" was identified as "The Virgin of the Poor." The book reports that "300 chapels, the over 3,000 monuments and shrines, and 25 churches throughout the world" were built in honor of her apparitions before one poor girl.

cures for illnesses. This history can then make it easy to see the link to "temple," although the separation means the "virgin" does not require huge buildings built in her honor. She only wants the people to have a sacred place to pray and worship the Lord, to whom her spirit will assist.

When this connection is seen, where appearances of the "Virgin" Mary have called for buildings being erected, the Roman Catholic Church has raised many "temples" named in her honor, without her appearance required. Many Catholic cathedrals and basilicas are dedicated to the name of "*Notre Dame.*" When one reads "*Mur sexe*" as supporting the main theme's "*grand cite,*" then a "city" anywhere in a nation deemed "great" (Christian), which is "Walled" and where children of both "sexes" have witnessed the "virgin," everywhere a large cathedral is named for Our Lady can be the focus. That broad view of all the "great" nations of the Christian world would support a theme of any large "city" with a "temple" dedicated to the "Virgin."

While Rome "will be" the "one" place that has been "wealthy" enough to build so many large "temples" across Europe, it remains the most likely choice. The advent of a globe-traveling pope, however, has made it possible to see a larger area covered. This could mean the "big city half in ruin," as shown to Sister Lucia and her two cousins, as well as Nostradamus' "great city thoroughly desolated" are not limited to Rome. That distinction can represent any walled city with a church dedicated to the Virgin Mary.

One such place is found in the old town of Avignon, France. That "Walled city" was the site of the exiled papacy in the 14th century (1309-1376). The Holy See had relocated there due to Rome having lost its influence in secular matters, in particular those involving England and France. Two popes of Rome had been ordered imprisoned by French King Philip. Pope Clement V was a friend of the French king, who agreed to be crowned in France, beginning a line of French popes. The palace built for the popes (*Palaise de Papes*) is in southern France, and is now the seat of the Archbishop of Avignon. During that century, Rome was a place "From the inhabitants one alone not will stay," as far as the heads of the Roman Catholic Church were concerned. The desertion was to France.

In Avignon, there is a "temple" dedicated to the "virgin." The name of this church is the "Cathedral (of) Our Lady with the Masters [Doms] of Avignon" (*Cathédrale Notre-Dame des Doms d'Avignon*). This is a possibility for the meaning of "*temple*," which then links to the word "virgin." Such a place shows how Sister Lucia did not specifically name where the "big city" was, as neither did Nostradamus tell specifically where the "*grand cite*" was located, here in quatrain III-84.

The Italian "temples" named for the "virgin" are generally called "*basilica di Santa Maria*," with the largest in Rome. Still, a cathedral in southern France, with another important one dedicated to the name of Mary is in Catalonia, Spain (near the Pyrenees), shows that this quatrain is not limited to only one site. There is a famous cathedral in Paris bearing the Virgin's title, and the University of Notre Dame, in the United States, is another. Such a span of possibilities then acts as an indication that much territory could be affected by the illegitimate actions of popes. All of Western Europe is shown to be attacked in *The Prophecies*, through the language of the quatrains and letters, meaning anywhere close to a "church" dedicated to the "virgin" will be where her people will be "violated."

The last word of line three is "*violee*," which is the rhyming mate to line one's "*desoleé*." The presence of an accent mark in "*desoleé*," and not one in "*violee*," when "*violee*" was spelled as "*violé*" (masculine) or as "*violée*" (feminine) in Randal Cotgrave's 1611 dictionary, acts to prove the ability to freely add an accent mark when needed. Prior to the invention of accent marks, words with multiple pronunciations would be spelled the same, thus confusing the reader as to meaning. As such, the past participle conjugation of simple verbs might have once simply ended with an "*e*," with the assumption that letter would be emphasized orally. The presence of accent marks was simply to assist in the verbalization of words.

The meaning of "*violée*" (as a simple anagram, switching the places of the last two "e"s) is then read to be, "violated; broken, transgressed, infringed; corrupted, defiled, deflowered; wronged, misused, abused."[80] As a stand-alone statement, there is certainly the aspect of "rape" to be considered, as the word strongly evokes imagery of "violent force" set upon another. Translations such as "deflowered" and "defiled" support that view of "violated," linking it to "*sexe*" as a "sexual violation." However, besides a statement of rape, one's rights can also be seen as "abused."

---

80 From Randal Cotgrave's 1611 French-English Dictionary, published online by Greg Lindahl. (http://www.pbm.com/~lindahl/cotgrave/search/96or.html)

As such, "rape" is an illegal "abuse" upon another; but one can be "violated" both literally and figuratively. When line three offers the past tense of a violation, this supports the use of "*cité*," in line one, as the past tense of a citation. Thus, the most general meaning of the words brings a focus on negative aspects of the law, as those "broken."

In this sense, when one "breaks" a law, one as common as speeding or spitting on a sidewalk, one has "violated" some statute that establishes the norms for a society. When the theme of quatrain III-84 is seen as religious, rather than secular, largely due to the words "temple" and "*vierge*," it becomes more natural to see "violated" in the light of God's Holy Law. In this way, "violated" states actions of the past, against that Law. This supports the main theme, where a "city warned" will find what "will be" if it lets "goodness" become "desolated." As such, "*violeé*" can be translated as "desecrated,"[81] where that which is sacred has been "violated."[82] That is a state where that which is holy has been given unto dogs.

The word "*violeé*" then can be read as an action upon the noun, "*vierge*," telling of a "virgin violated." This supports the deep-cutting scandals of Catholic priests having "abused" immature boys, with decades of "violated" children having lost their "virginity" through "rape." While their attackers were "Mature" adults, those children would themselves reach "Ripened" ages (from "*Mûr*"), wanting nothing to do with the "sexual" (from "*sexe*") predators that changed their lives for the worse. This is a repeated act, by multiple culprits, because line two states "not one only" (from "*un seul ny*") ones force "sex" in a "church," with virgins.

That history then cuts to the heart of the "Virgin" Mary, which can be seen identified by the "& *vierge*" acting as "*Vierge*." Her spirit has acted as protector and intercessor to the faithful of the Church, built by those who followed in the steps of Jesus, her earthly son. Because she has so frequently appeared before children born into the poorest of families, with very little education and usually weak religious upbringing, she has spoken to the elders of the Church through the mouths of babes. For children, the most pure representatives of humanity as undefiled "virgins," to be "violated, raped, wronged, defiled, abused, deflowered, and corrupted," such acts are against all moral Law and civil law. The acts

---

81   From the website *Wiktionnaire*, and a search of the word "*violer*." (http://fr.wiktionary.org/wiki/violer)

82   From the Free Dictionary by Farlex, under a search for the word "desecrate," with the reference shown as The American Heritage® Dictionary of the English Language, Fourth Edition. (http://www.thefreedictionary.com/desecrate)_

committed against each child, by those supposedly acting as men of faith, have been acts against the one Holy Spirit who has venerated the Church of Rome. The ampersand in line three makes this important announcement.

Prophecy is sourced in the Divine, where time ceases to exist, and where God knows all – past, present, future. The apparitions of the Blessed "Virgin" have been "to warn" the Church to do more to re-consecrate the lands of the faithful. She is able to do that by knowing the pitfalls that lay ahead of the Church, ones it certainly will fall into without her protection, responding to the prayers of the people. She has appeared in Portugal, France (southwest, southeast [2], and northeast [2]), Belgium (south, east), and Ireland (northwest central),[83] with each apparition finding wayward citizens and a Church unable to maintain the faith. Each time the Church has been challenged to prove to itself that its protector has indeed made herself known. Each time the people have been told to repent their sins and pray for those who have fallen into sin, asking to be forgiven.

Her appearance at La Salette, France (southeast) is where she was referred to as the Lady in Tears. Her tears were said to be the result of a lack of faith. According to the reports of the children at La Salette, the lady told them:

> "If my people will not obey, I shall be compelled to loose my Son's arm. It is so heavy, so pressing that I can no longer restrain it. How long I have suffered for you! If my Son is not to cast you off, I am obliged to entreat Him without ceasing. But you take no least notice of that. No matter how well you pray in [the] future, no matter how well you act, you will never be able to make up to me what I have endured for your sake."[84]

This is a statement of a "virgin wronged." She went on to explain to the children that "only a few old women" went to "church" regularly, and many went to "Mass only to poke fun at religion." She continued by stating, "During Lent they flock to the butcher shops, like dogs."[85] That ref-

---

[83] There are reports of her appearing in Japan, Egypt, Slovakia, Lithuania, Rwanda, Australia, Spain, and America, with these not being officially recognized by the Church, and some condemned by Vatican officials.
[84] A Woman Clothed with the Sun, Image Books, 1961, John J. Delaney (ed.), from the chapter entitled "The Lady in Tears," written by Msgr. John S. Kennedy, p. 93.
[85] A Woman Clothed with the Sun, Image Books, 1961, John J. Delaney (ed.), from the chapter

erence is one supporting the concept of "the animal in the man," where the Catholic faithful had become like a "dog given that which is holy."

It is a statement about how weakened Christians will have become, due to the secular interests of a Church more concerned with "wealth" and "possessions" (translations of "*bien*") for its own opulence, rather than to spend its own resources making sure the poor are seeped in religious belief. It is why, "Of them inhabiting" the lands claiming to be Christian (i.e.: Europe and the Western world), "one alone not will persevere" as believers in God's and Christ' promises of heavenly reward.

The apparition at Fatima continued that message of La Salette, 41 years later, by showing Sister Lucia and her cousins when the "virgin" would no longer hold the weight of the Son's arm. She would no longer be able to protect those unworthy of her love, no longer giving her reason to strain to keep Christ from striking anyone down. Fatima would expose the fate of a Church without the arm of Christ protecting it. That protection would only last as long as the Church served God. Its own faithlessness is then the true reason it will end, through acts of self-destruction.

From this view of a "virgin wronged," line three ends with a comma, separating it from line four. The first word of line four is the preposition, "*Par*," which means, "By, Through; Of, By reason of; For; On."[86] As such, the capitalization is introducing an important explanation how and why the "violation" of the "virgin" would take place. It also introduces further clarification concerning the "inhabitants" of the "city" where "one only not will stay."

That mode and reason is then found stated in the following word, "*fer*." In 1611, the word "*fer*" meant, "iron; also the head [tip-blade] of a pike, lance, arrow, etc.; also the tag [designation] of a point."[87] As a word stating a form of metal, it was stating the strongest metal from which weapons could be forged. As such, "*fer*" must be seen in the light of warfare.

The Power to take Peace from the Earth

---

entitled "The Lady in Tears," written by Msgr. John S. Kennedy, pp. 94-95.
86   From Randal Cotgrave's 1611 French-English Dictionary, published online by Greg Lindahl. (http://www.pbm.com/~lindahl/cotgrave/search/693r.html)
87   From Randal Cotgrave's French-English Dictionary, published online by Greg Lindahl. (http://www.pbm.com/~lindahl/cotgrave/search/436l.html). Additionally, a "tag of a point" may mean the aspect of a "barb" of language, where a comment is meant as a slap or insult; but it may also be relative to a "branding iron," where the end is designed to make a point of reference on an animal.

To begin to consider this context, it helps to know how this word directly reflects a 16th century world, much more than the other words in quatrain III-84 have, to this point. In the 16th century, "iron" was what swords were made from. Spearheads and lances were the common weapons of soldiers. In an epic story of warfare yet to come, 16th century vernacular must be understood to apply to our present, recent past and not too distant future. In that regard, the word "*fer*" is written 23 times in *The Prophecies*, and it is found in quatrains appearing in each *Centurie* except the seventh.[88] This frequency makes its use important to recognize.

With the word being relative to the dangerous aspect of weapons, it should always be read as though the primary intent is to focus generally on implements of destruction. These can range from simple swords, to rifles, tanks, and missiles, with all being forms of armament used by military personnel. The word "*fer*" is so often repeated because the main focus on the story of *The Prophecies* is our history of war, and the future aspect of more war. It tells of the use of "weapons," with the singular number, in "*Par fer*," implying multiple "weapons." The capitalization of "By" indicates the method of or reason for the deployment of a most important "weapon." Thus, the word "*fer*" assumes the importance of "*Fer*," by following a capitalized preposition.

As a major statement of the "violated," this statement is about some rule or law being "broken," which is relative to a "broken" agreement, one hinging on protections against the "misuse" of "weaponry" power. When the word "virgin" is read as a first experience, which importantly comes "By weapon," and in a place where such a "weapon" had never before penetrated, as an "undefiled" land, "By weapon" acts as an indication of a military "rape."

In the words of the Lady in Tears, and the statement said to the children of La Salette, the "violation" comes "By weapon," when the "Virgin" can no longer hold the arm of her Son up as a protection of Christians and their "cities." This "weapon" would be of the nuclear variety, which man has made in its lust for power, but unable to control the consequences of its own creations.

It is the development of a weapons that matches Revelations 6:3, when the second seal is opend and a red horse comes out. "Its rider was given powe to take peace from the world and to make people kill each other.

---

[88] From the webpage "Alphabetical Nostradamus Index," created by J. Flanagan, on the page entitled, "F-H Nostradamus Index." (http://alumnus.caltech.edu/~jamesf/nindex/fh_index.html)

To him was given a large sword." (NIV) The same symbolic "sword," or "*fer*," has already been developed, tested, used, and prolifcally produced by the major powers of the world, so the arm of Christ is the seal holding back the release of that destructive power.

When the use of "*fer*" can still be seen literally, in 16th century terms, such that a "pike, lance (or spear), and arrow" are the means by which the weapon is effected. The capitalization of "*Par*" elevates the level by which those projectiles are launched, to that much greater than being simply hand-thrown. This terminology still matches modern military arsenals, such that the "iron" individually on the tip of such "weapons" is now called a "warhead." The "spears" are fired by aircraft, ships, and ground troops (surface-to-air missiles), with bullets fired from rifles being the modern day equivalent to the "arrowheads," without need for shafts and feathers.

In this way, the first two words of line four are clarifying the "violation" and the "desolation" coming "To the inhabitants" of a "city warned." When fired upon "by warheads" of such magnitude that "one only" will be enough to cause mass fear and immediate evacuation, it will be too late. This will also mean "one city" being fired upon "By (a devastating) weapon" will "not" be the "only one." This is a sign of widespread "warfare."

It also clarifies how "There" ("*Là*"), where war will be initiated upon "the great" calling themselves Christian nations, they will have been "cited" or "warned" of some form of judgment being arranged for past errors against the Law of God. That judgment promised by Muslim nations, primarily over the issue of Israel, will be in the form of military retribution, "By weapon" (supplied by the enemies of the West, the remnants of the Soviet Union). The suprise element "will be quite" devastating, leaving those "cities desolated."

The statement, "*Par fer*," is followed by a comma, separating that overview from the next word, "*feu*." Another comma then follows the word "*feu*", such that this one three-letter word makes a statement about what follows the initiation of an assault, "By warheads." This makes it important to understand the full scope of meaning that "*feu*" bears, as it is in a position to make a statement of deep meaning.

The word "*feu*" has a primary translation that is relative to "fire," which can also mean "light."[89] In a quatrain with a religious theme, this then has symbolic associations to God and Christ, as the "light" that leads men away from darkness. Still, the same word (same spelling) also has a use as an adjective, meaning, "dead, deceased, departed."[90] This usage has the impact of identifying the present state of someone or something once living, but has since "died." This makes the word be synonymous with "late" or "defunct."[91] As a verb, "*feu*" can be seen as an interjection or order, such as made to troops in battle, to open "fire" upon an enemy. All of these meanings must be seen as having some bearing as a subsequent clarification of those "violated," who "not will remain," and who "will be quite desolated."

As the word "*feu*" follows the word "*fer*," there can be no denying its positioning makes it a natural subsequence of weapons use. As "fire," this depicts incendiary devices, designed to set structures ablaze. Certainly, historical documentation of the atomic bombs tested and used at the end of World War II showed superheated blasts set buildings, not completely blown away, on fire. There also is no denying the death toll that followed the use of those "weapons." Still, one can see how "violated" can be a state of abuse, which is then explained by a threat, "By weapon," rather than their actual use. This, then, makes "fire" become the command to initiate militarily actions relative to that threat.

In regard to this last potential use of "*feu*," it becomes important to realize the war of words that exist in the world today. For one, the nation of North Korea has "violated" the terms of the agreements it has with the United States, as well as the armistice with South Korea. It has done this "By weapons" tested (missiles), and the sinking of a South Korean ship, which killed over 40 sailors who were on board. There are threats made public, both those of prepared retaliation by the United States, and those of the North Koreans (as in retaliation to economic sanctions in place against them), which await someone actually giving the go ahead to launch serious attacks, "By weapons" of mass destruction.

While this threat posed by North Korea is real, and it has been confirmed that they possess the technology to make limited numbers of nuclear "weapons," the greater worry appears to be the direction Iran has taken towards similar development tactics of its own. This is where the United

---

89   From Randal Cotgrave's 1611 French-English Dictionary, published online by Greg Lindahl. (http://www.pbm.com/~lindahl/cotgrave/search/439l.html)
90   Ibid. (http://www.pbm.com/~lindahl/cotgrave/search/439r.html)
91   From a Wiktionnaire search for the word "*feu*." (http://fr.wiktionary.org/wiki/feu)

States and its allies have threatened Iran with pre-emptive strikes, while having already struck with computer virus attacks on their nuclear development computer systems. Having already imposed serious economic sanctions that effect the ordinary Iranian people, the United States can be the one giving the command to "fire."

Israel is most worried, due to the lack of direct American military actions that would disable Iran's nuclear facilities. It has been saber rattling, making its own threats towards Iran. The West sees Iran in violation of United Nations imposed limits on nuclear proliferation, seeking to restrict who is allowed to join that club. Should Iran gain possession of nuclear weapons capabilities, their coming "By weapons" that could be used in the war (*jihad*), one declared against Jews and Westerners, could be one declaring "fire!" beginning what most people feel would be Armageddon.

As this is all seen from the perspective of the past, where neither North Korea nor Iran has yet acted "By weapons" of major capacity, line four of quatrain III-84 is still an unfulfilled prophecy. However, the theme of the Virgin Mary's apparitions, where she has warned of Christians (Catholics) having "violated" her spirit, this too has been "By weaponry" developed since 1941, and that "weaponry" hasg been "fired," with many human lived "departed" as a result.

That historical development is what drew the Soviet Union into an arms race, deepening their views against religion, turning a nation that once stood strongly for the Russian Orthodox Church branch of Christianity into the evil atheist nation the Blessed Virgin warned the Church of Rome to re-consecrate, or see its own "desolation" be the result. Because the "virgin" was "violated" by the popes of the Vatican, the arms race did ensue, such that the Soviet Union became the antithesis to Christianity. It grew in power because it matched the developments of the United States, "By weapons." Pope John Paul II then publicly proclaimed the Fatima prophecy finished, while taking credit for defeating the Soviet "Wall" (the "Iron" Curtain) by prayer. However, that does not appear to be true.

If one is to believe *The Prophecies* is a truly divine work, then one will see how that collapse of the Soviet Union has been feigned. This is found in the story line that many quatrains tell, and the story is "paraphrased" in the letter of explanation sent to King Henry II. The nations formerly under Soviet domination will play a huge role in a coming war, while the Russians sit back and pretend to have nothing to do with the way the world has turned.

The Soviet Union's war against the United States, and the West, by 1989-90, had turned into one of economic strategies, which the West was winning. The collapse and subsequent release of the Eastern Bloc nations immediately became an economic burden the West gladly took on, seeing itself as benevolent victors. Even the Russians reached out their poor hands, in exchange for some classified documents, which proved they were sincere in their need. However, that war of economy is still being waged.

Iran has since become the surrogate of Soviet "weapons" technology, and Iranian oil money has helped Russia make a profit selling its "weaponry." The guise of Iran seeking to develop nuclear technology is nothing more than a misdirection ploy. Iran already has been armed "For" (alternate translation of "*Par*") use of major (capitalized preposition leading to a noun) "weapons" against a common enemy to both Muslims and Communists. The purpose of this armament is not to gain an edge in the business of verbal threats, but to deploy "weapons" of mass destruction, with the intent to cause the "death" of a Christian West.

When this aspect of *The Prophecies* is realized, the whole view from which quatrain III-84 is but one piece supporting that view, one can see how the violation in line three is shown in line four to be the major worship "Of weaponry" (viable translation of "*Par*" as "Of"), and not God. Thus, the "fire" for one's religion has been replaced by high-tech machinery, in the West, whereas the East sees the "fire" for their religion ignited more "By" coming upon significant "weapons." In both cases, it is not God lighting their way to war, but both being blinded from the true "light," with the Islamists seeking the "death" of Israel and America.

From this multifaceted examination of "*feu*," line four follows that one-word statement with another, which is "*peste*." In the Randle Cotgrave 1611 French-English Dictionary, the word "*peste*" translated as, "The plague, or pestilence; A death, contagion, infection; also, a pestiferous fellow, one that ruins or spoils others." The word "pestiferous" can mean someone who is contagious or carrying a disease; but, as a description of a person who "ruins or spoils others," the intent focuses on the definition of "morally evil or deadly," as "pernicious" (meaning, "destructive"

Chapter 6: Quatrain III-84

or "causing great harm"). Certainly, this word can easily follow the word "*feu*," as an indication of subsequence.

The key to line four is the first segment, "*Par fer*," where the only capitalized word of that line appears. Again, when a capitalized preposition (or article) is linked to a noun, the essence of importance flows to the second word. This means "*fer*" is as important as the modes leading to it, indicated by "*Par*" (By, Through, Of, By reason of, For, or On). Thus, the "violated" are so "by" a major "Weapon."

The flow from that, as a result, is "fire" or "dead" (both), such that the flow from that is "plague," still linked to the power of "weaponry." In today's age of "weapons" of mass destruction, the standard category of "contagion weaponry" is named biological (or germ) warfare. This is when the introduction of a "plague" into the midst of an enemy is purposefully administered as an act of war. The "plague" then spreads to wherever the enemy hides and kills all who come in contact with the infectious disease, if not treated quickly with medicines designed to combat that disease.

Still, when the "weapon" deployed is mighty enough, causing massive numbers of "dead," without people properly caring for the "dead," minimally through "fire" (cremation), the result (a subsequent event in the flow) would be a spread of disease caused by rotting flesh. This would compound the effect of the "weaponry" used, and increase the number of "dead." As such, the commas would reflect a separate element of despair, based on attacks "By weapons."

When one sees the theme of the Roman Catholic Church, and the "one alone" who presides over that "church" ("*temple*" translated as that) as the pope, one can see how "*peste*" could be placing a derogative description upon he who would have "violated" the trust of the Virgin Mary. As a subsequent aspect of an attack on Rome, this shows how leadership will have caused the death of Roman Catholicism. A series of popes will have acted secretively, as "pestiferous fellows," bringing spiritual ruin upon themselves and those faithful to those popes. Their actions will have brought physical ruin to the lands of Christianity, "By weapons."

Following the comma after the word "*peste*," quatrain III-84 concludes by stating "*canon peuple mourra*." When read all at once, in the context of the Vatican, as a separate segment of words, the relevance of "canon" stands out as, "A law; a rule, decree, ordinance, or canon of law."[92] This makes the "canon people" those who establish church laws, fitting the definition of "canon" as, "An ecclesiastical law or code of laws established by a church council."[93] That Law is based on the writings of the books of the Holy Bible.

The last word, "*mourra*," is the future tense form of the infinitive verb "*mourir*," which means, "to die, decease, depart this life; to perish; to decay."[94] As set in the future tense, the end of line four projects the end of those "people" associated with holy "canon." This falls in line with the vision shown by the Blessed "Virgin," at Fatima, Portugal, to the "virgin" children, one who would survive and become a "nun," Sister Lucia. It also fits the ecstatic trance of Saint Malachy, who was shown the end of the papacy.

Still, when the end of line four is seen linked to the capitalized beginning of that line, "By weapons" can allow one to see how a "canon" is also, "the gun termed a canon; also the barrel of any gun; and (more generally) any instrument or thing that is long and hollow, as the barrel of a gun."[95] This focus can then be separated from the word "people," such that the "people will die" because of a "canon" being "fired," rather than the "people firing" a "canon" ending up "perished."

When line four is seen as a string of related but separate elements, one is lead from an important "weapon," which is "fired," and which initiates "fire," causing "dead" humans. Those "dead" can be killed by biological "weaponry," such that they become "diseased" to the point of "death," or the number of "dead," unattended, can lead to a spreading "plague." This is then explained as "canon fire," as the mode of "weapons," which "will kill" the "people" targeted. Those targeted will then include Christian clerics, who live near Rome and manage the "canons" of the Roman Catholic faithful.

The importance of this quatrain is it states what "will be," from a perspective of the 16th century. The verbs "*sera*" ("will be"), "*demourra*" ("will remain"), and "*mourra*" ("will die") show this quatrain as a prophecy of

---

92   From Randle Cotgrave's 1611 French-English Dictionary, published online by Greg Lindahl. (http://www.pbm.com/~lindahl/cotgrave/search/156l.html)
93   From the online Free Dictionary by Farlex. (http://www.thefreedictionary.com/canon)
94   From Randle Cotgrave's 1611 French-English Dictionary, published online by Greg Lindahl. (http://www.pbm.com/~lindahl/cotgrave/search/647l.html)
95   From Randle Cotgrave's 1611 French-English Dictionary, published online by Greg Lindahl. (http://www.pbm.com/~lindahl/cotgrave/search/156l.html)

what will happen to bring about the end of the papacy and the Roman Catholic Church. This is in support of the prophecies of Saint Malachy (canonized in 1199) and all of the European Marian apparitions (19th & 20th centuries), in particular the one at Fatima. This says, to me, that it is still in our future, and thus to some degree controllable, based on our efforts going forward. The warnings of the "Virgin" Mary, repeated through Nostradamus (understood now), are for our benefit, as long as we act upon those warnings, from a position of faith.

Chapter 7
The Fourth "*Vierge*" Quatrain

Quatrain IV-35

In the fourth quatrain stating the word "*vierge*," found as 35th in Centurie IV, with the word appearing in line one. This placement makes it part of the main theme for the whole quatrain; and that is like the first quatrain examined, quatrain II-17. A difference here is the word is presented in the plural number, rather than the singular.

The Old French of Nostradamus is provided first, followed by my literal translation, in English.

> *Le feu estaint, les vierges trahiront,*
>
> *La plus grand part de la bende nouvelle:*
>
> *Fouldre à fer, lance les seulz Roy garderont*
>
> *Etrusque & Corse, de nuict gorge allumelle.*
>
> --
>
> The fire extinguished, the virgin ones will be betraying,
>
> There more great portion from there faction unheard of before:
>
> Lightening in weapon, spear them only ones King will be guarding
>
> Etruscan & Corsica, of night throat blade of a sword.

Chapter 4: Quatrain II-17

The main theme of this quatrain is divided into two segments, by the presence of a comma between the third and fourth words. Thus, the first segment states, "*Le feu estaint*," and the second, "*les vierges trahiront*." The presence of a comma marks a separation in occurrence, such that the part following is understood to have a subsequent focus. This is due to the purposeful ordering of each line in a quatrain, as well as a line's words and segments. Together, both segments of line one combine to establish the main theme of this quatrain.

As shown above, the translation of the two segments can be read as, "The fire extinguished" and "the virgins will be betraying." This makes "The fire extinguished" relative to "the virgins," or "them" [assuming the plural number] who are "virgin ones." The plural number agreement, as "*les*" to "*vierges*," makes "virgins" become singularly identified, when read as "virgin ones."

The singular number allows one to again focus on the singular use of the majority of the quatrains that present "*vierge*." Since quatrain IV-35 is the only presentation in the plural number, seeing the plural relative to "them" who are each a "virgin" is important. This makes an individual "vestal virgin," seen in the first quatrain of this book's "*vierge*" series, a link between this quatrain and the other. Quatrain II-17 states "*vierge vestale*" in that quatrain's main theme statement, in the singular number, with "*les vierges*" in the main theme here.

The vestal "virgins" were young girls, from two in number, to six. They were chosen by lot, from a pool of girls aged six to ten, thus they were prepubescent. Those selected were given temple status, serving in the temple for up to 30 years, at all time virginal. There was also a college of virgins, up to twelve in number, where young girls were selected to be prepared for temple service, like being backups. Those "virgins" would be trained for temple use, and then promoted to replace retiring "virgins," whenever that occurred.[96]

The temple of Vesta was located in the Roman Forum, at the foot of Aventine Hill (one of the Seven Hills of Rome). Because Vesta was the goddess of the hearth, the Vestal Virgins had to maintain an eternal flame dedicated to the hearth, along with taking vows of chastity. Both duties honored their "virgin" deity. The fire of Vesta was extinguished in

---

96   From the Wikipedia article "Vestal Virgins," under the subheadings, "Number of Vestals," and "Terms of service." (http://en.wikipedia.org/wiki/Vestal_Virgins)

394 A.D., on orders by Roman Emperor Theodosius I.[97]

This history does not explain a quatrain telling of the future, but it helps identify Rome as a place that identifies with "virgins" and an important fire. With quatrain IV-35 beginning with "*Le feu,*" the capitalization of an article makes the main theme line in quatrain IV-35 begin by focusing on "THE fire." The article can then transpose the importance to the following noun, creating the essence of an important "Fire."

The Rome implication is later supported by the capitalized, proper nouns found in line four, "*Etrusque & Corse.*" These can translate as the region of Italy now called Tuscany, with "*Etrusque*" translating to mean "Etruscan," or one of Etruria, which was between the Arno and Tiber rivers. The word "*Corse*" (capitalized) can be read as the French name for the Mediterranean island of Corsica (properly "*la Corse*"). Corsica is an island of French nationality, but it is just off the coast of Tuscany, which makes it a natural translation, following "Etruscan," which leads one to see this supportive of a main theme that is relative to regions of land between Rome and France. However, "*Corse*" can be read another way.

The modern translation of the French verb "*corser*" means, "to spice up," or "to increase." The past participle of this verb is "*corsé,*" which is the same spelling Nostradamus used, only without the accent mark. The systems for understanding *The Prophecies* allow for an accent to be added, a conclusion supported by the many words written leaving off the (one or more) accent marks (per word), as the proper spelling of the words are today. Since one is not limited to reading a capitalized word as a known proper noun, it is possible to read "*Corse*" as meaning an important state of "Spiced up," or something importantly being "Increased."

When the Old French translations for the word "*corser*" are seen to be, "to embrace, take, or hold by the body; to catch, take, or lay hold of the body,"[98] one can see how, following "Etruscan," one finds "Caught," or "Held," or "Taken," all referencing either one individual or group of people importantly "Caught" or "Held." In this case, line four is more focused on the region of Tuscany, as "Etruscan" is stated first, prior to an ampersand.

The ampersand announces the importance of the word "*Corse,*" with its

---

97   From the Wikipedia article "Sacred fire of Vesta." (http://en.wikipedia.org/wiki/Sacred_fire_of_Vesta)
98   Randal Cotgrave's 1611 French-English Dictionary," published online by Greg Lindahl. (http://www.pbm.com/~lindahl/cotgrave/search/243r.html)

Chapter 4: Quatrain II-17

capitalization a dual indicator of significance. This word still draws focus to the island of Corsica, but in a secondary level. This is determined because the verb further acts to explain some important (capitalization) action that has taken place on the mainland of Italy. To focus on Tuscany first, and then transfer the focus to Corsica makes line four more confused, especially when two nations are involved (Italy & France).

A Light Put Out

The realization of Italy, in line four, demands the first segment of line one be fully realized. When one closer inspects the words, "*Le feu estaint,*" one sees how the translation, "The fire extinguished," is a complete statement of three words. Whenever multiple words are read all at once, as the first attempt to understand the quatrains of *The Prophecies*, important statements are missed. Groups of words read together neglects the significance that each word has individually. Closer inspection finds that those three words have a profound effect on the theme of quatrain IV-35, when read slowly and separately.

Every line in each quatrain begins with a capitalized first word. The capitalization denotes a word chosen to imply significant importance. When the first word is a capitalized article (as is the case here) or preposition, the importance of capitalization directs to the following word. A capitalized article indicates the individualization of the noun the article precedes. In this case, "The fire" is placing focus on "THE fire," which announces an important "Fire." That makes the important factor be the word following the article, more than the article itself. That tends to minimize the importance of an article, meaning Nostradamus could have simple began the line with a capitalized "*Feu,*" in order to gain the same effect of meaning.

This means there is another way that a first word article gains its own importance. This comes when the article is found to have an alternative use. This is possible when the word "*Le*" can be read as a pronoun. In that case, "*Le*" can be read as identifying an important one of the masculine gender, as a significant "Him." When one does this, one must realize that such a reference to the general, as simply "Him," means "He" is so important that "He" is readily recognized. Further, if the first word of a quatrain introduces an important reference to "Him," then that quatrain should be placed along with other quatrains of the same context, in a

103

subsequent order where "He" is more specifically identified. However, in this reference to "Him," the second segment of words in line one, containing "virgins," will also act as an identifying factor; such that "Him" is related, in some way, to "virgins." This can be seen as the Pope, because it is "Him" who leads "nuns."

In the last line of quatrain III-84, we discussed the use of the word "*feu*," where that word is recognized to mean both "fire, light" and "dead, deceased," as nouns and adjectives. This was also discussed as having a Christian aspect, where Jesus Christ is the "light" and the way. Here, in quatrain IV-35, the importance of "*Le*" is linked to the word "*feu*," such that "The light" can again have the significance of Christ, with "Him" being the individual bearing that torch ("fire") for all Christians (Roman Catholics especially) to be led. Still, as a link to quatrain III-84, quatrain IV-35 can be seen as a reference to where one finds "A weapon," leading to "fire" in "The great city," causing it to be "desolated," where "one alone not will remain," with the "virgin violated."

Evidence of "*Le*" representing an important figure, like the pope, is found in line three, where the direct support for the main theme is always stated. In line three, the capitalized word "*Roy*" (spelled "*Roi*" now) is found, which translated as an important "King." In the case of The Prophecies there are few who will qualify as a national King of importance, with England being the only exception of merit. Because England now has a Queen, and has had one for many decades, the identification of "Him" as a King makes "*Roy*" a better identifier for the one known as the Bishop of Rome, the sovereign of Vatican City.

When line one is seen beginning with important focus being placed on the Pope, the second word, "*feu*" can be seen as "light," more than "fire." The leadership of the Pope is intended to act as the liaison of Christ, who is the "Light" ("THE light") of truth by which Christians are to be guided. However, this translation of "*feu*," while "light" and "fire" are the most frequently used, is not the only translation possible.

The same word, in Old French and present French, means, "dead, deceased, departed."[99] When this translation is applied to a reference to an important "Him," who is identified as "Pope," the implication is the death of that person. Reading "*Le feu*" as "Him deceased" means "THE light" for Christianity has been "extinguished," with the next word in segment

---

[99] Randal Cotgrave's 1611 French-English Dictionary, published online by Greg Lindahl. (http://www.pbm.com/~lindahl/cotgrave/search/439r.html)

one being "*estaint.*"

The third word in this main theme line is "*estaint,*" which does translate to state "extinguished." The accepted Old French spelling was "*estainct,*" which Nostradamus also used in his text; but French in the 16th century was beginning a period of refinement and change, with some words still accepted as proper to spell different ways.

The Old French version, "*estainct,*" is said to translate to mean, "extinguished, quenched, put out; spent, lost, abolished, utterly perished; consumed, come to nought."[100] This makes the word have the past participle effect, and convey the meaning that "He" is described (adjective use) as "dead," from acts that would be responsible for that demise. As such, his "fire" (noun use) had been "put out."

This view is then allowing one to see how Sister Lucia was shown such a death of a pope. In the vision she was shown by the Blessed Virgin, she recalled, "he was killed by a group of soldiers who fired bullets and arrows at him." In this sense, "Him," clarified in line three as the "Pope" (possible translation of "*Roy*"), under "fire" of bullets is "deceased," along with "THE light" of Christianity, being "utterly perished" physically and "A light extinguished" figuratively.

This them makes the second segment of words allow one to grasp Christian meaning of "virgins." That segment states, "*les vierges trahiront,*" where the plural article ("*les*") is both a link to "those" who "extinguished Him" and "them" who are "virgins" for "Him." When the plural word, "virgins," is linked back to the capitalized word "*Le,*" one can see Christ become visible as "Him" to whom "the virgins" (nuns) have sacrificed their virginity, being married to a Spirit with which "they" never experienced carnal knowledge. That becomes the "light" ("*feu*") which will lead "those" to become "virgins" to "Him." However, the last word is a statement of the third person plural future, such that after that "light" and "fire" has been "extinguished" a pause in time will occur; and afterwards, "them virgin ones" will be related to something that "will be betraying."

As an individual word, "*trahiront*" is the third-person plural form of "*trahir,*" the verb meaning, "to betray," or "to deal treacherously with."[101] This is then predicting a future when "betraying" will take place. That

---

100   Randal Cotgrave's 1611 French-English Dictionary, published online by Greg Lindahl.. (http://www.pbm.com/~lindahl/cotgrave/search/406r.html)
101   Randal Cotgrave's 1611 French-English Dictionary, published online by Greg Lindahl. (http://www.pbm.com/~lindahl/cotgrave/search/921r.html)

word, individually then links back to the word "virgins," such that what states "the virgins will be betraying" can also be read as linking "them" ("*les*") as the ones [plural number] who "will be betraying," with "those virgins" the ones [plural number] betrayed. In this later case, "*les*" is relative to "Him" and the "light put out," as "those" followers who will have been led into darkness.

As often is the case in the verbiage of Nostradamus' quatrains, plural words can represent those of a particular group or activity. In this regard, the word "*vierges*" can be seen as "*vierge-s*," meaning "virgin ones," as "those" ("*les*") ones dedicated to celibacy. That group is then "them" who are unaccustomed to that act of betrayal. It also can be seen as an act against "virgin ones," who will have never been in the position of not having "Him" to lead "them."

Those who will have contributed to the "Him" being "dead" (from "*feu*"), can then be seen as the same ones acting in treacherous ways towards those who are nuns, seeing "*vierges*" in religious terms. The use of "virgin ones" can be read as implying anyone, females and males, who will have never experienced a sack of Rome in their lifetimes. It can also be read as a statement of the children ("those virgins") who experienced Marian apparitions. All are linked to popes, who depend on that "light" of guidance.

The word "betray" has to be seen as at the root of the word "treason," which in French is "*trahison*." The definition for "treason" is then seen as a, "Violation of allegiance toward one's country or sovereign, especially the betrayal of one's country by waging war against it or by consciously and purposely acting to aid its enemies."[102] When this definition is applied to "*trahissant*," the present participle spelling, as "betraying," the later can be read as reference to a country's sovereign, which is the relationship the "Pope" (as "*Le*" identified) has to Vatican City.

Although Vatican City is a city-state, and thus a tiny principality, where the Bishop of Rome is the "King" of the Vatican, that city-state acts as the capitol of the nation of Christianity. In that sense, whenever there is a question of authenticity in holy and religious matters, such as proving apparitions, stigmata, weeping statues, images of Jesus on things, and even determining what books are written by prophets who were divinely inspired, the nation of Christ depends on the Vatican for divinely inspired

---

[102] From the Free Dictionary by Farlex online, sourcing The American Heritage Dictionary of the English Language, Fourth Ed. (2000) Houghton-Mifflin Company, used here through the right of fair use.

answers. However, when the time comes that "The light" of the pope has been "put out," then one can understand the "treason" the city-state and its leaders have committed, by refusing to listen to "the virgins" who sent warnings to the "Pope," from Christ the "King," instructing the Church to act.

One sees line one is separated into two parts by a comma, and that is then symmetrically balanced by line three also being found to be so divided. Because the supporting details to the main theme statement are found in line three, each half of lines one and three relate to one another. Thus, "The fire extinguished" is supported by "Lightning in weapon," with each being the first portions of lines one and three. Likewise, "them virgins will be betraying" is supported by "spear they only ones King will be guarding."

This means the second half of line three is directly supporting the theme of "them virgins," who will find a condition that "will be betraying." The second segment of words in line three states, "spear them only ones King will be guarding," but this must be broken down into individual statements, as was line one.

A "lance" becomes a clarification of the type of "weapons" that are identified in the first half of line three; but when "*lance*" is seen as "spear," this is still the "weapon" of show, currently displayed by the Swiss guard at the Vatican. As such, modern missile "lances" will be defended against by wooden "spears," which "will be guarding" the "Pope."

This helps support a theme where "Him" is that leader of importance; but the true significance is the "King will be guarding" the warnings of "the virgins." Due to this "guarding," the "Pope" "will be betraying" both "the children" and the "Virgin" Mary, all "virgins." This future tense, of "betraying" and "guarding," means the warnings will come after "Him," the "Pope," will have "extinguished" the "fire" of faith and devotion to Christ, the true "King." That "light" was "put out" at the turn of the 20th century, when the world went to war often, developing "weapons" of mass destruction, all of which the Vatican failed to take a strong stance against.

When the word "*Roy*" is read as meaning the "Pope," his principality being near Rome, in Italy, links that specific title to the Tuscany region named in line four, On one level, the "Etruscan" people are part of the population of Italy, and who, generally, "will be guarding" that "King." Conversely, the "Pope" is the one who "will be protecting" all Christians (especially Roman Catholics), supported by an entourage that includes "nuns." When this is applied to a theme of betrayal, one can get the sense of a leader who "will be misleading" those who "will be protecting" that reign. This makes "Him" a bad Shepherd who is leading a flock astray.

One can then see how, "He put out the light," and "those" under Him were the "virgins" of that betrayal. As a "King," more than "Pope," a religious head would turn into a political leader, willing to side with whoever paid the most reward. This makes "Him" be the one of importance who would lead followers, in essence, to being blinded from the "light extinguished" and the "fire put out." As such, Italy gave rise to a national "King" in the late 19th century, with King Victor Emmanuel II having spent a significant part of his youth in Florence, Italy, the capitol of the Tuscany region. Benito Musolini would make alliance with both the King of Italy and the Pope of Vatican City, allowing him to attempt colonial expansions into Africa and Greece. The Vatican became powerless when Italy united behind a "King."

A Form of Blind Injustice

Nostradamus wrote the word "*bende*" in line two, which in Italian means, "to blindfold" or "to bandage."[103] A reference to Italy can then be seen, through the switch from French to Italian, and then back to French. The French word of the same meaning is "*bande*," but the "*a*" is clearly made an "*e*" in the 1568 Lyon edition, as can be seen below.[104]

X X X V.
Le feu eſtaint, les vierges trahiront,
La plus grand part de la bende nouuelle: [105]

The secondary theme is then telling of the time when "There" (reading "*La*" as accented), Italy, will have "more" who will be deemed "great." When those who had been "great" have been reduced to just a "part"

---
103   From the website Wiktionary, under the word "benda." (http://en.wiktionary.org/wiki/benda#Italian)
104   In Erika Cheetham's book, The Prophecies of Nostradamus," which also used the 1568 Lyon edition as its Old French text source, has been modified to show the word "*bande*." That is incorrect. The same mistake is found in John Hogue's book, Nostradamus: The Complete Prophecies.
105   From .pdf files made available online for research purposes, by Mario Gregorio, and the website "Propheties On Line." (http://www.propheties.it/home.htm)

of the whole, those weakest will become "blindfolded," thus unable to see the "light." They will have experienced a "new" wound, requiring a "bandage" that is "novel" and "strange." As a result, the "Pope" will act "more lofty," playing a "role of" martyr, as "the blindfolded." This "new" play will put the faithful in the dark, betraying their trust in a way that had "never been heard of before" (translation possibility for "*nouvelle*").

This is then allowing one to see the vision shown to Sister Lucia, which she recalled in her letter to the Pope (1943, supposedly left unopened until 1960), as why the angels "gathered up the blood of the Martyrs and with it sprinkled the souls that were making their way to God." The capitalization of the word "Martyrs" makes her indicate the importance of recognizing who it was who will have been "put to death for devotion to religious beliefs," as defines the word "martyr."[106] This can then be applied to the meaning of quatrain IV-35, showing that the ones who maintained their faith, through devotion to the man who claimed to be the number one servant of God on Earth, will be killed for that devotion to that religious belief.

Sister Lucia saw the "Bishop dressed in White" leading "other Bishops," other "Religious" persons (including nuns), and "various lay people of different ranks and positions" up a mountain to a "Cross." This vision, seen by a poor Portuguese shepherd (eight years old), with no education and little knowledge of the hierarchy of the Roman Catholic Church at that time, saw the leader as "the Holy Father." That title is how Catholics refer to the Roman Pontiff, which has been a succession of men dating back to Saint Peter.[107] However, she began her vision by recounting how an "Angel" shouted "Penance!"

At that instant, Lucia saw, "an immense light that is God." It was later that she saw the "Bishop dressed in white," which she assumed was the "Pope." Her assumption could have a double meaning, if it is not wrong. She could have seen the Spirit of Jesus Christ, who *The Revelation* says will be in white when he returns, and who truly is the Holy Father linking all popes to God the Father. The symbolism of Sister Lucia's vision can be of "The light extinguished," which is the "light" of Christ. The call of the Angel is for forgiveness, for having lost touch with the "light."

---

106   From the Free Dictionary by Farlex online, sourcing The American Heritage Dictionary of the English Language, Fourth Ed. (2000) Houghton-Mifflin Company, used here through the right of fair use.
107   Per the Vatican website, under the heading "The Holy Father." (http://www.vatican.va/holy_father/index.htm)

Seeing her vision in this way makes the focus of *The Prophecies* be relative to the diametrically opposite position Nostradamus wrote the Church would find itself in the future (along with the Kings and Sects). This "anti-Church" is the one that is known to have sourced many well-publicized scandals, many involving "virgins," but which also includes the murder and cover-up of a Pope (John Paul I). That history means a real Shepherd has be replaced by Bad Shepherds for the faithful.

Sister Lucia told of a leader leading everyone up a hill to a Cross. That is the symbol of Jesus' death, which was a punishment used by the Romans, with the Seven Hills of Rome the symbolism shown those children at Fatima, Portugal. Instead of a religious leader shown leading faithful Christians to live like Jesus, the Pope symbolically leads the faithful to their deaths, where their "fire" of life is "extinguished." Thus, the prophesy of Sister Lucia is of that diametrically opposite position the Catholic Church will have placed itself in, sacrificing the will of God (to be found through a Good Shepherd, Pope John Paul I) for personal power and material gains (to be found in the profits from Sicilian Mafia money-laundering through the Vatican Bank).

After that murder of Pope John Paul I, all the minor scandals multiplied in scope. Twice, in 1981 and in 1982, Pope John Paul II had his life threatened by assassins, which is not something popes commonly worried about prior. God had been their bullet-proof vest. However, after the first assassination attempt took place on the aniversary date of the first appearance of Our Lady of Fatima (May 13, 1917), with the second attempt taking place at Fatima, Portugal, on the eve the feast of the Blessed Virgin (May 12, 1982), Pope-mobiles were found to provide better safety for popes.

The message of Fatima was for the Church to stand up against Communism, but instead of acting against that evil philosophy, a pope would eventually be chosen from a Communist nation, where religious congregations had been outlawed (Poland). Rather than fight evil, the Roman Catholic Church was overtaken by evil, making the Virgin's prophecy be for a Church to oversee a world that would go to ruin. The Church was too weak to stand up and act, when told to do so by a young Portuguese shepherd (a "nun"), so the prophecy waiting to be fulfilled, as seen by Sister Lucia, is still a work in progress.

In reference to the apparitions of Mary by others, the words "*les vierges*" can be seen as the multiple appearances by the Blessed Virgin to different young children (mostly girls), all of an age and history of virginity. Those appearances began in the 19th century, continuing into the 20th, after the Church had begun to show signs of decreased importance to the Christian populations of Europe. This means one can read, "The fire extinguished," as how the Renaissance and Age of Revolution (a.k.a. the Age of Reason) had succeeded in stripping the Roman Catholic Church of its power of influence over Christian kings (particularly in England and France), and subsequently over the Christian people. As such, its "light" had been "quenched."

That period of feebleness, when the Vatican put its light under a barrel, was when philosophies would sprout like mushrooms in the dark, leading to the usurping of all royal power by governments. Men raised the philosophies of politics as gods for the masses to worship, where freedom and equality were catchwords that led those movements. Nostradamus wrote of those "new Philosophers," from the perspective of a time when the Church was still Church.

The rise of Communism was the tip of that philosophical iceberg, beginning with Marxism (19th century) and culminating with the overthrow of the Czar in Russia (early 20th century). This timing matches the seeming rash of Marian apparitions, with the Virgin Mary appearing in several European places in the 19th and 20th centuries. She warned children to tell the Church to honor their Lord.

Told to suffer for her, "those virgins" were called liars, and persecuted terribly, before their unchanging stories were found to be truthful. After lengthy investigations, the Church finally recognized each of the visions as true, based on the miracles that followed the Blessed Mother's sacred appearances. Therein lies the "betrayal," for as much as was done to the children ("virgins"), the Church was moreso "betraying" the ultimate warnings of the Marian apparitions ("those virgin ones"). The vision of Sister Lucia shows how the Church would be continuing to fail her Son.

Because the word "*vierges*" appears in line one, support for that meaning coming from "virgin ones will be betraying" does not require every word of every line be interpreted. Still, it is useful to see how this quatrain links to the others discussed here, in the "virgin" series of quatrains. The context of lines three and four fit what has been stated previously; and there are key words that are repeated, showing links that go beyond the use of "*vierge*."

Line one of quatrain IV-35, as already mentioned, repeated the use of "*feu*," found in line four of quatrain III-84 ("*Par fer, feu*"). Line two begins by stating, "*La plus grand part*," where the word "*grand*" is another repeated word, found in line three of quatrain II-17 ("*Le grand conduict*"), in line two of quatrain III-44 ("*Apres grans peines*"), and line one of quatrain III-84 ("*La grand cité*"). Line three of quatrain IV-35 states, "*Fouldre à fer, lance les seulz Roy garderont*," where "*fer*" was found in line four of quatrain III-84 ("*Par fer*"), and the singular form of "*seulz*" was found in line two of quatrain III-84 ("*Des habitans un seul*"). These repeated words (not counting articles or prepositions) are establishing a contextual connection between these quatrains that have been pulled together by their use of the word "*vierge*."

Line one of quatrain IV-35 ends by focusing on the future condition of "betrayal," following that with line two's theme statement, "*La plus grand part de la bende nouvelle*." The capitalization of "*La*" should be seen as more important as an adverb ("*Là*"), introducing "There" or "Here" as the place of that "virgin ones treachery." That place is where "more" is found, with the transfer of importance (as "The more") identifying a place of wealth, even opulence. That identification is then confirmed by the use of "*grand*," such that it identifies where "great" people enjoy their wealth and power. However, this place is not where all enjoy such lavish lives, because only "part," or only a "portion" are so "noble," even though all ranks "of" (the preposition "*de*") people there are "part great," with all "parts" making up the whole.

A preposition is such a common word it is often difficult to look at their individual importance, as one-word statements. Still, the French word "*de*" can translate to mean, "of," but also "with," and the opposite directions, "to" and "from." To get a better feel for the multiple possibilities in line two, one needs to look ahead and see the second use of the word "*la*," this time in a lowercase presentation.

Symmetry is an element of the systems that is necessary to grasp, in order to best understand *The Prophecies*. In line two of this quatrain, there are two series of words surrounding the central preposition, "*de*." Both series begin with the word "*la*," with the first one capitalized (importance) and the other in the lower case.

Since I have already explained the translation of "*la*" can be read as the adverb "*là*," at this point one simply needs to be reminded that words repeated in the same quatrain will have different translations, as long as the repeated word has more than one translation possibility. As such, "*Là*" can translate as "Here," and "*là*" can translate as "there," a symmetrical arrangement that revolves around the word "*de.*" The result can be an indication as "Here from there" and "There to here," and vice versa, as a flow of directional movement.

This directional movement then allows one to see the importance of the lowercase "*la*," as an indication that "the faction new," or "the bandage fresh" (each possible from "*la bende nouvelle*") is on a lower level of existence than are "The more lofty part" or "The more great share" (each possible from "*La plus grand part*"). The direction movement is also an indication of one lesser group migrating to be at the same place as the "great," when one sees the "Here from there" and "There from here" possibilities.

This makes the secondary theme (line two) focus on a disproportionate "parts" standing between the "great." The "great," as a noun, as far as Nostradamus was concerned, meant the West, Western Europe, and/or the Christian world. The ones not "great" are then "the band" (a possible translation of "*bende*"), which can be seen as a group of misfits united, one that is "fresh" or "rare."

Because the two theme lines are difficult to understand fully, without more details added, line two ends with a colon, making the rest of the quatrain add clarification to this situation of treachery (main theme), due to a state of inequality (secondary theme). More directly, line two's statement of "*bende nouvelle*," particularly when "bandaged fresh" is read, can then be found expounded in line three's "Lightning," which comes "from" or "in" (from "*à*") the form of a "weapon" ("*fer*"). This tells of harm resulting from weaponry, and the reading of "band never heard of before," as an uncommon alliance, then explains who had that "Lightning in weapons" capability.

The repeating of words, such as "*fer*," seen in quatrain III-84, allow one to find contextual agreement between quatrains. Context expands into stories that develop plots. Once a plotline is established, it is unnecessary to repeat central themes to remind the reader what the overall context is. When quatrains are read individually as prophecies, as if written in a vacuum, not linking to other quatrains, the context becomes solely dependent on the wording of the quatrain. This causes quatrains to seem vague, confusing, and senseless. They are linked together in a proper order, meaning to analyze one quatrain without knowing the overall context is to interpret something out of context. By not recognizing how quatrains are linked by one word ("*vierge*"), and the context of that linkage is found in the repeating words, like "*fer*," poor conclusions are reached.

When "*fer*" was seen, in quatrain III-84, as explaining why "one alone not will remain," a condition stated in the secondary theme, a colon was found at the end of that theme line, just as line two in quatrain IV-35 ends with a colon. In quatrain III-84, line four not only added supporting details to that secondary theme, but also clarified that desolation state by stating, "*Par fer*," or "By weapons." Here, quatrain IV-35 is clarified by the word immediately following the colon, in line three, by stating "*Fouldre à fer*," or Lightning in weapons." This is context that expands the story while developing the plot further.

A Spear of Gold with A Point of Fire

When one connects the context of Rome being under attack and "desolated," this quatrain, linked together by the use of "*viegre*," is now clarifying the "weapons" are coming from the sky, as streaking bolts of "light," which quickly strike (all descriptive terms of "lightning"). The capitalization of "*Fouldre*," meaning a powerful "Lightning," linking to "*à fer*," meaning "in weaponry," is then comparable to the capitalization of "*Par*," meaning an important means "Through" which "weaponry" is deployed. This makes it possible to understand the context of "By weapon," where a capitalized preposition transfers importance to the following noun as the use of an important "Weapon." This is then furthered in context to be a "weapon with Lightning" ("*Fouldre à fer*" in reverse), or an important (capitalization) form of "Lighting in (a) weapon."

When one sees the context of quatrain III-84 linking to quatrain IV-35, then line one here can be seen as introducing "There light consumed" ("*La feu estainct*") matches "There great city" ("*La grand cité*") in that previous quatrain's main theme. When read as, "THE light" (capitalization of an article transferring that importance to the following noun, as "the Light"), this is explained in line three (the supporting details line for line one) as "Lightning" replacing the "Light" of Rome. That becomes a clarification (colon use) for how "extinction" or "utter destruction" (translation variations of "*estainct*") will be administered, via "The [Lightning] fire" (as from "*La [Fouldre] feu*") coming "in (a) weapon." This yields more detail when read as "[Lightning] by Weapon," using the description in quatrain III-84 with terms in quatrain IV-35, as "*[Fouldre] par Fer.*"

To see the main theme stating "There light extinguished," where the Vatican is a place for the "Light" of Christianity, served by "nuns," paralleling how Rome was the place of the temple to Vesta and her eternal flame, tended by Vestal "Virgins," the cause is then stated in the second half of line one. Knowing that attacks will come, "By weaponry," striking like major bolts of "Lightning."

This can be seen as the punishment of Jove, the Roman god (a.k.a. Juppiter [or Jupiter]), who had the epithet Fulgurator,[108] which is the Latin-based word that is at the root of the Old French term "*Fouldre.*"[109] As the god of all changes in the heaven, he had the power over lightning.[110] Due to Rome being the target in quatrain III-84 ("The great city will be quite desolated"), seeing the importance (capitalization) of "Lightning" as the power of a Roman god helps identify the place of attack in quatrain IV-35 ("There more great part").

Seeing this support for naming Rome at the beginning of line three, one can then look back to line two and see how "*la bende nouvelle*" also has that lean. The word "*bende*" is not French, but rather Italian, as the feminine plural of the word "*benda,*" meaning, "bandages."[111] In Randle Cotgrave's 1611 French-English Dictionary, a listing of "*bende*" referred one to look up "*bande,*" which includes the meaning, "a fascia, swath-band, or tie-band for a wound." Thus, the spelling "*bende,*" as Italian, is another hint that a quatrain about "virgins" is leaning one towards Rome, where "There more great part" will be found "with the bandages fresh."

Because a "bandage" is a sign of a wound underlying, and "Lightning in weapon" would create wounds, one can then see the French word "*bande*" being defined by Cotgrave as, "a band or company of soldiers'

---

108 From the website mythindex.com, under the heading "JUPITER, Roman Mythology Index. (http://www.mythindex.com/roman-mythology/J/Jupiter.html)
109 The etymology is stated to be from the Latin Vulgate word "fulgere," from classical Latin, "fulgur." From the website Wiktionnaire. (http://fr.wwiktionnaire.org/wiki/foudre) The word "fulgur" means, "a flash or stroke of lightning." From the University of Notre Dame, Latin Word Lookup. (http://catholic.archives.nd.edu/cgi-bin/lookup.pl?stem=ful&ending=)
110 From the website mythindex.com, under the heading "JUPITER, Roman Mythology Index. (http://www.mythindex.com/roman-mythology/J/Jupiter.html)
111 From the website Wiktionnaire, under searches for "bende" and "benda." (http://fr.wiktionnaire.org/wiki/bende and http://fr.wiktionnaire.org/wiki/benda)

a troupe or crew; a faction or combination of any other persons." This then identifies those who are opposite of "The more great" ("*La plus grand*"), as "the faction recent" ("*la bende nouvelle*"). The colon following this statement of a "band of soldiers rare," causing "bandage fresh," is clarified by the statement "Lightning in weapon." These are then the enemies of Christians, where "There more lofty part" is in Italy, just outside Rome in Vatican City.

To more specifically state the "weapon" containing important (capitalization) "Lightning," following a comma one finds the word "lance." This is a type of "spear," or "a weapon consisting of a long shaft with a sharply pointed end."[112] While this was a common "weapon" in the 16th century, one should be able to see the shape of a "lance" more commonly found in modern "weaponry," as that of missiles and rocket. Instead of a pointed head, tipped with "iron" (literal translation of "*fer*"), these now are identified as warheads. Still, there is the possibility of "lance" having its medieval meaning still in place in the 21st century.

The second half of line three states, "lance them only ones King will be guarding," which (when said all at once) is a symmetrical indication of major "Lightning" opposing a wooden "lance" as "weapons" in a battle. This brings to mind the presence of the Pontifical Swiss Guard, which has officially guarded Vatican City since 1506.[113] Besides swords, this military presence is known to stand at gates and doorways with spears, called "partisans."[114] This volunteer military is defined as, "A small force maintained by the Holy See, it is responsible for the safety of the Pope, including the security of the Apostolic Palace. The Swiss Guard serves as the *de facto* military of Vatican City."[115]

Despite the advancements the Swiss Guard has incorporated into its "guarding" techniques, having been lately trained in modern small arms use and non-armed defensive skills, one can still sum up the military defense of Vatican City as being a "lance." That is the "spear" held by "those only ones" who "will be guarding" the "Pope" (translation possibility of "*Roy*"), should it come under bombardment attack. The Italian military

---

112 Definition of "spear," by the website Free Dictionary by Farlex online, source: Collins English Dictionary – Complete and Unabridged, Harper Collins (last 2003), used here by Fair Use standards. (http://www.thefreedictionary.com/spear)

113 From the article on Wikipedia, entitled "Swiss Guard." (http://en.wikipedia.org/wiki/Swiss_Guard#History)

114 From the article on Wikipedia, entitled "Partisan (weapon)." (http://en.wikipedia.org/wiki/Partisan_(weapon))

115 From the article on Wikipedia, entitled "Swiss Guard." (http://en.wikipedia.org/wiki/Swiss_Guard#History)

will not be found "There," meaning "the only ones," weapons related, which "will be guarding" that "King, "will be wooden spears."

Since Rome is assumed to be the general target of attack, perhaps it is coincidental that *Santa Maria della Vittoria* (Our Lady of Victory) is a minor basilica in that city, which houses the sculture by Bernini, depicting the *Ecstacy of Saint Teresa*. Teresa of Avila was a Spanish mystic and Carmelite "nun" who experienced the Holy Spirit entering her in a vision of an encounter with an Angel. The Angel pierced her heart with a golden spear, and this encounter is that depicted by the artist Bernini.

Due to quatrain IV-35 being focused on Rome, where "nuns will be revealing" (alternate translation of "*vierges trahiront*"), and where the betrayal of "virgins" will come via "Lightning at head of a lance" (alternate translation of "*Fouldre à fer*," it is worth reviewing what Teresa said about this Angel with a "spear."

She wrote:

> "I saw in his hand a long spear of gold, and at the iron's point there seemed to be a little fire. He appeared to me to be thrusting it at times into my heart, and to pierce my very entrails; when he drew it out, he seemed to draw them out also, and to leave me all on fire with a great love of God. The pain was so great, that it made me moan; and yet so surpassing was the sweetness of this excessive pain, that I could not wish to be rid of it."[116]

Certainly, in this explanation, the words "spear," "iron point," and "fire" are relative to the use of "*lance*," "*fer*," and "*feu*" in quatrain IV-35. Saint Teresa was one of the Carmelite "nuns," and the ecstacy she experienced can be seen as a "virgin violated" (from quatrain III-84), due to the pain she reportedly experienced from the penetration of the shaft. The word "*lance*," when read with an accent mark above the last "e," becomes the past participle of the verb "*lancer*," meaning, "thrust through" and "pierced." Teresa experienced this activity. Thus, this quatrain tells of an unrecognized prophet telling how pain from spears should be spiritually experienced, as the soul being satisfied by nothing less that God.

The Vatican should know this well. Instead, the betrayal of the "virgins"

---

[116] From the Wikipedia article, "Ecstacy of Saint Teresa," under the subheading, "Sculptural group and its setting." http://en.wikipedia.org/wiki/Ecstacy_of_Saint_Teresa

will be rooted more from a lust for the material of the "spear," gold, rather than a desire for the ecstacy of the Holy Spirit. This is what will be bringing out the Angel Sister Lucia saw holding a "sword" (possible translation of "*fer*") and shouting, "Penance! The physical use of the weaponry of war is foreseen to be a reality, causing pain and "death" (alternate translation of "*feu*").

The Union of Tuscany & Corsica

Line three does not end with any punctuation, meaning that line four is a direct continuation of the statement, "lance them sole ones will be protecting." This then leads to the capitalized word "*Etrusque*," which translates as, "an inhabitant of Etruria" (an "Etruscan"), which is the region of Italy known as Tuscany. The definition of "*Etrusque*," as an "inhabitant," allows this word to link quatrain IV-35 to quatrain III-84, where line two states," *Des habitans un seul ny demoura*," saying, "From the inhabitants one alone not will remain." When one reads in line three of quatrain IV-35, where it states, "*les seulz*," translating as, "them only ones," a connection is made, "Of the inhabitants" will be "them only ones." This makes the "one alone" be an important statement about an "inhabitant of Tuscany," an "Etruscan," who "will not remain" there. The context of two quatrains combine to suggest not only an important desertion by one, but also that not one in all of Tuscany will remain there.

While "Etruscan" is a proper noun, capitalized naturally, the French can use a lowercase spelling to indicate the culture surrounding the "Etruscan" people, such that an individual inhabitant of Tuscany is not necessarily the primary focus in line four. The capitalization can be showing the importance of a region (and culture) that is a "part" of Italy, on the same coast as Rome (just to the north). This is then an important indicator of the Italian defense of Rome and Vatican City, as that which "will be protecting" (alternate translation of "*garderont*") the culture of Christianity, Italy, and Western Europe (all those "parts great"), located physically in the Italian region of Tuscany, where Florence, Siena, Arezzo, Lucca, and Pisa are located. Each of those places can be identified as "Etruscan."

Following the identification of an "Etruscan" focus on the "only ones" who will be defending" (alternative translation of "*gardeont*") the "Pope" (alternate translation of "*Roy*"), is an ampersand. That symbol acts as a signal for something important to follow. The word following is "*Corse.*"

The word "*Corse*" can be read as "*la Corse*," meaning "Corsica." This is another element of symmetry, where the two words surrounding an ampersand are equally similar (regions of land) and different (Italy and France). In a translation reading "Corsica," one is focusing not on the mainland of Europe or the nation of Italy. One's attention is drawn to a Mediterranean Sea island, one which is "part" of France, while being closer to the coast of Italy than France. As such, the symmetrical focus leads to the place where the Ligurian Sea, the Tyrrhenian Sea, and the Mediterranean Sea all border, the island of Corsica.

Again, in the lowercase, the French word "*corse*" is an indicator of that "Corsican," rather than the island itself. This matches the use of "Etruscan," such that the capitalization leads one to see the importance of "Corsican" culture and nationality, where the "inhabitants" of Corsica are French, Christian, and Western European (another "part" of the "great").

When the ampersand is seen as a major conjunction, joining "Tuscan AND Corsican," one is seeing the defense of Rome and Vatican City as a joint venture between Italians and the French. This is a theme developed in other quatrains, beyond the limitations of the word "*vierge*," which prophesy a time when French troops ("*bande*") will move onto Italian soil, in defense of Italy. This has never happened in history, although the French have fought in places like Tuscany, long ago,[117] when the two nations had been enemies.

The theme supported by "Etruscan & Corsica" is not of a French invasion of Italy, but a joint military action, defensive in nature. It acts as a continuation of "the only ones" who "will be guarding" Italy and the "Pope." Line four of quatrain IV-35 is referencing this theme, as having been an alliance that will be already in place at the time when "spears" will counter "Lightning weaponry." It will be a time when hostilities between nations make danger fill the air. A period of standoff will prevail, with posturing, through unified strength representative of an alliance between France with Italy, designed to prevent war, rather than initiate it. However, without a real feel for aggression, a renewal of what the Nazis called "*Blitzkrieg*" will take the French and Italians completely by surprise ("Lightning war").

---

117   When "*Roy*" is read as an Italian "King," Napoleon was King of Italy as Emperor. Napoleon was of Corsican descent. The "King" of Sardinia, Victor Emmanuel I, had his palace in Turin, in the Piedmont region of the Italian mainland, but was forced out by Napoleon. He would return to Turin in 1814, after Napoleon had been defeated.

Because line four is adding the supporting details to the secondary theme of line two, one can see how "From more great part to there" (possible translation of "*Là plus grand part de là*"), is foretelling of troop movements to Tuscany ("*Etrusque*"), importantly (ampersand use) from France ("*Corse*"). This would be an act like a "bandage" (translation of "*bende*" as "*bande*"), which would be "unheard of before" (translation of "*nouvelle*"). Additionally, one can see how a "narrow strip" ("*bende*" as "*bande*") "will be guarding" ("*garderont*") the "Pope" ("*Roy*"), between the Tuscan mainland and the island of Corsica. That "band" is called the Tyrrhenian Sea.

That sea also can be seen as a "gorge" or "canyon" (translations of "*gorge*") between the central mountains of Italy (the Apennines) and the mountains that form the island chain of Corsica, Sardinia, and Sicily. This makes the water between the "throat" or "bottom of the mouth" (translations of "*gorge*") the channel through which ships must pass in order to reach the "breast" or "bosom" (alternate translations of "*gorge*") of Italy, which is Rome.

When this water course is seen as an important area "defending" the "Pope," through which French troops would sail to Italy and enter into Tuscany, one can then see "*Corse*" differently. Following an ampersand (denoting importance) and being capitalized (importance), the word "*Corse*" can be seen as the third person singular form of the verb "*corser*," meaning "to spice up, to increase."

In Old French, the meaning of "*corser*" was "to embrace, or to take hold of." The past participle is formed by simply adding an accent mark, as "*Corsé*," such that "*Corse*" shows a build-up of military strength in Tuscany, where French troops have embraced those of Italy. This, again, is a stop-gap measure, a "bandage" on a wound that will have already occurred. As a show of strength (the importance of ampersand introduction and capitalization), "they" will be "the only ones defending" the "Pope."

The problem with this act of unity, where two "parts great" join in defense, is highlighted by the comma after "*Corse*." This denotes a separation of time, after Tuscany has been "Increased," then "from darkness" (translation of "*de nuict*") the attacks of "Lightning" will occur. The sea will provide the place for naval assaults by missiles (implied by "*lance*"), which will cut the "throat" of this "Increased" defensive effort, like with the "blade of a sword" (translation of "*allumelle*").

The indication coming from, "the only ones Pope will be guarding" ("*les seulz Roy garderont*"), is that "only" Italian forces will be left to defend Rome. The weak link in the chain of command of this alliance becomes that place least expected to be attacked. Rome may be assumed to have an international defense against attack, as its mystique as a renowned city. As "part" of the "great" cities, like Paris and New York, even Mecca, it may be thought to be beyond one's approach, through hostility. The result will be as if a wooden "spear" were up against a bolt of "Lightning."

This analysis is supported by many other quatrains, making it possible to see the words of quatrain IV-35 add to and support that story line. The key to remember is the word "*Roy*," where neither republic, Italy or France, has a "King." This makes the word indicate a "Pope," a translation consistently found supported in the context of other quatrains, When this is combined with the use of "*vierges*," the "King" can only be Christ, if not the "Pope."

This translation is also supported by the preliminary theme, when seen to state a time when "Him" ("*Le*" as a pronoun) will have "extinguished the fire," or "put out the light" (from "*feu estaint*"). When "He" will be found "dead, deceased, and departed" (from "*feu*") having "utterly perished" (from "*estaint*") as a vehicle of Christ (a theme from quatrain III-84), this identifies a Church that has become diametrically opposite of its intended goal.

This means the theme of "guarding" and "Lightning weaponry" will be an eventual result of the Vatican having not acted on the warnings of "virgins," who passed along directions from the Blessed "Virgin." In this way, quatrain IV-35 expands on the story line of Marian apparitions to "virgin," while also expanding on the story line of the fall of the Roman Catholic Church, and the Western world's identity as "great."

Chapter 8
The Fifth "*Vierge*" Quatrain

Quatrain VI-35

In the fifth quatrain stating the word "*vierge*," the 35th in Centurie VI, Nostradamus wrote the only capitalized version in *The Prophecies*. The word is found at the end of line two. The whole quatrain follows, first in Old French and then in my English translation.

> *Pres de Rion, & proche à blanche laine,*
>
> *Aries, Taurus, Cancer, Leo, la Vierge:*
>
> *Mars, Jupiter, le Sol ardera grand plaine,*
>
> *Boys & cites, lettres cachez au cierge.*
>
> ---
>
> Nearby with Black, & neighboring to white wool,
>
> Aries, Taurus, Cancer, Leo, the Virgin:
>
> War, Expansion, him Sun will burn great plain,
>
> Spear & warned to appear ones, letters hidden ones from the ceremonial church candle.

Quatrain VI-35 is a popular one, as it attracts those interested in astrology. One can see verbiage relative to astrological signs filling up line two; and in line three is found the names of two planets and the Sun. Due to this focus on celestial entities, the main theme often has been translated as if it tells of the constellation Orion, in the Milky Way. However,

Chapter 8: Quatrain VI-35

popular translations like that say nothing of value, as far as meaning is concerned, regardless of how much the words of this quatrain can catch the eye of astrology students.

My translation, on the other hand, makes understanding possible, while still being of interest to those studying astrology. In this vein of interest, "*la Vierge*" is how the French designate the astrological sign Virgo (the Virgin), and that reading would naturally follow a statement that included other signs of the zodiac. However, there is little gained from that translation.

There are two word in "*la Vierge*," which means it should not be read simply as Virgo. Even though that translation would match the other signs listed, the use of French is a change of language, from the Latin spelling that are naming the astrological signs, "Aries, Taurus, Cancer, Leo." I do not make that translation because "*la Vierge*" (even in the lower case, "*la vierge*") is also how the French identify "the Virgin" Mary. By leaving the wording intact, as "the Virgin," it is possible to see how line two clearly ends with a word with at least two reading possibilities.

That is important, as a problem arises when one reads line two simply as the names of zodiac signs. When read all at once, line two means very little, other than a statement of timing. The timing is indicated by the Sun's yearly movement into (and through) each sign, as seen from a geocentric perspective (from earth looking out), where the constelations become a fixed backdrop for the earth's circling of the sun.

Around March 23, the sun crosses the equator (the Vernal Equinox), it astrologically reaches the cusp of "Aries," staying in that sign until it leaves and enters Taurus, around April 20. Around June 21, the sun enters Cancer, and stays there until entering Leo, around July 23. The sun leaves Leo for Virgo around August 23, and does not leave that sign until around September 22-23. From the information given, this timing of the sun's relationship with the earth (Spring and Summer for the Northern Hemisphere) means nothing more.

As the string of words representative of astrological signs are stated in line two, they must present a secondary theme, one that is relative to the main theme in line one. Additionally, the use of commas creates a series of separation points, such that each word is making its own statement, which needs to be understood more than simply known what days mark each sign. Each word is also capitalized, making each one-word statement important; and each word is Latin, although accepted French representing astrological signs.

Beyond those obvious clues, one sign is missing in this series of zodiac signs (Gemini), which makes a statement in itself. One must understand why that omission was made. This series of words and commas ends with a colon, meaning that line three is expected to reveal some clarification about the meaning of the French words, "*la Vierge*." This means that for one to understand quatrain VI-35's secondary theme, one needs to examine the other lines and draw that meaning back to words that, on the surface, appear to be only signs of the zodiac.

The main theme states, "*Pres de Rion, & proche à blanche laine*," which basically translates to state, "Near to Rion, & close with white wool". I have underlined "Rion" because it is not a word clearly known, although people have improperly turned this word into Orion, the name of a constellation, named for a Greek mythological hunter. It would make more sense if Rion were read as the Arthurian nemesis to Arthur, King Riense (a.k.a. Rion). There is also a town in the French region Aquitaine, named Rions, but (again) one must be careful adding letters to the words of *The Prophecies*, but neither a mythical king not a French town makes sense in a main theme.

Beyond realizing that a capitalized word needs to be solved, one can see how this main theme is divided into two halves. This is determined by punctuation breaking it in two, but not simply with a comma. One finds a comma-ampersand following "*Rion*," such that an important word ends the first segment of words, and following a break (comma use) importance is stressed (ampersand use), relative to the second segment of words.

In standard syntax, the redundancy of a comma (meaning use of the word "and" was stated by symbol) and an ampersand (a symbol for the word "and") together would indicate an ignorant writer. There are many places where Nostradamus demonstrated his ability to seperate segments with just a comma, or just an ampersand; but there are many times he chose to use this double symbol combination. Knowing the systems of Nostradamus allows one to see how the first half of line one is separate from the second half, allowing the ampersand to introduce the importance of a co-main theme, beginning with the word "*proche*."

Chapter 8: Quatrain VI-35

A two-part main theme was seen in quatrain IV-35 ("*Le feu estaint, les vierges trahiront,*"), but that separation did not include an ampersand. Thus, that quatrain's line one acted as one main theme with two points of focus. Here, however, quatrain VI-35 is stating two main themes, separately but equally in their relationship to one another.

The ampersand makes the first word of the second main theme, "*proche,*" act like a capitalized word, although in the written in the lowercase. This, in effect, makes it match the significance of the first word of line one, the capitalized "*Pres.*" Both "*Pres*" and "*proche*" have similarities in meaning, such that both can translate as "near." Therefore, each co-theme is introduced by words stating the importance of proximity.

The Symmetry of Color

In the systems of Nostradamus, elements of symmetry are important to recognize, especially when the words of a quatrain are unclear or confusing. Whenever an ampersand is present within a line, a condition for symmetry is always present.

In quatrain IV-35, line four had an ampersand between the first two words, with a comma after the second word. The comma separated those two words from the rest of that line. The two words, "*Etrusque & Corse*" were discussed as being symmetrical, as two capitalized words offering similar characteristics (two regions of land), while also offering differences (lands of two different nations).

In the main theme of quatrain VI-35, the comma is between the word "*Rion*" and the word "*proche,*" but an ampersand is also placed in between. The presence of an ampersand between the two words (actually between the comma and "*proche*") severs the direct relationship the two words have. In that way, "*Rion*" and "*proche*" become asymmetrical. However, symmetry still exists, but from one segment of words to the next.

The ampersand then is connecting the two sets of words that surround it. This means that one can look for something that reflects a similarity from one half to the other, or one can look to find something that reflects a complement of a similar generality. As stated, both halves begin with words of similar meaning, such that "*Pres*" means, "near, by, near upon, and almost touching," while "*proche*" means, "near, neighboring, adjoining, and close unto." Still, that similarity seems somewhat lacking, as the color stated in the second half ("*blanche*," meaning "white, or hoary") needs some balance reflected by the words "*de Rion*," which follow the word "*Pres*."

That balance can be seen by turning the unknown word, "*Rion*," into a known word. That is accomplished when one sees the word as a simple anagram, where "simple anagram" is defined as an easily solved letter scramble. While anagram use has to play a role in solving some difficult unknown words found in *The Prophecies*, it should be as a last resort; and is should only be done so an unknown word adds clarity where none existed before.

As such, "*Rion*" can be seen as being a known French word, simply spelled backwards. Just by reversing the order of the letters, the French word "*noiR*" appears. This can then be converted into "*Noir*," so the capitalized letter is maintained in the first position, rather than specific to the "r." The word "*noir*" means, "black, sable, dark, and obscure." That makes "Black & white" become the central focus placed upon two co-themes, with two symmetrical colors surrounding an ampersand.

In the quatrains of *The Prophecies*, not counting this spelling, Nostradamus wrote the word "*noir*" twenty-six times (in variations: masculine, feminine, and plural).[118] Conversely, he wrote the word "*blanc*," or "*blanche*," seventeen times (in the same variations as found for *noir*).[119] This frequency is important to recognize, especially when this work is discussing the importance of the word "*virgin*" (in variations), because it appears seven times in the quatrains (this is the fifth discussed). These frequencies make the combination found in the main theme here important to understand, as Nostradamus wrote words of "color" metaphorically, more than as a literal description of color.[120]

The word "red" (in variations) appears no less than 34 times, making it be a major part of the theme in *Les Propheties*. The colors red, black and white symbolically represent religious beliefs (which will be discussed more latter). As The Prophecies is relative to a future involving religious

---

[118] From the Index of the Centuries by M. Nostradamus, prepared by J. Flanagan, page titled, "N – P Nostradamus Index." (http://alumnus.caltech.edu/~jamesf/nindex/np_index.html)

[119] From the Index of the Centuries of M. Nostradamus, prepared by J. Flanagan, page titled, "B & C – Nostradamus Index." (http://alumnus.caltech.edu/~jamesf/nindex/bc_index.html)

[120] Technically, black and white are not defined as colors, but more a totality of color, such that black is the presence of all color and white is the absence of all color. Paints, chalks, and crayons, of black and white pigmentation, are then used by artists to depict shading (black) and lightening (white).

conflict and persecutions, those colors should be expected to have more presence in the verbiage. As such, "yellow" is the least important color, having only slight religious merit, found written only once (stated in the plural number – "*jaunes*").

Other colors, such as "green" ("*vert*") and "blue" ("*bleu*"), have non-religious purposes, and they also appear infrequently (green – 4; blue – 2).[121] Thus, the frequency of "black" and "white" are to be recognized as regular characters, or major entities, which appear regularly in the story plots. The main theme of quatrain VI-35 is addressing opposite sides of a religious conflict as the co-main theme statements.

With "*Rion*" translated as "*Noir*," some could see a main theme about "Black & white" as being about race; but, while not completely wrong, race is not the primary intent. The use of words of color, in particular "black," "white," "red," and "yellow," denotes those of "religious sects," or groups of people who have the same general beliefs about religion. As such, "black" represents those who follow Islam, and "white" represents those who have Judeo-Christian beliefs. The color "red" denotes those with no religious beliefs, as atheists (in particular the political philosophy associated with Communism); and the color "yellow" denotes those who have polytheistic religious beliefs.

To some extent, a racial comparison can be made between European-descended Christians and the Caucasian race, commonly referred to as "whites." The same comparison cannot be applied to Arabs and Muslims, even though a similarity may be found in finding African Islamists being represented as "black" people. The preponderance of "red" uses in the quatrains shows that race is not the intention of colors, as it is best understood when linked to atheist political views. As such, Communists, of both Russia and China, have been termed "Reds." This acts to lead one away from race in a "Black & white" statement of theme.

When this aspect of color is realized, the first half of the main theme line is stating, "Near to Black." Due to the color associations, the word Islam (a capitalized proper name) can be substituted, making line one begin with a focus that is, "Near to Islam." The word "*Pres*," due to its capitalization, is placing important focus on something that is "Near, By, Close unto," or "Almost touching. " Because proximity is "Near," it is not an

---

[121] Nostradamus also used words that depict the colors "gold," "silver," "brass" [or "bronze"], "gray," "green," "blue" [azure], and "brown," which have metaphorical values that do not primarily pertain to religious beliefs.

actual part of that something, but importantly "Close by." Such importance of proximity can then be seen as a strategic placement. That strategy is then relative "to" (from the preposition "*de*," meaning "of, with, to, and from") something identified as importantly (capitalization) "Black" (when "*Rion*" is read as an anagram for "*Noir*").

There are several ways this can be viewed in order to make an important theme statement make sense. In one sense, the "Black-white" contrast, where "Black" equates to Islam, can place focus on where Islam finds its home base, in the Middle East. This could be a setting such as Saudi Arabia (as it is known today), since Mecca is found there; but it could also be every Muslim nation in that region of the world, where the religion of Islam reigns. That could make line one's initial statement of theme be on the proximity of those "Near to the Middle East," but not part of Islam ("Black"), instead being either Christian or Jewish ("white"). This could infer the presence of Israel in what was Palestine, while also indicating (to a lesser degree) Christian elements in Lebanon, Turkey, and Armenia.

Another place where the same focus can be seen is North Africa, which is Islamic, with the other nations of Africa having an increasing influence of Muslim factions. While there are Christian and Jewish pockets within Africa, those can be considered one with the whole, such that "Near to Islam" is less strategically significant. The importance of being "Near" is better represented by the islands of the Mediterranean and Aegean seas, where Christian settlements in Greece, Cyprus, Crete, Malta, and Sicily are of strategic importance as buffer zones "to" the "Muslim" world. In this way, one sees how those of the "white" world are equal in importance, but separate form the other, while being quite "Near" and "neighboring unto" one another.

This brings back memories of the last quatrain discussed (quatrain IV-35), where the concept of a French military presence was prophesied to enter Italy, as part of an alliance. This has yet to occur, at any time in prior history. The main theme of quatrain VI-35 is now seen to support that alliance, as the French being in Italy would be for strategic purposes. Being "Near to Islam" would be on the peninsula of Italy, including its islands (and the island of France – "Corsica"). That positioning would put a defensive line "Closer unto" any danger that may arise "with North Africa" or "from the Middle East."

From that perspective of a defensive movement, from France into Italy, where the purpose would be to show strength by strategically getting "Close to Muslim" nations, the importance (ampersand placement) is then that those "Black" (Islamists, Middle Eastern Muslims, and/or North African jihadists) will have significantly built up their own strengths "near to white" nations. Each half of the theme is separate, but of equal importance, as one causing the other and one being a reaction to the other. They exist because of each other, and while both are already in proximity to one another, the importance becomes an unnatural closeness, such as would be the French entering Italy to help defend it from attack.

This bring out the importance of understanding the last word of line one, "*laine.*" The word "*laine*" is one of those French words that only has one translation, which is "wool." While there may be some uses that would imply "wool" in various textile applications, it is still understood to be the hair of sheep that has been sheared for that purpose. This singularity of translation becomes important to see "wool" as synonymous with "fleecing," which has a connotation as "fraud." This aspect would be seen in the metaphor, "a wolf wearing sheep's clothing." However, there is another way to look at "*laine.*"

There are instances in the quatrains of *The Prophecies* where the words in print do not have marks that match the proper spelling, either accent marks or apostrophes. Because these instances can only be understood by assuming the marks (adding them to the written word), it is allowable to add marks to achieve understanding, although it is not allowable to remove any marks that do appear in print. Such a possibility comes from the addition of an apostrophe when the written word begins with an "*l,*" "*d,*" or "*s,*" which are commonly abbreviated forms of "*le-la,*" "*de,*" and "*se,*" with the missing vowel replaced by the apostrophe mark. This makes "*laine*" possible to be read as "*l'aîné*" (Old French as *aisné*) or "*le aîné,*" meaning "the oldest" or "the older (brother)."

Regardless of how "*laine*" is read, it becomes relative to the word "*blanche,*" which means, "white." Those who have read the Milky Way into this quatrain have turned "white wool" into a description of our galaxy, which is senseless as a main theme focus. When one puts "white" and "wool" together, one is reminded of the nursery rhyme "Bah, bah, black sheep have you any wool?" This makes "wool" more likely a reference to the animal from which "wool" comes from, which is sheep. This, in turn, can be seen as relative to Christianity, due to pastors and priests being shepherds to their flocks. Again, when "fleece" is seen as "white," in the sense that the robe of a church leader can be seen as one of "white wool," the second half of line one's main theme is focusing importantly on something "close unto with white wool."

According to *Catholic Encyclopedia*, a "pallium" is a vestment mantle made of "white wool" (the part not silk), and the word is defined by the Free Dictionary by Farlex as, "A vestment worn by the pope and conferred by him on archbishops and sometimes on bishops." As such, one can see this having a Christian aspect, as referencing the papacy, due to its leaders wearing garments made from "white wool."

When one sees the same association that the word "white" bears, as Christians in general, the same leadership model is still conveyed when "*laine*" is read as "*l'aîné*." The word tells of "the elder brother," where Christians denote each male as a "brother," with females being "sisters." Since God is the Father of Christ, all Christians are brothers and sisters of Jesus. This would make a leader, such as a pope, be the highest-ranking "brother," as the "elder brother," with Saint Peter being the "oldest brother" of the Roman Catholic Church. This allowance, for a pope to be "the eldest," is then supported through him being described as one who wears vestments of "white wool."

Christianity and Latin

This aspect of "wool" and an "elder" ends the main theme line, with a comma at the end separating it from the secondary theme of line two. When one sees the secondary theme line stating "*Aries, Taurus, Cancer, Leo, la Vierge*," the presence of five capitalized words must be recognized as a series (each followed by commas of separation) of important stand-alone statements. Those statements are made from words that are readily recognized as astrological, but one must also see that the names of the first four signs are Latin. The use of Latin in *The Prophecies* is a direction to seek a higher level of meaning, rather than the mundane and normal. Such a higher level of meaning is then religious in nature, because Latin is the official language of the Roman Catholic Church.

When Latin is recognized, the capitalized words of line two can then be translated to state, "Ram, Bull, Crab, Lion, the Virgin" (with the French of "*la Vierge*" remaining the same as previously translated). Immediately, the first word, "Ram," can be seen as a continuation of the sheep theme of "wool," while also being an important (capitalization) statement about the leader of a flock. This could make "Aries" morph into meaning a "Pope," who would be one wearing the "white wool" of a pallium. This interpretation would link a religious theme to the two co-themes of line one, where "Black" and "white" are symbolic of the religions of "Islam" and "Christianity."

When the first word of line two establishes the direction and focus of the line two theme, the importance (capitalization) of "Ram" is then followed by an important "Bull" (the translation of the Latin word "*Taurus*"). Still, "Taurus" is the proper name for a mountain range in Southern Turkey, and that capitalized spelling, in Latin, can be seen as identifying that mountain range (moreso than the astrological sign). This means Turkey, or Asia Minor is "Neighboring with Black" (the Middle East) and "close by to white" (partially in Europe), as Israel and ancient settlements of Christians. This proximity goes along with the history of Christians in Armenia, who are part of Turkey's legacy (in a negative way).

From this ability to see "Taurus" as a reference to Turkey, one can then see how "Close" to Europe has a symbolic link to a "Bull." This comes from recognizing there is a mythological way to see "*Taurus*" as representing the European Union.

That comes from the story of Zeus being attracted to the Phoenician princess Europa. In order to abduct Europa, Zeus appeared in the form of a "white bull," which caused her to want to sit on its back. The "white bull" then swan to the island of Crete, where Europa became the first queen of that island. Crete is "Close by" Turkey, while being in Europe. From this story, the whole of Europe identifies with this connection to the supreme god, Zeus, and to this day the "white bull" is a symbol of the EU.

The European Union Residence Permit Emblem

From the Wikipedia article "Symbols of Europe" Permission to copy is granted by the GNU Free Documentation License

From the secondary theme being established as a series begun, from the Pope of Rome (the "Ram" of a Christian flock), to all of Europe (the "white Bull" and the Europa mythology), the movement indicates a spread of influence. This makes "Cancer" be seen two ways. One is as the zodiac sign that sets a timeframe between late-June and late-July, when the Sun enters "Cancer." The capitalization can then indicate an important entity that has a "Cancer" birth date. The second way is to read the word "cancer" as capitalized for importance. This word has a definition (from its root, the Greek word "*karkinos*," meaning "crab") as a "creeping tumor." The capitalization is an indication that the spread of influence has become importantly diseased.

When I state that "Cancer" can be seen as an astrological identifier for an entity, this is reading it as the astrological sun sign of an individual. Cancer is the sun sign reference for birthdate, such that the capitalization is not placing importance on the personification of the Latin name for a zodiac constellation, but on an important individual known as being born under that sign. On the grandest scale, an individual is a nation born. One such important nation, known to have July 4, 1776 as its birthday (the sun in the sign of "Cancer") is the United States of America. This makes the reference in line two extend the spread of influence from Europe to the New World of Nostradamus.

In *The Prophecies*, the word "Aries" appears in the poems four times, one here in quatrain VI-35. The word "Taurus" appears three times, again with one in this quatrain. The word "Leo" appears six times in the verses, with another six uses of "lion (s)" also found. The word "Cancer" appears seven times in the quatrains.[122] Additionally, the word "Cancer" is found in the letter of preface to *The Prophecies*, which adds significance as that letter outlines the storyline of the whole of the quatrains.

Because this work is focusing on the seven times "*Vierge*" (capitalized in quatrain VI-35) is found written, the multiplicity can be seen as placing focus on major characters in the stories. The United States is a major player, as in Europe ("Bull") and the Vatican ("Ram"). By "Cancer" being mentioned eight times overall, one certainly must realize that the United States was born with the Sun in that astrological sign.

When one sees "Cancer" as an importantly (capitalization) spreading dis-

---

122   All numbers referenced from the website "Alphabetical Nostradamus Index," which is an Index of the Centuries of M. Nostradamus, prepared by J. Flanagan, posted on the Caltech alumnus website. (www.alumnus.caltech.edu/~jamesf/nindex/indextop.html)

ease, reaching out like the legs of a "Crab," America's history can be seen as likewise slowly spreading. It has grown from an original thirteen colonies, to a continental 48-states. All of that growth took land away from those who with lived off the earth (Native Americans), thus the spread of that individual "Cancer" killed all along its path. The same growth has spread to additional territories, with some being added as states (as of now - Alaska and Hawaii). There is a tendril of grasp in still more possessions held in the Caribbean Sea and Pacific Ocean, with America's influence felt around the globe.

There are certain aspects of the symbolism behind the sign of the "Crab," which identifies America as hard-shelled, striking out with a big pincher, while worrying about its soft inner self. Nationality and issues of heritage are usually important for "Cancer" natives, and America likes to advertise itself as the land of the free and home of the brave. Somewhat in this regard, the story of *The Prophecies* is focusing on this spread of the United States, defending its actions as important for national security, but more so as a global power. Its international presence, while argued for worthwhile purposes, has not always been seen as welcomed.[123]

As far as the growth of Christianity is concerned, following line one's co-themes of Christianity and Islam, followed by line two's beginning with the "Ram" who is "Pope," America represents a "Cancer" that takes pride in its separation from the Roman Catholic Church. America's history has purposefully crept away from Rome's religion, and the influence of the "Pope," who was known to have had too much influence over governments and rulers. This should be viewed as a major "Cancer" upon Christianity, despite its claim as being the most Christian nation on earth. That will be the key "Cancer" that spreads into those lands of Islam, as the United States will enter by force, voicing the greatness of democracy and freedom, but being identified as a Christian Crusader.

Seeing how repetitiveness is vital to realize, the focus placed on "Leo," following "Cancer," makes an important "Lion" be relative and subsequent to the "Crab," as a "Cancer" upon Christianity. Such an important "Lion" should then be seen as the nation most symbolized by that creature in heraldry. That country is Great Britain, the father of America. The "Cancer," as a disease, can then be seen as linking to that heritage, although each nation would become important, individually.

---

[123] The growth of the United States has a long line of forced participation, from the American Civil War, to the Indian Wars, and military occupations due to other wars. These, too, were not as welcomed as American History would have one believe.

When this series of important individual identities is seen leading to "Leo," as the "Lion" nation, the secondary theme is developing a cast of characters that relate to the main theme of "Close unto with Black AND near to white wool." This can now be seen as developing a history of Europe, led by a Roman pope, as Christians with strong ties to the Holy Land surrounding Jerusalem. That history can be seen as dating back to the first Crusades, where European knights ventured into Arab land to capture and hold the Holy City. These war efforts made some wealthy (the Church of Rome and various orders of knights, especially the Knights Templar), and somewhat fueled westward exploration, as a search for new riches. That, in addition to the rise of philosophical thoughts that led Christians further away from Rome's influence, gave rise to the greatest Christian warrior nation (the United States of America), who would follow in the footsteps of the father (Great Britain). America's "Lion" father would be firmly entrenched in world affairs, including those concerning the Middle East and its Islamic beliefs.

All individual histories of each capitalized word, in Latin, show the religious (Christian) development in each element. The progression from Rome (the Pope "Ram") to all of Continental Europe (the "Bull" of Europa), then the colonization of the West (the "Cancer" U.S.A.), and the Great British Empire's influence around the world (the "Lion" of England), is a representation of the spread of Christianity. By the time the "Lion" has grown to an empire, the main theme is reflected in the British control of Muslims and the creation of the new State of Israel ("Near with Muslim & neighboring to white").

It is important to remember that line two offers a series of capitalized words, with the first four being Latin words. This takes the meaning well beyond the astrological name of signs and the simple translations of the Latin to English (or any other language). Each word brings forth symbolism that is associated with "Ram," with "Bull," with "Crab," with "Lion," and with "Virgin." This means that a great number of thoughts can be expressed simply by placing individual focus on each word. Additionally, each word can be seen as having multiple symbolic uses in a religious context, in particular those of Christianity, Judaism, and Islam.

All of the references to the land creatures have associations with biblical passages, which has allegory and metaphor meaning, beyond the literal. What must be seen as the rule of guidance, as a systemic element required for understanding *The Prophecies*, is the order of presentation,

Chapter 8: Quatrain VI-35

where the use of commas separates each, such that order represents a flow of sequence. One's full scope of symbolic meaning leads to the next, establishing a relationship pertaining to the secondary theme, while also being relative to the main theme of Christianity and Islam.

With this in mind, one can see how quite a lot can be written about the possibilities that are offered in line two of quatrain VI-35. It may be possible that everything is true and, as truth, adds much depth of understanding to the total meaning of this verse. Since the focus of my work here is not my intent to present every possible interpretation of line two, I will pare the possibilities down to a perspective relative to "*Vierge*" as the "Virgin" Mary. Because a historic timeline can extend back to the first Christians in Rome, the point is to see how a Christian theme can be read into line two here. Thus, the line begins by focusing on a "Ram," a protector of a flock of sheep, and the ending focusing on "the Virgin," the protector of the Church of Rome, where the "Ram" sits.

The end focus of line two is "the Virgin," with "*la*" being transformed to "*là*," making the last segment state "there Virgin." In either case, the importance (capitalization) is the Blessed "Virgin," the mother of Christ and the protector of her son's church. This means that all of the apparitions of her have all occurred in Christian nations. The first in Central America (Mexico), then under Spanish Catholic control, with the others recognized by Rome as being in Western Europe (France, Belgium, and Portugal) and Ireland. This means the sequence developed in line one leads to a focus on the warnings of Mary.

Because "*Vierge*" is the only capitalized use in all of *The Prophecies*, it acts as more than the appearance of the Blessed "Virgin" to a series of youths. Because it is a capitalized word in French, breaking a string of words in Latin, it places focus on France as a Catholic nation, one where multiple Marian apparitions have occurred. Her appearances in Belgium have been in the parts where French is the official language. Because Nostradamus was French, the secondary theme can be seen as leading one towards the divine prophecies of the one whose Nostradamus' name honors (Our Lady). As such, Rome (the "Ram"), Europe (the "Bull"), America (the "Cancer" nation), England (the "Lion"), and France ("there" where the "Virgin" appeared) are targets of the danger warning that came from "the Virgin" (all Christian nations whose people need to repent).

The secondary theme line ends with a colon following "*la Vierge*." This means a clarification or example will be found in line three, where the first capitalized word a direct continuation from the colon.

Line three, which systemically supports the main theme statement directly, supports the issue of "Black & white," while also making "*la Vierge*" (and the rest of line two) make more sense. As such, line three states, "*Mars, Jupiter, le Sol ardera grand plaine,*" where it must be recognized that "*Mars*" and "*Jupiter*" are Roman gods, with "*Sol*" the Latin word for "Sun." While all those words are Latin, words that have been absorbed into the French language, the words "*mars*" and "*sol*" are French, unconnected to those Latin roots. Because there are three capitalized words, each is addressing a significant issue, and when Latin is seen as the base language, that significance bears the higher meaning supporting a religious theme.

Wanderers on the Solar Plain

Due to both Latin and French being sources of meaning, line three can be translated several ways. I have presented line three as stating, "War, Expansion, him Sun will burn great plain," where "*le*" is read as a pronoun. The same words can also be seen as stating, "Weapon, Justice, the Land will be inflamed great flat." In this translation is found astrological metaphors for the planets "Mars" and "Jupiter." The metaphor allows the statement to make sense, as symbolism can greatly expand the translation possibilities. I will explain some of this as I get to those references; but, in the mean time, it is important to go one word (or segment) at a time and develop this clarification of "the Virgin" carefully.

As a clarification for "*la Vierge*," following the colon at the end of line two, "*Mars*" must be understood as a Latin word first. The Romans called their god of agriculture and war, "*Mars*." Thus, the word (in lowercase Latin) means "War." The capitalization raises the importance of "war" to a major state of "War." The religious elevation makes this be seen as "Holy War." As a clarification of "there Virgin," where "*la Vierge*" is referencing the apparition of the Blessed "Virgin" in Fatima, Portugal, "War" can be seen. Sister Lucia wrote that "the Virgin" was accompanied by, "an Angel with a flaming sword in his left hand; flashing, it gave out flames that looked as though they would set the world on fire."

In that statement, one must recognize that in Old French the word "*mars*" bore the alchemic meaning of "iron," the metal from which "weapons" were made. Thus, "a flaming sword" would be an important (capitalization) "Weapon" that "will burn." Thus, from "the Virgin" is a warning that is double-edged. It states to the Church, "Use the flaiming Sword of Christ to defeat communism, or have the Weapons of Satan defeat you."

When "*Mars*" is seen as a capitalized version of the French word "*mars*," as meaning a major form of "Iron," the metal, one must be reminded of the use of line three in quatrain IV-35. That line stated, "*Fouldre à fer, lance les seulz Roy garderont*," which can translate to say, "Lightning in iron, spear them only ones King will be guarding." The word "*fer*" also states the metal "iron," which symbolically is stated as "weapon." In that statement, there was a connection to "Lightning," as found in the capitalized word "*Fouldre*." This is important as "*foudre*" was also found in line three of quatrain III-44 ("*Le foudre à vierge sera si malefique*") and it has been discussed how the Roman god "Jupiter" was known as the "Fulgurator," as an epitaph for Jove's use of a "Lightning" bolt as a weapon.[124]

This becomes important because "*Mars*," after the separation of a comma, is followed by the word "*Jupiter*." The letter "J" was not commonly used in Old French, as it is today. This means the actual spelling in *The Prophecies* and in the 1611 Old French dictionary was "*Iupiter*," with "J" represented by an "I." Both the French and Latin spelling for Jupiter show it spelled with an "I," with Latin containing a double "p," as "*Iuppiter*." The meaning of all spellings focuses on the "Roman supreme god"[125] of mythology, with the French word including its alchemical metal connection, as "tin." Because line three, here in quatrain VI-35, means little when translated and interpreted as "Jupiter" (the god) or "Tin" (the metal) a symbolic translation makes more sense.

This is where "Jupiter" should be seen as an astrological statement, where the planet represents metaphor of human life, more than as a physical body orbiting the Sun. Beyond seeing "Jupiter" as a follow-up to "War" or "Weapon," as "Lightning" (the "Weapon" of "Jove"), the astrological shows how this "War" will be followed by an "Expansion" of significance. This is because astrology sees "Jupiter" as the planet representing "growth, expansion, and abundance," where there is motivation to extend beyond one's normal limits. When this metaphor is capitalized

---

124   Original reference is found on page 70 of this text. From the website mythindex.com, under the heading "JUPITER, Roman Mythology Index. (http://www.mythindex.com/roman-mythology/J/Jupiter.html)
125   From the University of Notre Dame "Latin Dictionary and Grammar Aid," on the web page "Latin Word Lookup." (http://catholic.archives.nd.edu/cgi-bin/lookup.pl?stem=jup&ending=)

as of significant importance, one see how "War" and "Weapon" use will be seen as breaking all limitations placed on their use prior. It represents an "Expansion" of major proportions, with a "Spread" that will be well beyond any prior history.

Certainly, nuclear "Weapons" presently represent those of the greatest scope of danger and fear, such that negotiated limitations have been placed upon their reductions, testing, and who may develop them in the future. This means that "Jupiter" represents a "Wealth" to those possessing them, which is another symbolic meaning behind the planet "Jupiter," as it generally symbolizing "Good luck" and "Wealth." This is key to understanding because when the Soviet Union dissolved, those regions and new nations possessing nuclear "Weapons" were in need of economic assistance for survival.

There were reports of missing nuclear arms in all the confusion created by the transition from captive to free governments, with record keeping being a low priority. After some stability was gained, the danger existed that newly freed poor nations would use their nukes to attract capital investments. Those who would seek to purchase those "Weapons" would be suddenly finding the "Luck" changing in their favor. One such country is Iran, whose public pursuit of nuclear power has caused relations between them and the West to be strained further.

The concept of "Justice" is another important metaphor for "Jupiter." The planet is astrologically seen as ruling both the ninth and twelfth houses, which are the two areas of life where religion is most relevant. Thus, "Jupiter" represents God (12th house), the metaphysical, and Temple, the physical, where a king (or pope) metes judgment, based on the Law. Following the concept of "Weapons" and/or "War" is then the concept of "Justness" and/or "Judgement." This conveys a wide scope of meaning, all of which can directly apply to the main theme of "Black & white," "Islam & Christianity."

For whatever symbolic interpretations that come from the astrological and mythological association coming from "Jupiter," a comma separates it from the next segment of words, such that it stands alone as a one-word statement (separated by a comma from the first word of line three, "*Mars*," itself a one-word statement). The words that follow begin with "*le Sol*," which can be translated as "the Sun." This translation then becomes primarily Latin (although French does allow for that meaning),

Chapter 8: Quatrain VI-35

because the personified (capitalized) presentation meant the Sun god of the ancient Romans.[126] This has a Christian meaning, relative to *The Prophecies* use of Latin and the symbolism present throughout the story lines.

In the quatrains, Nostradamus wrote the word "*sol*" twenty-three times (in lower and uppercase).[127] In addition, he wrote the French word most commonly used to mean "sun" ("*soleil*") a total of thirteen times, and the word "*solaire*," which can mean "sun," another four times.[128] The "Sun" has to be seen as a counter to the "Moon," and these two celestial orbs are the matches for the color usage of "Black" (Moon) and white ("Sun"). Thus, when one sees "the Sun" as the translation, especially here in line three of quatrain VI-35, where line three is adding supporting information to the main theme in line one, the reference is to Christ. That is enhanced further when "*Sol*" is seen as Latin, which brings out a higher meaning in interpretation.

The color usage of "Black & white," where color is the wrong term because the words are representative of the absence of light ("Black") and the presence of light ("white"), means light is the key point of the symbolisms of Islam and Christianity. Much can be said along these lines, but it can be summed up by the *Holy Bible* calling Jesus "the light and the way," just as "the Sun" lights a clear path to follow. Conversely, "Black" and darkness, symbolized by the Moon's dimmer reflection of light, becomes the symbol for Islam. This symbolism is reflected in many flags of Islamic nations.

This means line three's use of "the Sun" can be equally relative to a statement about "him Christ." This translation adds clarification to "Ram," the initial focus of line two, as "him" (the pronoun "*le*") who is the greatest (capitalization) "Christian" in Rome (the Latin use of "*Sol*"). Since "Ram" follows "there Virgin," the transitionmis then to whom the message of Fatima was sent. It was for "him" to act from faith in "Christ."

Still, the word "*sol*" is a common French word, which primarily means, "the soil, ground, land, foundation, or bottom of a place; the floor or low-

---

126   Per the Wikipedia article entitled "Sol (mythology)." The god named "Sol" was most frequently called "Sol Invictus" (the Unconquered Sun), but was later associated with the god Janus. (http://en.wikipedia.org/wiki/Sol_(mythology))
127   From the website "Index of the Centuries of Nostradamus," prepared by J. Flanagan, under the heading, "Alphabetical Index of Nostradamus," and sub-headed "Q-S Nostradamus Index." (http://alumnus.caltech.edu/~jamesf/nindex/qs_index.html)
128   Ibid.

139

est story of a house," but also "sun." In a series that begins with "War" or "Weapon," which is then shown to be an "Expansion" on "War" and/or a "Growth" of "Weaponry" capacity, it follows that a statement is made that begins focusing on "the Lowest level." That can then be seen as a statement of who will possess this military power. It will be a most important (capitalization) minor power (such as Iran, North Korea, Pakistan, Venezuela, etc.) who will then possess the major "Foundation" ("*Sol*") "Weapon" ("*Mars*") enabling "him" (a leader of said power) to attack an important (capitalization) "Land" ("*Sol*").

As a clarification for the symbols of line two ("Ram" – Vatican; "Bull" - Europe; "Cancer" – USA; and "Lion" – Great Britain), those would be potential targets of the "War Expansion." This would mean that those forces of "Islam" ("Black") will be vitally (capitalization) "Near," after having gone "to" (or "Near" after having gone "from North Africa") the places strategically (preceded by an ampersand) "neighboring." In addition, they will have strategically placed their allies "with" the people who are "Christian" ("white"), in order to "fleece" them ("wool"). That will take place throughout the West, where Christianity has spread; and it will be done by the use of major "Weapons" on a "Grand" scale. Those attacks will set up an assault that will take place on "Land," with "Ground" troops.

The capitalized word, "*Sol*," is not a stand-alone statement, as were "*Mars*" and "*Jupiter*." Beside the pronoun/article ("*le*") that precedes "*Sol*," the rest of line three continues to state, "*ardera grand plaine*." That translates to say, "will burn great plain." When this is seen as the direction "him Christian" and/or "the Foundation" will take (due to a future tense verb), the action of burning should be seen as related to the series of events relative to "War" and "Expansion."

The future tense verb, "*ardera*," is rooted to the infinitive verb "*adroir*," which means, "To burn or be on fire; to be inflamed or kindled; (hence) also to be very earnest; or hot in a matter; to love exceedingly; desire fervently, covet vehemently, long for very much; also to inflame or set on fire." This sense of use, where physical flames and symbolic passion are the intent, shows that the "War" is heart-felt, as would be a Holy "War." It also shows that the "Weapons" used will cause "fire," which will spread greatly ("Growth"). As this segment of words follows two one-word statements, separated by commas, one can see how "him" is he who will be ordering the attacks to commence, as the one atop of the strategy command. In that view, it will be "him" who will be targeting "Christians" ("*le Sol*") "fervently" ("*ardera grand*").

Once again, the use of "*grand*" must be seen as a noun, rather than an adjective, where its use identifies those who are known as rulers of greatness. This is most commonly focused on the West, most specifically the United States and "Great" Britain. Here, line three is clarifying line two, and identifying the "Ram, Bull, Crab, Lion." The use of "*grand*" confirms those symbols as being "Rome, Italy; Europe; the United States; and Great Britain" ("*Aries, Taurus, Cancer, Leo*").

This, again, "will be" where "the Land" will "be set on fire." While this scope would indicate a "burn" of tremendous size (as one could describe as "great"), more is gained from seeing the noun usage referencing places known to be "great." This link allows that word to have a more specific connotation.

The use of the word "*plaine*" has to be seen as the feminine form of the word "*plain*," which can also be a noun or adjective. According to the website Wiktionnaire, the word "*plain*" meant "full (not empty), in both Old French and Middle French.[129] When this meaning is applied to the statement in line three, one can see just how extensive the "fire" will "Expand," as "full" would imply everything "will be inflamed."

Still, the Randle Cotgrave dictionary (1611) shows the noun as, "A plain; a spacious piece of (level) ground, without house or tree upon it." The adjective use is then said to be, "Plain, flat, even, smooth, without wrinkles, without rubs." This usage would then be an indication of such an "Expansive" blast that it "will burn" (from a "Weapon," like a nuke) so widely that nothing will be left standing. This would mean that "*Sol*" could also be an indicator of buildings leveled to their "Foundations" or "Lowest levels."

As line three follows the colon at the end of line two, following "*la Vierge*," that clarification or example can then be seen as described by Sister Lucia. In her letters she wrote, "Well, the secret is made up of three distinct parts, two of which I am now going to reveal." She said this first revelation would be of Hell. She continued to write:

> "Our Lady showed us a great sea of fire which seemed to be under the earth. Plunged in this fire were demons and souls in human form, like transparent burning embers,

---

[129] From the website *Wiktionnaire*, under a search for the word "plaine," then linking to the root word "plain." (http://en.wiktionary.org/wiki/plain#French)

> all blackened or burnished bronze, floating about in the conflagration, now raised into the air by the flames that issued from within themselves together with great clouds of smoke, now falling back on every side like sparks in a huge fire, without weight or equilibrium, and amid shrieks and groans of pain and despair, which horrified us and made us tremble with fear. The demons could be distinguished by their terrifying and repulsive likeness to frightful and unknown animals, all black and transparent."[130]

Certainly, to a young girl with no knowledge of what future technologies would bring, a vision of a nuclear holocaust would appear to be "under the earth," rather than how the surface of the earth could become. The description she gave would fit the details that can emerge from line three, when one interprets based on knowing the systems for understanding *The Prophecies*. She clearly depicted a place where "great burning" is "fully" about.

Still, she gave a similar vision of desolation in her third secret, revealed in another letter. There, she told of the angel with a sword that flashed and gave out flames that seemed capable of setting "the world on fire." However, she went on with some key verbiage:

> "And we saw in an immense light that is God: 'something similar to how people appear in a mirror when they pass in front of it' a Bishop dressed in White 'we had the impression that it was the Holy Father'. Other Bishops, Priests, men and women Religious going up a steep mountain, at the top of which there was a big Cross of rough-hewn trunks as of a cork-tree with the bark; before reaching there the Holy Father passed through a big city half in ruins and half trembling with halting step, afflicted with pain and sorrow, he prayed for the souls of the corpses he met on his way; having reached the top of the mountain, on his knees at the foot of the big Cross he was killed by a group of soldiers who fired bullets and arrows at him, and in the same way there died one after another the other Bishops, Priests, men and women Religious, and various

---

[130] From the website "Fatima Secret – Message and Commentary," on the page entitled "The Message of Fatima, Congregation for the Doctrine of the Faith." (http://www.ewtn.com/fatima/apparitions/third_secret/fatima.htm)

lay people of different ranks and positions."[131]

In this description, look at how, "we saw an immense light" can be interpreted from "*le Sol*," where "him Sun" could be taken as Jesus, "the Son" of God. Next, she details "a Bishop dressed in White." This matches the use of "*blanc*" in line one, and makes "*le Sol*" be "the Christian," or "the Bishop" who Sister Lucia said they had the "impression it was the Holy Father." To her, the Holy Father meant the Pope, who does wear "White," and is the Bishop of Rome. When she detailed his walk up a steep mountain, through a city in ruins, and tells of "soldiers who fired bullets and arrows at him," all of this relates to the vision of line three in quatrain VI-35. It depicts a major time of "War," with an "Expanse" of "pain and sorrow" that will cause "him," the "Christian Ram" to pray for those who died because of his failure to respond to "the Virgin."

Seeing line three as continuing the theme of Islam and Christianity, through the warnings of "the Virgin," first for Christians to return to the fold and stop angering Christ by dishonoring the Church, and second by the Church dishonoring Christ by not reconsecrating Russia, as instructed by the Blessed Mary through the apparitions at Fatima. This means that Russia is behind the rise of "Islam" in this quatrain, after Russia became a lost sheep not recovered, when it became caught in the thorns of Communism.

The power that the Muslim nations will have in the future of Nostradamus will come from the remnants of the former Soviet Union. As such, Communist Russia is "Neighboring to Muslim nations, AND" it can pretend to be "close" to the Western nations (once it feigned a collapse), because "in" Russia are the old churches of "white" Russia, the Russian Orthodox churches of the Christian Czars. Once it begins to say its people have retained their Christian beliefs, the Russian Wolf will be wearing Christian "wool."

When the main theme is read in that way, line two's "Ram" ("Aries," in Latin) becomes the Polish pope who was a Cardinal in Communist Poland. If the secondary theme is seen as the corruption of the Church of Rome, with hidden Communist influences, the flow of the secondary theme then shows that spread to all of "Europe," then to the "United States," and finally to "Great Britain." In each place where covert influ-

---

[131]   From the website, "Fatima Secret – Message and Commentary," on the page entitled "The Message of Fatima, Congregation for the Doctrine of the Faith." (http://www.ewtn.com/fatima/apparitions/third_secret/fatima.htm)

ence becomes imbedded, under the guise of wearing "Christian wool," the migration of Muslims will follow because both share a common enemy.

Once the Soviet Union collapsed (1989-1991), a great flood of Islamic refugees began filling "Europe" (especially coastal Italy and France), with their increases felt in the "United States" (the terrorist acts of the 1993 and 2001) and "Great Britain."

This flow of anti-Christian peoples became the first step towards the conditions and changes represented by "*Mars, Jupiter, le Sol ardera grand plaine.*" If one sees those words translated somewhat differently, using other astrological metaphor for the names of planets, line three can also state "Action, Fortune, the Base will be inflamed substantial smooth." In this translation, rather than the attacks of "War," one can see the planning for that intent, where those plans are "Initiated" ("*Mars*") and "Funded" ("*Jupiter*") such that a "Foundation" ("*le Sol*") is built through fiery words that rouse support and volunteers. The target has to be seen as the "West" ("*blanc*") due to the repeated use of "*grand*" (in many quatrains), but due to the opponent being so "big," the planning itself must likewise be "substantial" and "wide scale" (all alternate translations of "*grand*"). When that has happened, with everything put in place, the difference between the two sides will be "even."

Again, this relates to the later coming of a "War" ("*Mars*") and all its devastation. Thus, the planning is implied by the words of "the Virgin," when she warned what would come should Russia not be reconsecrated. This means the Russians will be an integral part of that "War," as the one "great," through its network of spies in the West and its supply of "Weaponry." Its allies will be those who have not found economic success in the world (commonly termed "third-world" nations), such that Eastern Europeans and Africans (non-Muslims) will join as mercenaries, reaping the spoils ("*Jupiter*") of "War." The Muslim world will also be in alliance with Russia, using its oil wealth to purchase the technology of "War" to fight a hated enemy with people willing to die for that cause.

Hidden by a Wax Seal

This leads one to line four, following a comma after "*grand plaine.*" The capitalized first word is "*Boys,*" which is accepted as "*Bois,*" where the vowels "*y*" and "*i*" are seen as interchangeable. The word "*Bois*" commonly meaning "Wood," however it can also translate as, "a staff, lance, or spear," where the word is figurative of a weapon made of a central shaft of "wood." The capitalization can then transform this simple weapon into a major "Weapon," which can be used as a projectile, like a "Spear," which in modern military terminology would be seen as a "Missile."

Since the word "*Boys*" is separated from the rest of line four by an ampersand, it acts as a one-word statement of importance. As the first word following line three, and immediately after the word "plain," a translation as "Missile" makes sense. Line three tells of an "even" state having been reached by the opponents of those "great" ("*grand plaine*").

A "level field" ("*plaine*") is then relative to the "War" ("*Mars*") of line three. The "West," found in line two's series of capitalized words, supporting the use of "*blanc*" in line one, and the use of "*grand*," has enjoyed a collective superiority in "Nuclear ICBMs," since before the breakup of the Soviet Union. It has been the secrecy of such "Weaponry" that has led to fears on both sides, with strategic arms limitations treaties being agreed upon. Still, the breakup of the Soviet Union has upset this "level field." Rather than Russia (the sub-theme of line one) being the one who "will burn" the "West," the ones with no "Missile" ("Muslim" Iran), or only a few ("Muslim" Pakistan), "will burn" their enemy, the West, by way of surprise possession of nuclear "Missiles."

For as much sense as "*Boys*" makes, through "Wood" morphing into "Spear," then "Missile," there is something else to consider. In all of the quatrains of *The Prophecies*, the word "*bois*" appears seven times, in six total quatrains.[132] Of those seven appearances, this use in quatrain VI-35 is the only one capitalized AND it is the only one spelled with a "y," rather than an "i." This difference should be recognized as meaningful, just as "*la Vierge*" is the only capitalized version of "*vierge*" in all *The Prophecies* and it also has more than one meaning.

As explained before, one of the systems required to recognize in order to best interpret anything written by Nostradamus is that of symmetry. Symmetry is found surrounding ampersands, and the word "*Boys*" appears before an ampersand, which I will go into more deeply shortly. However, symmetry can be found between lines of a quatrain, in many

---

[132] From the website "Index of the Centuries of Nostradamus," prepared by J. Flanagan, under the heading, "Alphabetical Index of Nostradamus," and sub-headed "B-C Nostradamus Index." (http://alumnus.caltech.edu/~jamesf/nindex/bc_index.html)

ways.

For example, the use of astrological signs, in line two, is symmetrically balanced by the use of astrological planets in line three. There is also an ampersand in line one, which is now found to be symmetrical to the ampersand in line four. All of this represents signs that can be interpreted more deeply, giving support, clarification, and details that otherwise would be missed.

One point of symmetry that I feel is important in why "*Boys*" is spelled with a "*y*" is the presence of the word "*Rion,*" in line one. When I discussed "*Rion,*" I explained it should be read as a simple anagram, such that when spelled backwards it becomes "*Noir,*" meaning "Black." Because of that change, and the systemic element of symmetry, the "*y*" can be a signal to see "*Boys*" not as "*Bois,*" but as another simple anagram to complement the first.

This does not necessarily mean the "*y*" has to remain a "*y,*" because the "*i*" and "*y*" are often found interchangeable in *The Prophecies*. What was learned from the anagram in line one was that the capitalized "*R*" was not maintained in the changing of "*Rion*" to "*Noir.*" The capitalization remained fixed in the position of the first letter, meaning the "*y*" of "*Boys*" can still change to an "*i.*" Still, it would be best to maintain the "*y,*" if possible, to avoid any concept of rules being changed to make a word be altered to fit a preconceived notion.

On thing that must be realized is the possibility of combined words, especially when the letter "*s*" is part of an anagram. That letter is often abbreviated before a word, with an apostrophe added. That can be done in this case, where one can find "*s'Oby*" as the rearrangement. The "*s*" is short for "*se,*" meaning, "oneself, itself, or themselves." The main word in this case is the proper name of a Russian river, the Ob, also spelled "Obi." The River Ob flows north, emptying into the Arctic Ocean, from the Altay Mountains in southwestern Russia. The River Ob flows through the Western Siberian "Plain," such that seeing it identified from the letters "*B-o-y-s*" would have the "great plain" be compared to that of the one in Russia.

Another three-letter word that can be formed, with the forth letter separated as a 1-letter word (in French), yields "*y Bos,*" where the word "*y*" means, "there," or "on it." The word "*Bos*" is Latin, meaning "Cow, Ox, or

Chapter 8: Quatrain VI-35

Bull." This, of course, would be symmetrical to the Latin word "*Taurus*" meant "Bull." The inference in line four, when seen as "there Ox" of a "great plain," in a quatrain focused on where "Black & white" are "neighboring," is on the coastal "plain" of Israel.

"There," the Biblical Israelites constantly had to overcome the co-inhabitants of the "Land" of Canaan, where the Ugarit people worshipped a god named Ba'al Hadad.[133] He was supposedly the son of El, and both Hadad and El were associated with the "Bull." From Syria, to Phoenicia, to Israel, "there" is a coastal "plain," that region of people can become the supporting focus. This rearrangement of the letters published could give an indication of the Middle East as the focus that "will burn."

The last possibility (as I see it) where the "*y*" is maintained is not an anagram at all. Instead, it is a switch of languages, from French to English. This means that "*Boys*" is not "*Bois*," (French) but "Boys," an English word for male youths. When one realizes how Nostradamus often added an "*s*" to verbs, making that an indication of those who acted in the way of the verb, the same can apply to a noun. As such, "Boys" can be interpreted as "Boy ones," or those who are known through associations with "Boys."

When the first word of line four is seen as supporting the first word of line two ("Ram"), this could be an indication of the scandals that have hit the Vatican ("Ram" = "Pope"), where priests have long abused young males sexually. In that sense, "the Foundation" of the Church (trust in priests) "will burn" from their uncontrollable "lusts" for "Boys" (from *ardoir* as "to love exceedingly; desire fervently, covet vehemently, long for very much"). This, in turn, will reduce those seen as "great" (Christians, on a holy level) as "plain," or reduced to a flat status, no different from any flawed human being filled with sin.

Two more anagrams are possible, both of which change the "*y*" to an "*i*," with both using the same letter order. The difference is one hyphenates two letters, as a prefix to the last two letters, while the other sees all four rearranged letters as a new word. The simple anagram comes from simply switching the two central letters, as "*B-y-o-s*" (from "*B-o-y-s*"). The hyphenated word (with the "*i*" substitution) becomes "*Bi-os*" (meaning "Two-bones") and the whole word becomes "*Bios*" (Greek rooted, meaning "Life"). Again, both changes can add to the interpretation of quatrain

---

[133] From the article posted on Wikipedia, entitled, "Baal," under the subheading "Hadad in Ugarit." (http://en.wikipedia.org/wiki/Baal)

VI-35.

When one sees "*Boys*" transform into "*Bi-os*," the importance (capitalization) of "Two-bones" becomes the symbol of the "Crossbones." By definition, "crossbones" means, "a representation of two bones placed crosswise, usually below a skull, to symbolize death."[134] The symbol is one of danger, and as such one finds the symbol of a skull and "Crossbones" as a warning, one that everyone will be able to recognize. In this sense, the importance of that symbol is relative to what "will burn" those in "great" nations, resulting in an "even" application. This can represent significant "Weapons" of "Poison," which are of biological and/or chemical design. Additionally, when one sees the association of the "Crossbones" to piracy on the high seas, this can also be an indication of surprise naval attack. In all cases, this fits the theme of "War," especially one that will "Expand" beyond all previous accepted limits on acceptable means of "Warfare."

Finally, when the letters "*B-o-y-s*" becomes rearranged to become the word "*Bios*," this is the Greek word meaning, "Life," or "Living." According to Strong's Concordance, the transliteration ("bios," derived from βίος) also means, "manner of life, livelihood," and is seen as representing "the period or duration of earthly life."[135] Still, in Randle Cotgrave's 1611 dictionary, he lists the word "*bios*" as used in French to denote, "God,"[136] with Cotgrave denoting this to be more often used in Gascon (a dialect of Catalan) and Rabbinic (the language of rabbis developed after 600 A.D., incorporating Greek philosophy into Jewish tradition).

When "God" is seen as the giver of "Life," this then is a good link back to "Ram," where a "Pope" is mankind's link to "God." When "*le Sol*" is seen as "the Sun," and when this is seen as "the Light" of the Son, Jesus Christ, the focus becomes a form of anger that "will burn." The anger is from a lack of vigor from the Church, which had become "flat" and "plain."

This was seen in the La Salette apparition of "the Virgin," where she told the two children there that she was holding the arm of "the Son" back. That action of mercy was to keep Christ from striking out at those who claim to be "great" in his name, as a warning to change. This means

---

134   From the Free Dictionary by Farlex, in a search for "crossbones." [Fair use from the source: Random House Kernerman Webster's College Dictionary, 2010] (http://www.thefreedictionary.com/crossbones)
135   From the website Study Bible, in a search for the Strong's Concordance of "bios." (http://studybible.info/strongs/G979)
136   From Randal Cotgrave's 1611 French-English Dictionary, published online by Greg Lindahl. (http://www.pbm.com/~lindahl/cotgrave/search/115l.html)

"Christians" will be far from elevated towards "God." Instead, they will be "plain" and indistinguishable from any other human being.

The one connection that Christians, Muslims, and Jews all share is faith and belief in the same One "God." All believe in the stories of the Old Testament, relative to the times before the returning of the Jews from captivity in Babylon. Thus, the history they believe includes those stories of "God" punishing the world, through a Great Flood and the destruction of Sodom and Gomorrah. From beliefs in this power of "God" to improve the conditions of "Life" on earth, each feels a sense of superiority, through being backed by "God," leading them to act to confront and destroy evil. Thus, a Holy "War," foretold by "God," will be seen as the ultimate test of who really does have "God's" support, when each sees the others as flawed in their faith and in support of evil.

Due to there being multiple possibilities that can be considered when finding "*Boys*" spelled as it is, with a "y," and because all make some sense with the verbiage leading up to its appearance as the first word in line four, the key is found in it preceding an ampersand. Because the two words surrounding an ampersand represent a symmetrical relationship,[137] the word following "*Boys*" will help identify which translation becomes the primary intention. The second word in line four is "*cites*," which we have seen before (in the singular number – "*cité*"), in the main theme statement (line one) of quatrain III-84 ("*La grand cité sera bien desoleé*"). Thus, the symmetrical relationship of line four is between "*Boys & cites*."

Immediately, the appearance of an "s" at the end of each word can be an indication of the number of the symmetrical arrangement. As "*cité*" is either a "city" or "one cited," or "one warned to appear," the addition of an "s" means multiple "cities" or multiple people "warned." If "*Boys*" were to remain intact, as the intended word to translate, it would be similar as a multiple of "Boys"[138] (an indication of English-speaking nations). As a symmetrical opposite, the singular number "Spear" is countering multiple "cities," indicating the same "Weapon" targeting many places.

When one sees the anagram "*Bios*," where Randle Cotgrave stated this was a rabbinic word meaning (capitalized) "God," the use of a rabbinic word in a religious-themed quatrain elevates the use of "God" to Bibli-

---

137 When two words are only separated by the ampersand symbol, there is a direct symmetry involved, either two synonymous words or two antonyms, for example: fire & ice; or, fire & water. When a comma and an ampersand separate the two words, the symmetry is less obvious.
138 The word "boy" is English, although French will use "*boi*" to mean a youth in English-speaking countries. As it is not a true word in French, I have not written about this above.

cal (Old Testament) references. When one sees the translation as Greek, where "*Bios*" means, "Life," then one can see how the New Testament can play a role as well, making the meaning fit a Christian theme.

When this combination surrounding the ampersand is read as, "God AND cities," all Biblical stories where worship of the one "God" (Jewish and Christian) is established in "cities," this acts as a focus on the West. That is where the letters of the Apostles began the initial spread of Christianity to the "churches" in "cities" around the Mediterranean, this supports "Aries" as symbolizing important "Beginnings." It then also reflects and the extent that the Church of Rome continued that influence to Europe and beyond, with buildings to "God" erected in the "cities." However, when "God" is directly connected (the ampersand connection) to multiple "cities," then one has to consider the story of Sodom and Gomorrah, which were called the "cities of the plain." That story fits a quatrain telling of a destruction that would be a more "Expansive" ("Jupiter") than any form of "Weaponry" ("*Mars*") known to mankind, until the advent of nuclear bombs.

When that link is made to "God," one realizes how the story tells of Moses bargaining with "God," because "God" has "warned to appear" ("*cité*") a complete destruction of "those" (as "*cité-s*," read as "cited those") two "cities." The destruction would be due to the total state of corruption in the humanity there. Moses argued that if multiple people were found to be good in those "cities," then it would not be necessary to destroy good to punish evil. In the end, Sodom and Gomorrah were destroyed because Aaron was the only good person, since his wife looked back and was destroyed, and his two daughters made Aaron drunk so he would have sex with them.

The point of the story was not that two "cities" would be destroyed by "God," but that "God" would give prior "warning" to "those" who's "Life" was in danger. This relates line four to line two (a systemic relationship where line four directly supports the secondary theme of line two), where "the Virgin" has been the source of this "warning to appear" before "God," as faithful peoples. That "citation" was given by the Blessed "Virgin" at Fatima, Portugal, while she also warned in her apparition at La Salette, France. The vision allowed to Sister Lucia and her cousins was of destruction, as Sister Lucia's writing detailed: "a big city half in ruins and half trembling with halting step, afflicted with pain and sorrow."

Chapter 8: Quatrain VI-35

When this relationship is developed, seeing "*Boys*" as "*Bios*," then the importance (capitalization) of "*Bi-os*" can be seen, as a very toxic relationship ("Crossbones" as "Deadly") linked to "cities." Based on the "warning" given to "those," it has since become common knowledge that the nuclear defense shields of a "Doomsday" ("Crossbones") scenario would be to have major "cities" targeted as the places where destruction would have its greatest impact, either as pre-emptive or retaliatory strikes of "Warfare." These strikes would be made by a single "Missile" ("Spear" or "Lance"), such that each successful strike would level a "city" and its surrounding towns.

When the letters of "*B-o-y-s*" are rearranged to show "*Oby-s*" or "*s'Oby*," the translations become, "Ob River ones" or "themselves [of the] Ob." This then shows why "the Virgin" would "warn those" of the Vatican to reconsecrate Russia, as that is where the "Ob River" is located. The "plain" of the "Ob" (a.k.a. "Obi" or "Oby") River, in Western Siberia, is where the majority of the former U.S.S.R. staged its second line of ICBM defense,[139] as well as where nuclear waste has been dumped over decades, so that the Ob River system is threatened by radiation "Poison."[140]

Certainly, there are "cities" located along the path of the "Ob River," making them the "Obi ones." The "Ob cities" include Novosibirsk (Russia's 3rd largest city), Kamen-na-Obi, Barnaul (over 600,000 inhabitants), Surgut (over 300,000 inhabitants), Kolpashevo, and others.[141] This interpretation would act as an indication of the source for "Weapons" ("*Mars*") with "Expansive" ("*Jupiter*") power, being flowed into the hands of Islamic nations, such as Iran, Afghanistan, and Pakistan.

The source of the "Ob" River is "Close to Islamic" Kazakhstan, with a route from there, through Turkmenistan, reaching Iran. A shorter route would pass through Kazakhstan, then smaller Uzbekistan, reaching Afghanistan. That point of entry in Afghanistan would then be "Next to Islamic" Pakistan. This, of course, would be originating from Asian Russia, which is "neighboring with European" ("white") Russia; and the transfer of such dangerous "Weaponry" would be without the West observing, such that the "wool" would be pulled over the eyes of those "white" (Christians).

---

139   From the article posted online, "The Cold War Atomic Intelligence Game, 1945-70." (https://www.cia.gov/library/center-for-the-study-of-intelligence/csi-publications/csi-studies/studies/vol48no2/article01.html)

140   From the article posted online, "ENVIRONMENT – RUSSIA: Radioactive Lake Threatens Arctic Disaster." (http://www.wentz.net/radiate/lake/)

141   From the Wikipedia article, "Ob River," under the subheading, "Cities along the Ob." (http://en.wikipedia.org/wiki/Ob_River)

As far as "wool" is concerned, knitting from yarn that keeps one warm is a major concern, especially in the colder regions of the Northern Hemisphere. The hair, underwool or under-fur of a Muskox (the source of "qiviut woolens"), keeps them warm to minus-50 degrees Fahrenheit.[142] Russian women have passed on their knitting techniques to those natives of the Arctic Circle, where Muskox thrive. In this case, the "white wool" can be seen as not representing the color of the animal's hair, but a statement of the color of the snows of winter, and the "wool" necessary to stay alive. The Musk ox of Russia (of the *Ovibos* genus) became extinct from over-hunting in the 1880s.[143] However, it was successfully reintroduced "there" (from "*y Bos*," as "there Ox), from places it still thrived, in the 1970s. Another introduction made successfully in Siberia in the mid-1990s and early 2000s.

As you can see, some possibilities have more impact than others, with the element of "Wood, Spear, Lance, Staff" (translations of "*Bois*," from "*Boys*") being symmetrically associated with "cities" and "those warned to appear." The symmetry is one of opposites, in the sense that "Missile" (a modern warfare form of a "Spear") is a specific, versus a general "warning" that tells of mass destruction of many people. The deeper one ponders the letters, "*B-o-y-s*," the more details emerge to expand and clarify a theme of issues between "Islam," "Christianity," and Communist Russia, those "nearby" in sheep's clothing, with plenty of "Missiles" to lend, and of whom "the Virgin warned."

The comma at that follows the word "*cites*" then separates that symmetrical combination from the remainder of line four's statement. The last segment begins with the word "*lettres*," such that the word can be a statement not to overlook the spelling presented in "*Boys*," to focus on the uniqueness of the "letters." It also is a reflection of what "the Virgin" said, because line four directly supports the secondary theme in line two, making a statement about the "letters" Sister Lucia wrote about "ICBM" destruction that was "warned to appear" via Russia (albeit indirectly, through Muslims). Because "letters" is the first word to follow "those warned to appear," the "letters" are relative to "those warnings."

This is then further supportive of the "letters" written by Sister Lucia, stating the "warnings" sent from the Blessed "Virgin," during her ap-

---

[142] From the article posted online, "Muskox Yarn: The Cashmere of the North," from the website *Knitting and Beyond*. (http://knittingstuff.com/435221-Muskox-Yarn-The-Cashmere-Of-The-North.html)
[143] From the commercial website *David Morgan*, advertising products available, made from "Qiviut – Wonder Wool of the Arctic." (http://www.davidmorgan.com/qiviut.html)

paritions at Fatima, because they have become commonly known as "concealed" or "hidden ones" (from plural form of the past-tense verb "*caché*"). The word "*caché*" means, "hidden, concealed, kept secret; in covert; and conveyed away."[144] As Nostradamus did not accent the word "*cachez*," the addition of an accent mark is permitted; but, even without that need, the word "*cache*" (unaccented) means, "hiding hole, hidden corner, or nook out of the way."

The "-z" ending is then an indication of multiple things "concealed" in the same hiding place, rather than multiple places of concealment. This means the plural number is experssed as the number of things "hidden," reading the "-z" as an additional word, yielding "hiding hole ones" of "those" in the "hiding hole." This perfectly tells of the "letters" sent to one pope, who "concealed them" for later popes to consider. It also explains how the third part of the "letters" sent by Sister Lucia is called the "secret" third "letter.

The remainder of line four says, "*au cierge*," which says, "in the big wax candle," "at the big wax candle," "to the big wax candle," "from the big wax candle," and/or "with the big wax candle." This has been a confusing element of quatrain VI-35, because "*cierge*" only has the meaning of a "candle." It makes it appear that some papers ("*lettres*" can mean paper "documents," such as written "epistles") have had wax poured over them, trapping them inside the wax, or that "big wax candles" have "letters" - individual elements of an alphabet - secured to them. However, this misses the esoteric and religious aspect of "big wax candles."

The word "*cierge*" more specifically means a "wax candle used in religious rites."[145] This definition, in a quatrain whose theme is religious, allows one to see how a "candle" is synonymous with its use in Christian churches, and specifically in the Roman Catholic Church. Because each word of every quatrain bears its own weight of importance in interpretation, reading that "letters" are to be found "hidden in the candle" is reading too much at once. Certainly, the "letters" are more than one, and "those" are "kept secret. However, reading each word separately lets one see how multiple "letters" are "kept secret" multiple times.

Because the "letters" of Sister Lucia were sent to the pope, they were

---

144　From Randal Cotgrave's 1611 French-English Dictionary, published online by Greg Lindahl. (http://www.pbm.com/~lindahl/cotgrave/search/149l.html)
145　From the website *Wiktionary*, from a search of the word "cierge." (http://en.wiktionary.org/wiki/cierge)

sealed by the Bishop of Leiria (Portugal), keeping them "hidden" from view to everyone but the pope. After Pope John XXIII broke the seal, which was from the "wax" dripped from a lit *"cierge"* and stamped by a ring, his returning the "letters" to privacy, for a later pope to assess, he too would repeat the sealing process. The act of using a "candle" is what "concealed" the "letters."

Pope John XXIII (a "Ram") was presented the "letters" to read on August 17, 1957, but he decided to pray about the matter and had the "letters" resealed and returned to the archives. The pope would drip the "wax of a ritual candle" over the envelope, and stamp the impressionable "wax" with the papal ring. The story of the "secret letters" of Fatima is that multiple popes resealed them, until March 25, 1984, when Pope John Paul II (another "Ram") unsealed the "letters" for the last time. In response to that opening, Pope John Paul II made a declaration of consecration to the whole world, in regards to the "letters" he had read from Sister Lucia. In the year 2000 the "letters" would be made public (after the fall of the Soviet Union), when Pope John Paul II declared the issue settled. However, after having been "kept secret" 40 years beyond the recommended exposure date, the "letters" were "hidden with the big wax candle," as a seal.

The 1611 French-English dictionary shows the word *"cierge"* with instructions to see the word *"poincte."* That word then indicates a special meaning to be, "the middle-size wax candle used in churches," while adding, "the biggest being termed Cierge, and the least Bougie."[146] This can be a reference to the act of Pope John Paul II, who on May 13, 1984 lit a "candle" for each of the two children of Fatima who had died a year after having witnessed the apparition of "the Virgin."

In the sermon he read that day in Fatima (in Portuguese), he stated the "red dragon" is what Sister Lucia was referring to in her "letters," and the red dragon represented evil. He said evil is a constant enemy of the righteous, and therefore a continuing battle that is never over. In other words, Pope John Paul II ceased any further papal action, as directed by "the Virgin,"to challenge the Russians and Communism through her instructions to little Lucia. Pope John Paul II deemed the problem to be resolved.

When one does a search of "Secret Third Letter of Fatima," on the Inter-

146 From Randal Cotgrave's 1611 French-English Dictionary, published online by Greg Lindahl. (http://www.pbm.com/~lindahl/cotgrave/search/739r.html)

net, one finds many sites that promote a cover-up (a form of "*caché-z*"). Many cites reasons to not believe the official release of the "letters" of Sister Lucia, by Rome, as authentic. Some offer their opinions as to what the actual third "secret letter" stated, which is not what was released. The point of all this conjecture here is to show that quatrain VI-35 is releasing those "secrets" by the words of "the Virgin" being reflected in the details of Communist revenge. That philosophy will operate unopposed through the hatred that has been established between Christians and Muslims.

Chapter 9
The Sixth "*Vierge*" Quatrain

Quatrain VIII-80

The sixth quatrain stating the word "*vierge*" is found positioned as the 80th in Centurie VIII. This is the third of three quatrains that have the word "*vierge*" in line one, as part of the main theme statement (the other two being quatrain II-17 and quatrain IV-35). Following quatrain VI-35, where the word "*cierge*" ("big wax candle") was used, quatrain VIII-80 repeats that word. From this prefacing, quatrain VIII-80 can be found stating (in Old French, followed by my English translation):

> *Des innocens le sang de vef le & vierge:*
>
> *Tant de maulx faitz par moyen se grand Roge*
>
> *Saintz simulachres trempez en ardant cierge*
>
> *De frayeur crainte ne verra nul que boge.*
>
> ---
>
> To them innocent ones a lineage from widow him & virgin:
>
> So much from hurtful ones acts for occasion them selves noble Requested
>
> Sacred ones likenesses household wines at burning big wax candle
>
> With terror doubt of not will perceive not any that fished.

Chapter 9: Quatrain VIII-80

In the main theme for this quatrain, line one presents *"vierge"* as the last word of line one, separated from the rest of the line by an ampersand. The ampersand preceding *"vierge"* has the effect of making the word be read as if capitalized, like *"Vierge,"* due to the importance the ampersand inflects. This makes quatrain VIII-80 mimic the capitalization found in quatrain VI-35.

One can also see that a colon follows the word *"vierge."* The rules for reading punctuation in *The Prophecies* mean line two (minimally) will clarify the one-word statement ending line one, which is about an important "virgin." This means the secondary theme for the quatrain should be an example of the main theme, while presenting a seperate focus on that theme. The supporting details for the main theme are always found stated in line three, such that the main theme must find those details clarifying as well.

When one looks at the eight words written in line one, *"Des innocens de sang le vef le"* (7) *"& vierge"* (1). Of those, four words become the foundations upon which the other words are fastened. Those four words are *"innocens,"* *"sang,"* *"vef,"* and *"vierge."* On the most common level, those four words translate as, "innocent ones," "blood," "widow" or "widower," and "virgin."

When one sees how it has already been established that the word *"vierge"* has a consistent placement in quatrains that tell (at least partially) about warnings given by Marian apparitions, regardless of the spelling case, "virgin" has to be seen as having a strong connection to Christianity, and to the Roman Catholic Church. By realizing that religious theme direction, it is easy to see how "innocent ones" (as *"innocen[t]-s"*), "blood," and "virgin" all have religious connotations as well. That should help guide one to an expectation of a main theme that is related to Christianity, in some sense.

The word *"innocens"* is proper Latin, meaning "harmless, inoffensive, innoxious, blameless, guiltless, or innocent" (masculine, feminine, and neuter gender, in the singular number, nominative and vocative cases).[147] One of the systems of *The Prophecies* concerns the use of foreign languages (i.e.: anything other than French), especially when Nostradamus was moved to write in Latin (the foreign language he used most frequently). The use of Latin is a hint to the reader that the word, in some way, has

---

[147] From the website *Wiktionary*, in a search for the term "innocens." (http://en.wiktionary.org/wiki/innocens)

a religious element that should be noticed. As such, several popes have taken the name Innocent (13) and the church recognizes a day named the Feast of the Holy Innocents. That day is set aside to honor the children murdered by Herod (as mentioned in Matthew 2:16-18), in his attempt to keep Jesus from being born.[148] Children, it should be recalled, are the "innocent ones" to whom the Virgin Mary has most often appeared.

The Widow, Him, and the Virgin

The spelling of "*innocens*" can also be recognized as an abbreviated form of the French word, "*innocent*" (as seen in popes taking that spelling as a name). The French word has the same meaning as the Latin, with Randle Cotgrave adding, "faultless and without offence."[149] The "s" can then be seen as making the word plural, as "innocent ones."

This aspect of the lower case spelling can then be seen as less indicative of a proper noun (like Innocent, the name); but one must realize that "*innocens*" follows the capitalized preposition-article combination first word ("*Des*"), meaning the importance of capitalization progresses to the first noun following. Thus, the initial focus of importance is "Of the innocent ones," "To the innocent ones," "From the innocent ones," or "With the innocent ones." In this case, "the article "the" is connected to the capitalization in the plural number, as "them, they, or those." This is due to "*Des*" being a contraction of "*De+les*," a plural article; and it makes the preposition state an important direction relative to "The innocent ones."

While not a direct definition of "innocent," "pure" is a word that is synonymous.[150] When this is understood, "those" (a plural number pronoun from "*les*") who have been deemed to be "pure ones" are the Cathar people. As discussed previously, the Cathar people did not name themselves, so they were not properly named Cathars. They were describes as "pure ones" by those who lived with and around them, due to the nature of the lives those people lived. Again, the name Cathar stems from the Greek word "*kathoros*," which means "pure."[151] Realizing this possibility means that "*Des innocens*" can relate to southwestern France, where the

---

148 From the New Advent website, on the page titled, "Catholic Encyclopedia: Holy Innocents." (http://www.newadvent.org/cathen/07419a.htm)
149 From Randal Cotgrave's 1611 French-English Dictionary, published online by Greg Lindahl. (http://www.pbm.com/~lindahl/cotgrave/search/551r.html)
150 From the website *Wiktionary*, in a search for the term "pure." (http://en.wiktionary.org/wiki/pure)
151 From the Free Dictionary by Farlex, in a search for "catharsis." [Fair use from the source: American Heritage Dictionary of the English Language, 4th Ed., 2000] (http://www.thefreedictionary.com/catharsis)

Chapter 9: Quatrain VIII-80

Cathar people lived.

Relative to this concept of peoples in a specific region of the world, the word "*sang*" follows "*innocens*." This word most commonly translates as "blood," but it is also regularly used to denote, "stock, race, kindred, lineage, parentage, especially of kings, in whence we also use the words blood royal."[152] As one can see, this is directly read as a word denoting "bloodline," in the literal sense. However, in terms of the Christian religion, since one sees "*innocens*," "*sang*," and "*vierge*" in that vein, the "blood" can easily represent "the new Covenant" with Christ.

This would be how one would have to view the Cathar people, as they were deemed Gnostic Christians. They were quite possibly from the first infusions of new Christian "blood" into France. Thus, the word "blood" matches the context of a Christian theme, relative to "innocent ones."

As also discussed earlier, the three Biblical Mary figures are celebrated as having landed in France, as passengers on a raft without a mast. These were mostly Jews, making them the "blood" of Christ as well. In that history, the one passenger that did not match the Jewish "lineage" model was the girl, Sarah. She was either an Egyptian maidservant or an infant child, said to be of dark color. As a youth (servant or baby), Sarah represented the "blood" symbolizing the spirit of "the innocent ones" of childhood. Thus, she was "innocent blood."

If theories about this historic arrival on the shore of France are true, where Sarah is believed to have been the offspring of Jesus, through Mary Magdalene, line one could be confirming that parentage. The arrival of the "blood" of Christ is symbolic of the Holy Grail, as Holy "Blood."

Arthurian literature states the word "*Sangreal*," which is translated to state, Holy Grail. That word can be read as "*Sang real*" ("Holy blood") and/or "*San greal*" ("Holy grail").[153] This would mean "the innocent" youth, Sarah, was pregnant with the "bloodline" of Jesus the Christ. There are those who believe the Cathar people migrated to that region of France, due to the historical pilgrimage of the Roma took (from Eastern Europe), with many settling in that area. These would be Paulican converts to Christianity (as well as Armenians), who could also have Jewish "lineage."

152   From Randal Cotgrave's 1611 French-English Dictionary, published online by Greg Lindahl. (http://www.pbm.com/~lindahl/cotgrave/search/847r.html)
153   From the Wikipedia article "Holy Grail," under the subheading, "Origins." (http://en.wikipedia.org/wiki/Holy_Grail)

When one then looks to the third important word of the main theme statement, the word "*vef*" can mean both "widow" and "widower." Randal Cotgrave listed both as masculine nouns, with one stated to mean, "widower," and the second to mean, "widow, widow-like, of or belonging to a widow." The word "*vef*" was also referenced by Cotgrave in his translation of the word "*veuf*," which he said meant "widow" (the modern translation is "widower"). Additionally, Cotgrave translated the word "*veufve*" as "a widow," without referencing "*vef*." Those were the masculine and feminine spelling in Old French, with the modern French equivalents now "*veuf*" and "*veuve*." The word is rooted in the Latin word "*vidua*" (feminine gender, nominative and vocative cases), and the English translations of this word show how a "widow" can also be "an unmarried woman," inferring an old woman without a husband.[154]

From these meanings, one should then be able to see how nuns are symbolically married to Christ, and many Christians, of both genders, seek to be in the same relationship. In those cases, both men and women are left alone while their marriage partner is away. This is a figurative definition of "widow." In any case, a "lineage" is protected by just one partner, with the one generating this "bloodline" no longer alive, or at least living on the physical plane.

This means the three important words of the main theme of quatrain VIII-80, leading up to the ampersand, are projecting a flow of "innocent ones," relative to a "blood" connection with a marriage, where the husband has gone away, leaving a "widow" behind. This is certainly reflecting on a religious "lineage," especially befitting the model of the Holy Grail, which was the chalice that held the "blood" of Jesus, and the Holy Blood that caused those who spoke in Old French and Old English to remark how "*sang*" was often used to denote royal "blood."

With the focus set on the important words of line one, it now becomes important to recognize the repeating of the other words that connect the important ones. Those words are "*de*" (meaning "of, to, from, with") and "*le*" (the article "a, an, the" or the pronoun "him"). Line one began with a capitalized version of "*De*," with it combined with the plural article, "*les*" (meaning, "them, those, they," in the plural number). From that beginning, the important words are connected with two other "*le*" presentations and one repeating of "*de*." While the words are not as im-

---

[154] From Wiktionary open-content dictionary, under the word "vidua." (http://en.wiktionary.org/wiki/vidua)

portant (on the surface), they are important to realize their impacts on the important words.

In the systems of *The Prophecies*, the repeating of words means each representation has a different translation, as long as the repeated word has multiple uses. As such, repeated words never mean the same thing. The preposition "*de*," for example, often can show movement and transition, as "from – to," or "to – from." The word "*le*" has been discussed previously, such that it translating as the word "the" means it has little reason for being written, unless it is capitalized, showing the importance of "one," being "The" noun of focus or "An" important one. It has much more meaning as an indicator of a male presence, as the pronoun "him," when presented in the lower-case spelling.

In line one of quatrain VIII-80, the presence of two "*le*"s means other options may need to be considered. One is the addition of an accent mark, making "*le*" become "*lé*." Read with the accetn mark, the word means "width, breadth, broad, wide, large." The other is to see a generic pronoun as the translation, as "it" rather than "him." These option mean line one can translate to show, "From them innocent ones broad lineage to widow him & virgin." Inversely, the same words can state, "To those pure ones it bloodline from widow him & virgin."

This begins to shape a theme of movement, with a "lineage" established by "him AND a virgin." The most recognized birth to a "virgin" is that of Jesus to the Blessed "Virgin." This fits a religious theme established by the four important words in line one. That theme leads one to see "Of the innocent ones" as the descendants of early Christianity.

When the word "*le*" is seen accented, so that it represents a "wide" scale and "breadth" of scope, it becomes the spread of the "innocent ones." On that most basic level, where the name Innocent honors children killed, such that "innocent one" or "pure ones" are indeed youths, that spread can be seen as a phase of progeny, which is then explained as "*sang*," or a "lineage." This "bloodline" or "race" (defined as a group characterized through the transmission of genetics) stems "from" ("*de*") one who is a "widow." As a "widow" of "him" who has died, she had minimally one child through which the genetics (DNA) of "him" passed through her, his "widow."

The ampersand that precedes the one-word statement, "virgin," then emphasizes this state as of particular importance. Besides the noun definition as one without experiencing sexual intercourse (as a child would normally be), or one decidedly shunning sex (as "chaste"), the adjective meaning allows the word to project a pure state (a reflection on "innocent ones") as well as an event happening for the first time. In that case, "virgin" bears the important (ampersand introduction) focus as a beginning that is relative to "him," with "him" descending from a "widow."

This would be enough to make the statement be of the Blessed "Virgin," the mother of Jesus, bearer of the Immaculate Conception. On the other hand, it can be a reflection on an "unmarried" state (seeing "virgin" as "nun"), where an offspring was the result. It can even indicate a second immaculate conception, to a different mother, who would herself conceive without sexual intercourse, bearing an heir to "him."

Once these possibilities are brought to one's consciousness, one has to then look at the importance of the symmetry surrounding the ampersand. That symmetry represents either a balance of opposites, or a balance of similarities. In this case, "*vef le & vierge*" does both.

The combination of "*le & vierge*" shows the opposite of sex, when it translates as "him AND" her, a female "virgin" (the noun gender of "*vierge*" is feminine). When the pronoun is seen as the balance opposite a noun, one can see how the word "*vef*" not only retains its ability to mean "widow," it is most likely to be the "widow" of "him." This means the union between a husband and wife, where a female "widow" means the wife of "him," her deceased husband, is linked importantly (ampersand use) to the word "virgin." The implication is a marriage without sex ("virgin"), which still produces a "bloodline."

This identifies "him" as Jesus, who was "him" of the "virgin" Mary. Still, because the death of Jesus did not make Mother Mary a "widow," the implication is that Jesus had a wife. That would most likely be Mary Magdalene, who was referred to as Jesus' "companion" (per the Gospel of Philip).[155] A "companion" can be defined as "a domestic partner," or one who lives with another.[156] The Gospel of Philip used the Greek word "*koinonos*" (transliteration), which translates as, "a partner, associate, comrade; sharer (in anything); one in fellowship with," in addition to

---

155   From the Wikipedia article "Gospel of Philip," under the subheading, "Mary Magdalene." (http://en.wikipedia.org/wiki/Gospel_of_Philip)

156   From the Free Dictionary by Farlex, in a search for "companion." [Fair use from the source: American Heritage Dictionary of the English Language, 4th Ed., 2000] (http://www.thefreedictionary.com/companion)

"companion."[157]

This causes conjecture that Jesus was indeed married. This is certainly not unusual, as it was standard for all adult male Jews (Jesus was 30-33 years of age during his ministry) to be married. He would have then been expected to have had a sexual relationship with his wife, for the purpose of having children. To be unmarried and to practice celibacy, at his age, would have been scorned.

When one sees the two-word combination, "widow him" as opposite the ampersand, linking to the word "virgin," one sees how "his widow & virgin" can be read as Mary Magdalene and the Egyptian maidservant, or baby of dark complexion. In either case, there was a progeny with Mary, who was a "virgin," as a youth. A marriage between Jesus and Mary Magdalene can also be seen as one that was not consummated by physical sexuality, such that Mary Magdalene was a married "widow & virgin." This would have allowed her to have born the baby of Jesus through another "virgin" pregnancy, such that his earthly wife ("widow," upon his death) would become a continuation of "him" through another child born to a "virgin."

Seeing this ending to the main theme of quatrain VIII-80, one can then see how the prepositions and articles complete a theme that can state, "To the children (innocent ones) extensive lineage from widow him & virgin." This religious theme directs the entire quatrain, so the rest of this quatrain will support that theme. This support is enhanced by the colon at the end of the main theme line, symbolically stating that line two (the secondary theme, minimally) will clarify or give an example of the "virgin" and the connection to "a bloodline of widow him."

The Men Who would be Kings

Line two states, "*Tant de maulx faitz par moyen se grand Roge,*" which can translate as, "So many with evils done ones through medium themselves lofty (I) Govern." As a clarification of the main theme, specifically stemming from the one-word statement of importance (ampersand use), "virgin," line two appears to place focus on the Church of Rome, who venerates Mary as the Blessed "Virgin." When the whole of line one is seen as clarified in the secondary theme, such that the main theme is

---

157   From the website *Bible Study Tools*, from a search of the word "*koinonos.*" (http://www.biblestudytools.com/lexicons/greek/nas/koinonos.html)

about a "bloodline" of Christ, line two places focus on the growth of leaders that would be "Kings" of Europe.

The first word of line two, the capitalized "*Tant,*" shows an importance that will be "So, As, So great, So much, So many; As well, As dear, As worthy; In sort, and In such manner,"[158] which states an important expansion of the "bloodline." The spread of a Christian "lineage," as well as "Royalty" to "Rule" over those Christians, and a "Church" with a "Pope." All would spread to such a degree that it can be summed up as "So great."

This expanse is then seen to not be all good and wonderfulness, as "*Tant*" is followed by "*de maulx faitz,*" which together says, "with evils done." When the first word of line two is shown leading to those words, it becomes a secondary them focusing on "So many" from the "widow, him AND the virgin" in a world filled "with evils" ("*de maulx*"). This is a statement about need for this "bloodline," as a continuation of the Biblical "lineage" begun with Adam, leading to Jesus Christ.

As such, the "lineage" would be continued in France (and beyond). This would be followed by the spread of the Roman Catholic Church, as the replacement for the Roman Empire's holdings. This can then be seen as the conflict between Gnostics and the Church, and the Crusades and Inquisitions brought on by the Church, in the name of Christ. This can be seen as "So many" acts "with mischiefs done." Still, The wording of line two also sets up a secondary theme that warns of how "So many" dedicated to the "virgin" (the kings of Europe and the popes) will have succumbed "to evils," causing them to perform "evil deeds" and "hurtful acts."

The word "*maulx*" is an Old French spelling of the modern word "*maux,*" with both representing the plural number of "*mal.*" The word "*mal*" can mean, "trouble, difficulty, pain, evil, or badly,"[159] where Randle Cotgrave added, "mischief, hurt, harm, damage, wrong, displeasure, annoyance, grief, sickness, naughty, bad, ill, lewd, hurtful, uneasily, and ill-favoredly (among others)."[160] Randle Cotgrave also listed the word "*mau,*" where he listed its translations as, "An evil, mischief, damage, annoyance, pain, grief, sickness; bad, ill, and naughty," meaning "*mal*" and "*mau*" are dif-

---

158   From Randal Cotgrave's 1611 French-English Dictionary, published online by Greg Lindahl. (http://www.pbm.com/~lindahl/cotgrave/search/897l.html)
159   From the website *Wiktionary*, in a search of the term "mal." (http://en.wiktionary.org/wiki/mal#French)
160   From Randal Cotgrave's 1611 French-English Dictionary, published online by Greg Lindahl. (http://www.pbm.com/~lindahl/cotgrave/search/60or.html)

ferent spellings for the same word. Cotgrave also separately listed the word "*maulx*," as "mischiefs; see Mal."[161] This means "*maulx*" must be seen as a properly spelled Old French word.

A potential problem with that spelling may come to light with the spelling of the next word, "*faitz*" (these spelling are according to the 1568 Lyon edition). The word "*fait*" is an accepted spelling for the third-person present form of the infinitive verb "*faire*" (meaning "to have," with the 3rd pers. present = "has"), while also representing every past tense version, as "had." The word "*fait*" is also a noun, meaning "fact." The plural number of that word is "*faits*," and not "*faitz*," although it might be thought that "*faitz*" translates as "facts." The problem arises when one sees Randle Cotgrave list "*fait*," but rather than translate it, he refers one to look up the word "*faict*," the Old French spelling for both noun and verb now spelled "*fait*."

The question then arises, "Why would quatrain VIII-80 have an Old French word ("*maulx*") be followed by a modern French word ("*fait*"), when there are many spelling of "*faict*" throughout *The Prophecies*? In the 1566 Lyon edition of *The Prophecies*, line two shows "*maux faits*," where the "*l*" has disappeared and the "*z*" has changed into an "*s*." Differences like this are why I disregard the 1566 edition, as it appears to have printer edits that were unapproved. The only reason for a reprint two years later, after Nostradamus' death, would be if it were ordered through instructions given to his assistant (Jean Chavigny, a.k.a Chavignard), to make sure the manuscript was reproduced "as is." This means there is purpose for the two words spelled the way they are in the 1568 edition.

One aspect of Nostradamus spelling "*maulx*" as Old French can be seen as having it represent a simple anagram. While retaining the essence of "evils" and "mischiefs," it is able to expand in meaning when the "*l*" is allowed to become an article attached to "*maux*," as an abbreviated prefix. This makes "*l'maux*" a combination word to consider, which would make its spelling relative to modern French.

The exception then becomes the use of a "-*z*" at the end of "*fait*." Common throughout the quatrains are plural endings being added to past-tense verbs, with the plural number letter, "-*z*," acting to indicate those who have acted in line with the verb. This makes the use of "*fait*" not readable as the noun ("fact"), more than it is as the past participle of

---

161   From Randal Cotgrave's 1611 French-English Dictionary, published online by Greg Lindahl. (http://www.pbm.com/~lindahl/cotgrave/search/617l.html)

"*faire*." The spelling "*faitz*" then becomes "those" who have "done" or "those" who have "acted." It is still possible to see "*fait*" as the noun, such that "facts" is more applicably read as "those" who are known in "fact," or historically documented, and without dispute.

Seeing this detail coming from the spelling of words means line two can be seen to present a statement that says, "So many of the evils those done," and/or "So much with the mischief ones those (in) fact." This then leads to the words "*par moyen*," which can translate to state, "by reason of way," or "through medium."

In the last case, where "medium" is used, the definition becomes, "Something, such as an intermediate course of action, that occupies a position or represents a condition midway between extremes."[162] Following the word "act ones" ("*faitz*"), where "evils" preceded it, the "intermediate" between "evil" and the "widow, him AND virgin" (the holy good on earth) is a priest for the One God, or an Apostle for Christ. This implies the "acts" by the "mediums" for Christ, those filled with the Holy Spirit, will have been persecuted or stripped of their roles.

The next words written are "*se grand*," where once again the word "*grand*" is presented in the text of *The Prophecies*. Whereas the word "*grand*" must be viewed in the overall theme as those nations of "greatness," through wealth, power, and international glory, the most common indication is of Christian nations. This level of "greatness" is then attributable to the blessings of Christ and God. In a quatrain whose main theme is Christian, this would be such an indication. However, as line two is setting up a secondary theme to the "bloodline" and "lineage" of Christ, as the "mediator" for Jesus and the Blessed "Virgin," there is an air of "loftiness" and "stateliness," as well as "power" bestowed upon "those" (plural number in "-*z*") who "act" for God and Christ.

Thus, "those" will see "themselves" ("*se*" in plural number) as "great," while others (plural number) will see "oneself great" ("*se grand*" in a singular sense). In the latter sense, the common people will be conditioned to believe they are looking upon a leader appointed by God. The best example of this is the deification Roman Emperors heaped upon "themselves," which has been a deification model used by the Roman Catholic Church.

---

162   From the Free Dictionary by Farlex, in a search of the term "medium." [Fair use from the source: American Heritage Dictionary of the English Language, 4th Ed., 2000] (http://www.thefreedictionary.com/medium)

Chapter 9: Quatrain VIII-80

The word "*Roge*" is not a word in French, which means it needs to be looked at more closely. Despite the attempts of some to turn "*Roge*" into a misspelled version of "*rouge*," (meaning "red," a color worn by Cardinals, but not popes), that is not supported by logic. One does not have the right to add letters as needed, in order to fit a preconceived notion. Logic says that since Nostradamus stated *The Prophecies* were sourced by divine inspiration from God, where all comes from perfection, misspelled words are impossible. Therefore, the letters of "*Roge*" need to be rearranged, as a simple anagram, in order to turn a word that is not a known into one that is known.

As an anagram, "*R-o-g-e*" easily converts into "*Rego*," where the "*e*" and "*o*" swap positions. The word "*rego*" is clean Latin, as a form of the verb "*regere*," meaning, "to rule, to govern, to guide, to direct, to administer."[163] The form "*Rego*," as the first person, singular, present, states, "I rule, I govern, I steer, I guide."[164] That means the capitalization has the effect of changing the word into a proper noun, as one individual important enough the be "King" or "Ruler."

The Latin language, as indicated by its use in *The Prophecies*, according to the systemic rules, is an indicator of the language of the Church of Rome. Adding that to a main theme having clear religious (Christian) direction, the word "*Roge*" can then be seen as indicative of the position held by a "Pope."

When this is taken into consideration, one can see the secondary theme being developed within the scope of the main theme. As a clarification to or example of a "lineage" of the "virgin," where the main theme established a Christian "bloodline" born from "him" and a "widow," importantly resulting in a "pure child," this is now possible to see both European "Kings" (main theme) and Roman "Popes" (secondary theme) as the themes of quatrain VIII-80.

Since the times of the Jesus' death, resurrection, and ascension, when Mary Magdalene was made "his widow," to the time of Nostradamus, "So many" Christians will have filled southern France (Cathars) and given rise to a "bloodline" of kings (the Arthurian myth). This rise will have also been enhanced by the influence of the popes of Rome, with the Avignon

---

[163] From the Notre Dame University "Latin Dictionary and Grammar Aid," in a search for "rego." (http://catholic.archives.nd.edu/cgi-bin/lookup.pl?stem=rego&ending=)
[164] From the website *Wiktionary*, in a search for the term "rego." (http://en.wiktionary.org/wiki/rego#Latin)

Papacy affecting that influence during the 14th century. During that century, the genocide of the Cathar people occurred, as commanded by the Church (before leaving Rome), under the name of Albigensian Crusade (named after the people around the city Albi, in southwestern France, where many Cathar people lived and thrived). But those "evils" would not be the only "acts" of persecution "done" by "those" (plural number) under the influence of a "Pope," as a series of Inquisitions would take place, as well as waves of plague, where "So much ills" took place in the name of good.

The secondary theme leads one to see "So many of bad ones made ones through moderation itself great King." This is the Church being elevated to a level of godliness on earth, with "moderation" seen as conversion, rather than move, die, or both, in order to maintain different beliefs. Nostradamus' family found that possible because of they believed Jesus "himself" ("*se*") as "great" ("*grand*") and truly the "King" ("*Rego*"). They adopted the family name that honored the "Virgin," as a family ("bloodline") venerating "Our lady."

Still, reading "So many of bad ones" gives an indication of a number of "hurtful" elements that were seen to have "caused, acted, exploited, effected, and/or committed" against the "virgin." In light of the recent scandals that have faced the Roman Catholic Church, in particular those involving priests and bishops around the world, "harms made" involving male children, who were "innocent ones" and still "virginal." They were able to make such advances without much resistance, because they were seen "As worthy" of trust, "by reason of" ("*par*") their being seen as "mediators" ("*moyen*") to the "great King," or Christ the "King."

The scandals worsened due to "themselves" (plural meaning of "*se*") being part of the "grand" church, knowing the "power" (derived from the meaning of "*grand*," as "mighty") and "loftiness" of the church's "substantial" holdings must be protected by the "Pope." Thus, nothing was done to reprimand those who were "So many," doing "So much harm." This makes the secondary theme be one of a downfall of the institution dedicated to the "virgin."

Because line two ends without any punctuation, it is continued without pause in line three. The first word of line three then directly relates to "*Roge*," or the first person singular present statement of "I Govern." The first word of line three is capitalized, showing the importance of that chosen word. That word is "*Saintz,*" which is making a important distinction about officially declared "Saints," or the "ones" (plural number of "*-z*") deemed to be "Saints" by the Roman Catholic Church.

Those destined for sainthood have their names recommended by individual "Popes," but many of the designated "Saints" have themselves been "Popes." Because the first thirty-five popes have been deemed "Saints" (74 total popes have been canonized, 73 from the first 109 popes), this first word of line three furthers how sincere "Holiness" (from "*Saintz*") is relative to how one individual "Rules" ("I Govern"). Additionally, the spelling, as "*Saintz,*" is in the masculine gender, plural number, designating a "lineage" of "popes," in particular those in the early Church.

At the time Nostradamus wrote *The Prophecies* (1554 -1555), the last Roman pope to be canonized as "Saint" was "Saint" Celestine V, who served as pope in 1294 A.D.[165] He was the 74th pope to be named a "Saint," as the 192nd in line after "Saint" Peter. In groups of 50, 48 of the fist 50 popes were deemed "Saints." Of the second 50, the number dropped to 21. The third group of 50 only has three canonized. The fourth group only has one (he served between 1566-1572), although six have been beatified (given the name "Blessed"). The fifth group of 50 also only has one canonized (his term was 1903 – 1914), with two beatified. The remaining group of popes only numbers 16, with Pope Benedict XVI the current one in that position (not counting antipopes).[166]

Since Nostradamus wrote *The Prophecies*, there have been two popes made "Saints." The canonization of Pope Pius V occurred in 1712, 140 years after his death in 1572. The other to be canonized was done by Pope Pius XII, in 1954, only 40 years after Pope Pius X died, in 1914. This means that since the lifetime of Nostradamus a 331-year span bridged the service of those two popes (1572 – 1903). However, things seem to be changing.

Since the canonization of Pius X, Pope John Paul II beatified Pope John XXIII and Pope Pius IX (1846-1878). Both of those distinctions took place on September 3, 2000. Pope Benedict XVI has since proposed Pope John Paul II be "fast-tracked" to sainthood, having a nun claim she was healed of a disease by praying to his spirit (she later recanted that claim). Pope

---

[165]   From the New Advent website, under the page title, "Catholic Encyclopedia: List of Popes." (http://www.newadvent.org/cathen/12272b.htm)
[166]   As of early 2013, a second pope has been appointed, supposedly making one a quitter or an antipope, but they live happily together in Vatican City. The call the new one Pope Francis the talking mule? That may or may not make the total 267.

John Paul II was beatified anyway, but he has not given the "Saints" membership card just yet.

In other words, the 20th century has found a renewed interest in promoting popes as "Saints" and canonization in general. Pope Pius XII (canonized 39 people, including one pope). Pope John Paul II canonized over 100 people, but he reigned over 27 years. The new antipope, Pope Francis of South America has only had papal rule for a couple of months and he already has figured out over 800 people are worthy of being deemed holy. After centuries of popes simply holding the highest position in the Church, as "moderators" or "mediums, they have begun to see "themselves great" enough to see holy when they look at it. Even though one might presume it takes a "Saint" to know one, perhaps all the 20th century popes will be deemed "Saints" by Antipope Francis.

Drinking from the Cups of Wolves

This recent trend must be seen as explained by the second word in line three, "*simulachres*," which means (in the plural number), "images, pictures, or counterfeits of a man or woman; the figure, semblance, resemblance, likeness, form, or proposition of anything represented."[167] As a stand-alone statement, one has to see how the word points to something that is a copy of an original, with "likeness" implying something not of its own right. The word "counterfeit" more strongly states something that is false, rather than bona fide and legal tender. The modern French spelling, "*simulacre*," translates as "statue, idol; phantom, specter; and travesty, mockery."[168] This means that when the word follows "Saints," it is making a statement about "Popes" who would be "Saints" being a "mockery" of the Church, "counterfeiting" the true meaning of a leader filled with the Holy Spirit.

That then leads to the next word, "*trempez*," which has two uses. One is as the plural form of the masculine gender noun, meaning, "household wine, small wine for servants, made from water added to the bottom lees or grounds of good wine." The second is as the feminine gender, first person present form of the verb "*tremper*," meaning, "the temper of a weapon; also a dipping; steeping; seasoning, tempering; also the temperature, disposition, or composition of the mind; the mood, humor, or

---

[167] From Randal Cotgrave's 1611 French-English Dictionary, published online by Greg Lindahl. (http://www.pbm.com/~lindahl/cotgrave/search/869r.html)
[168] From the free multilingual dictionary Wiktionary, under a search for "simulacre." (http://en.wiktionary.org/wiki/simulacre)

temper wherein it is."

Without the "-z" ending, the word can also be accented, indicating the past-tense of that verb, where one finds the meaning to be the "ones" (plural ending to past-tense verb) who "dipped; moistened, wet; steeped, soaked; seasoned or tempered."[169] Keep in mind the standard letter indicating the plural number is "-s" (added to the accented masculine form) and not "-z." This means the "-z" ending is significant.

When line one states in its theme, "To the innocent ones him blood," the Catholic communion, or eucharistic rite, can be seen as symbolizing that "blood." The serving of holy wine, as the blood of Christ, is then clarified in line three (the supporting details line for the main theme), telling of "counterfeited Saints" serving "counterfeited wine" (the "dregs") to the "innocent ones." When the word "*trempe*" bears the meaning of "dipping" one can see the communion service where some will dip the sacramental wafer (the bread) into the wine of the communion cup. The spirit consumed is not the best offering, but of the lowest quality.

Still, "*trempez*" acts as identifying the mental attitude of the "Saints," who might see their position as one giving each the power to wield the sword of Crusader. In modern French, "*trempes*" has a noun usage, where the colloquial meaning is "beatings" and "hidings."[170] That could be seen as an indication of "Saints" "hiding" their true "emotions" towards Christ and the "virgin." It can also indicate the people served are being punished, as through a ritual "beating" conducted by "those" (the plural "-z") pretending to serve Christ.

When the word is read as "*trempé-z,*" where it is a past participle of the verb "*tremper,*" the plural ending turns the word into a noun representation of the "ones" who "*trempé.*" That meaning becomes "those" who "dipped, moistened, wet, steeped, soaked; seasoned, tempered." This extends to the sacramental rites of baptism and all use of holy water, which is blessed by pretenders. That means nothing they touch changes states, from the physical to the spiritual. This describes the "counterfeit Holy men" as "seasoned counterfeiters," or "those practiced in the art of deception.

This later meaning (apologies to *The Rolling Stones*) relates to the state-

---

169   From Randal Cotgrave's 1611 French-English Dictionary, published online by Greg Lindahl. (http://www.pbm.com/~lindahl/cotgrave/search/927l.html)
170   From the free multilingual dictionary Wiktionary, under a search for "trempe." (http://en.wiktionary.org/wiki/trempe)

ment in quatrain VI-35, where line four told of "letters hidden," where "letters" sent to the pope were subsequently "hidden" away in the archives vault. That link makes line three of this quatrain (VIII-80) focus on the events of Fatima, Portugal (1917), which were warnings for the Vatican to confront Communism and re-consecrate Russia.

That warning was "hidden" because the Vatican was no longer the home of true "Saints." That place only protected those pretending to be holy men. Without the support of Christ the "King" in their "hearts" (the meaning of "*moyen*" as "in the midst of," which is within one's heart), they would be "hiding ones" ("*trempez*"), from fear of confrontation, lest they be exposed as faithless.

The next two words of line three state, "*en ardant*," which can translate to say, "into burning." The use of the word "*ardant*" can then be seen as repeating a word seen before in this series of "virgin" quatrains. In quatrain VI-35, line three had its final segment state, "*le Sol ardera grand plaine*," which was said could translate to state, "the Foundation will burn great plain." Here, in quatrain VIII-80, line three follows "Holy men … counterfeits … those dregs" with words that then continue, "into burning."

The verb "*ardoir*" is the infinitive verb that is the root for both "*ardera*" (quatrain VI-35) and "*ardant*" (quatrain VIII-80). As such, "*ardoir*" means, "to burn, to be on fire; to be inflamed or kindled; (hence) also to be very earnest; or hot in a matter; to love exceedingly; to desire fervently; covet vehemently, long for very much; to inflame or set on fire, as in the Proverb, "*L'argent ard gent*."[171] That idiom translates as, "Money burns many.[172] When one sees how "*ardera*" represent the future tense form, quatrain VI-35 is stating, "him [the] Foundation [or Lowest level of a house] will inflame." Thus, the use of the present participle, "*ardant*," in quatrain VIII-80 says, "Holy ones [who are] counterfeiting dregs [are] inflaming." Both forms are referring to an "exceeding" level of "fervor," relative to the Roman Catholic Church.

The small word "*en*" states the transition from "*trempez*" to "*ardant*," or from "seasoned ones" to "inflaming." The word "*en*" can have several uses in French, one being as a simple preposition, stating "in, into, at, on, and upon." As a stand-alone statement, "*en*" can then be showing the

---

171   From Randal Cotgrave's 1611 French-English Dictionary, published online by Greg Lindahl. (http://www.pbm.com/~lindahl/cotgrave/search/063l.html)
172   From a listing of "French Proverbs stated in Randal Cotgrave's 1611 Dictionary," under the heading, "Money, the lack thereof, and the business world," and published online by Greg Lindahl. (http://www.pbm.com/~lindahl/cotgrave/search/063l.html)

direction that will be found taken by the "Holy men" who will be "counterfeit ones," and "hiding ones." This means "*en*" could be an indication of a transition "into" their rank, and once established with high-ranking positions "in" the Church they would be able to then substitute watered down wine to the believers. This entrance, "in" with the Church that had "Saints" before anyone took the time to deem them as such, becomes a purposeful sham "upon" Christianity, a true religion spread by the acts and deeds of real "Holy men." Still, there was another use of "*en*" in Old French.

According to the Randal Cotgrave 1611 dictionary, he detailed one use of "*en*" as, "Relating to a thing meant or mentioned before," used as "thereof; any or none thereof." Line three of quatrain VIII-80 states "*trempez*," or "seeped ones," before the word "*en*." That use could then translate as, "thereof," making "those dipped" (plural number with "*-z*") be the focus or concern of that "burning."

One can then see the word "*trempez*" meaning "baptized ones," as "one dipped into" the water of a baptismal font. That ritual has been performed by "Holy men," especially "Saints," who have been "steeped in" the Holy Spirit, more than ordained by teaching practices (seminaries), learning only to baptize the flock with water. When one finds that element prior to the use of "*en*," it leads one to see "*ardant*" as the result of that "dipping" and "tempering."

When one admits the main theme is religious, in particular relative to Christianity, with the "blood of the widow him AND virgin" an indication of the spread of Christ's message to France, before the Church of Christ in Rome took over for the Roman Empire and its emperors, one has to see "burning" in a Christian context. While the aspect of "burning" can be seen as an emotional "fervor," it can equally be seen as a form of punishment, such as "burning" at the stake (an earthly decision as appropriate justice) and "burning" in hell (a heavenly decision as appropriate justice). While the present participle makes it possible to see an actual physical fire "burning," just as quatrain VI-35 made it possible to see something that "will burn great plain," the physical does not capture the expanse that the symbolic allows. Therefore, the greatest danger to be found in line three of quatrain VIII-80 is the acts of the shepherds, not only "burning" their souls in eternity, but also "burning" those souls of the flocks who blindly follow them, as "Holy men."

The word "*ardant*" stands alone, as its own statement about "burning, enflaming, and/or fervently desiring." It then leads one to the last word of line three, which is "*cierge*," or "candle." As revealed in the analysis of quatrain VI-35, where the word was found in line four ("letters hidden ones in the candle"), we learned that a "*cierge*" is the name of a Roman Catholic ceremonial "candle." Randal Cotgrave described the word as being the "biggest middle-sized wax candle used in churches" (from referencing the word "*poincte*"). Because quatrain VI-35 offers the wax of a "candle" as the papal seal on the "letters" of Sister Lucia, the same focus can be shown on line three here, and its use of a "burning ceremonial candle."

According to the systems required to follow, in order to understand *The Prophecies*, line three is where the direct supporting details for the main theme (line one) are found. This means the introduction of an important (ampersand preceding) "virgin," the "burning candle" is supporting that theme. The main theme begins by stating, "From the innocent ones [to] him [their] blood." The main theme separates "virgin," and shows it an important word to consider, by the ampersand.

The Blessed Mother Mary gave Sister Lucia and her cousins a glimpse of a future that was the end of the Church. At the beginning of the third secret exposed, she wrote, "we saw an Angel with a flaming sword in his left hand; flashing, it gave out flames that looked as though they would set the world on fire." This was a warning by the "Virgin" (ampersand acts to capitalize), of "burning" to come.

Sister Lucia also wrote in her third secret letter, "two Angels each with a crystal aspersorium in his hand, in which they gathered up the blood of the Martyrs and with it sprinkled the souls that were making their way to God." Not only does this match the main theme, as depicting how "innocent ones," Christians, died for "him," Christ, by spilling their "blood," it explains the use of "*Saintz*." To realize this, it is important to see how "Martyrs," as personified by capitalization, is the same as "*Saintz*."

A "martyr" is defined as, "One who chooses to suffer death rather than renounce religious principles."[173] As such, capitalizing the word then makes it properly identify Christians who have been deemed "Saints" because of such a sacrifice. In this regard, on May 12, 2013, Antipope

---

173 From the Free Dictionary by Farlex, in a search of the term "martyr." [Fair use from the source: American Heritage Dictionary of the English Language, 4th Ed., 2000] (http://www.thefreedictionary.com/martyr)

Francis named 802 new "Saints."[174] Of those "Saints" named by Francis, 800 were "Martyrs of Otranto" (Italy).

Turkish invaders in the 15th century beheaded 800 citizens of Otranto because they refused to convert to Islam. These 800 are not listed by their names, individually, as their "likenesses" (form of "*simulachres*") is as a group. They have been collectively known as the "protectors of Otranto" since being beatified in 1771. Still, because their path to sainthood stalled (for 236 years), Pope Benedict renewed the canonization process in 2007, announcing those "Saints-to-be" on the same day he told the world of his resignation (February 28, 2013). Antipope Francis was then given credit for the actual canonization, almost as if he and his Vatican cohort were "dipping" into the beatitude bucket looking for "dregs" from whom to take credit.

The Lampstand will be Removed

Because the main theme statement (line one) ends with a colon, and because lines two and three do not end with any punctuation, the three subsequent lines act as one clarification. This means line four continues the clarification of the main theme, while systemically supporting the secondary theme. It still continues the flow of the supporting details of the main theme, from line three. When the use of "virgin" is seen as the warning from the Marian apparition at Fatima, and the "innocent ones blood" being relative to martyrdom of Christians, line four continues the element of "burning thereof candle" with "*De frayeur*," or "From terror."

The use of "candle" (as a "big wax candle used in religious rites") has been shown to act (when combined with "letters," in quatrain VI-35) as a ceremonial "candle" used to make a papal seal on an envelope. Here, the use is still relative to the Roman Catholic Church (due to their veneration of Mary), but the focus is not so much on the "dripping" of wax as it is on the "burning" that will have set "upon" the Church. As such, a "candle" becomes an instrument of time, where a "burning candle" can only yield light so long, before it burns out. The saying, "burning the candle on both ends" means one is hastening towards that time when the "candle" will no longer have use. When that imagery is seen, line four is then addressing the collapse of Christian leadership by shifting to the introduction of a time importantly (capitalization) "With fear."

---

[174] May 13 is the date of the first of the apparitions at Fatima, and that date is recognized as a Marian feast day, known as Our Lady of Fatima.

It is important to recognize that the word "*De*" is a repeated word in this quatrain. It is presented in line one as "*Des*" (capitalized plural combined form), and in line two as "*de*" (lowercase). This means that all three translations will not have the same translation at the same time. If line one begins "To the innocent one," and if line two continues, "So much from," then line four is limited to beginning as "With" or "Of," the other translations of "*de*." The capitalization, as "With," means an important accompaniment follows the "burning in candle." This is "With terror," which is the emotional reaction Sister Lucia felt, so much that when she was shown the "burning" of Hell, she wrote, "I think we would have died of fear and terror."

Fire has been a consistent theme throughout the quatrains containing the word "*vierge*." Quatrains III-84 and IV-35 told of "fire" ("*feu*"), and quatrains VI-35 and VIII-80 mention "will burn" and "burning." The repeating of "*cierge*" in quatrains VI-35 and VIII-80 is likewise important to recognize, as a "candle" is a way to use "fire" as "light." In all of the quatrains of *The Prophecies*, the word "*cierge*" only appears three time. Two have been in this series containing "*vierge*," and while the other quatrain does not reference that word, it does use "temple," ("*temple*") "lamp" (as both "*lamp*'" [French] and "*lucerne*" [Latin]), in addition to "*cierge*." This usage can be an indication of the light of a "candle," as represented by a "lampstand."

In John's *Book of The Revelation*, chapter 2, a message is sent to the church in Ephesus, which says, "remember from where you have fallen, and repent and do the deeds you did at first; or else I am coming to you and will remove your lampstand out of its place." (Rev. 2:5, New American Standard Bible) In the letter written by Sister Lucia, she said, "pointing to the earth with his right hand, the Angel cried out in a loud voice: 'Penance, Penance, Penance!' And we saw in an immense light that is God," This shows how the vision shown to the Apostle John was of the same end shown to Sister Lucia, relative to when the "burning candle" is not yet extinguished, before the lampstand is removed. The result, as witnessed by the "innocent ones" in Fatima, was an end shown to take place if forewarning is not heeded.

Thus, it will be that removal that will come "With fear" and "Of horror," to those who will have not heeded the warning, as they will be of no faith. The word following "*frayeur*" ("fear, dread, fright, terror, horror, and/or scaring") is "*crainte*," meaning "doubt of, doubted" (as well as "dreaded, feared, awe of, and/or redoubt"). This is an indication that Christ fulfilling His promise will come as a surprise. No one will have taken the warning of John seriously, nor will they have seen the prophecies of Nostradamus as having any merit, and they will have disregarded the warning of Mary, the "virgin," through the "innocent ones," with Sister Lucia a "nun" (variation of "*vierge*").

The aspect of "doubt" can then be seen reflecting the "Pope," as a supporting detail of "*Roge*," which has been seen as an anagram for "*Rego*," meaning "I rule, I guide, I govern, and/or I steer." This "doubted" is related to "terror," as the institution of the Church not recognizing a threat of "terror" against it. It will be casting "doubt" on itself, due to the scandals that will have caused "horrors" to "innocent ones." The point of all that will be "doubted, dreaded, and/or feared" is that "neither" side "will see" the truth. The warnings of a doomed Church, from the "virgin" (Lucia and Mary), will not allow the truth be known (the secret letters sealed from view). The vision shown to three "innocent ones" "will not be viewed" by those truly faithful to Christ ("him" of the "virgin").[175]

Another negative follows "not will see" ("*ne verra*"), such that "*nul*" means, "none, not one, not any." The scope of "not will view" is then stated to be a complete lack of vision and acceptance of sight, by anyone. The word "*nul*" can also mean "of no value," which is a statement of something seen being something that "will not (be) perceived" as valuable or worth acting upon. This is the documented history of the warnings received by the Vatican, from Sister Lucia.

This reading of line four, to this point, shows an extension of the "burning candle," as the light by which one can "see," by which one can read letters. The association of the "*cierge*" to religious rites and Church presence means line four is presenting the importance (capitalization) "Of that" which has been written (later use of "*que*," as a reflection back on "that" before), which should be "feared" and "dreaded," should it ever come to pass.

Line four is then foretelling of a time prophesied that will be known but not recognized when it comes. It will be a time when one is blind to seeing, as "that" which one "will see" will be "blank" (alternate translation of

---

[175] The line of popes who will have seen the letters of Sister Lucia did include Pope John Paul I, who did immediately initiate actions to correct the errors of the Church, or to right the Bark. However, he was assassinated after only 33 days, forever dooming the warning of Fatima to a hidden state that "not will see" the light of day.

"*nul*"). It represents a time when the one who should "see" for the people (those reading by the "candle of religious rites") will be "idle" (alternate translation of "*nul*"). It is saying "that" state of ineffectiveness "will see nothing," because the lampstand will have been removed.

The last word of line four is "*boge*." This word can be seen as Ancient French (a language prior to the Old French of Nostradamus), related to the word "*bouge*," meaning, "A big bag (made of a jute cloth)," as well as something akin to a "knapsack" (French "*cartable*").[176] According to Randle Cotgrave, the word "*bouge*" meant, "A budget, wallet, great pouch, male, or case of leather, serving to carry things in behind a man on horseback."[177] This would make it also akin to a "saddlebag." In the context of line four, within the theme of line one, this can only be a symbol of material things being the focus of the Church, rather than spiritual goals. However, this should not be seen as the primary intent of the word "*boge*."

The word "*boge*" is a matching rhyme to the last word in line two, "*Roge*." I have already addressed that "*Roge*" is not a word, and through seeing it as an anagram, it morphs into "*Rego*." Because the quatrains of *The Prophecies* so often have symmetry, it is almost systemic to see a word like "*boge*" as also needing to be rearranged, simply to match "*Roge*" being rearranged. The rhyme then becomes less an issue, because the rearrangement is.

In this regard, the letters "*b-o-g-e*" can simply be rearranged to become "*gobe*," where the last letter should be accented, as "*gobé*." This is the past-tense form of the infinitive verb "*gober*," meaning, "To ravine, devour; feed greedily, swallow great morsels, let down whole gobbets."[178] A "gobbet" is said to be the diminutive of the French word "*gobe*," meaning "mouthful," with "gobbet" being "A piece or chunk, especially of raw meat; and a small amount of liquid, a small drop."[179] The past-tense form can be read as "swallowed up," "gobbled up," or "gulped down."

If this translation is read into line four, it shows a state that is hard to "swallow." It shows a ravenous state that had been "feared" and "dread-

---

[176] From the website *Wiktionnaire*, from a search of the term "boge." (http://fr.wiktionary.org/wiki/boge)
[177] From Randal Cotgrave's 1611 French-English Dictionary, published online by Greg Lindahl. (http://www.pbm.com/~lindahl/cotgrave/search/128l.html)
[178] From Randal Cotgrave's 1611 French-English Dictionary, published online by Greg Lindahl. (http://www.pbm.com/~lindahl/cotgrave/search/493l.html)
[179] From the Free Dictionary by Farlex, in a search for "gobbet." [Source: The American Heritage Dictionary of the English Language, 4th Ed., 2000] (http://www.thefreedictionary.com/gobbet)

ed" coming true, despite all language to the contrary, casting "doubt" on prophecy. Pope John Paul II supposedly gave the Catholic faithful a bitter pill to "swallow," when he consecrated the whole world (which included the Soviet Union), thereby putting an end to all speculation about the secret letters sent to the pope, by Sister Lucia in the 1940s. All that was to be "feared" was set aside, with all to be in "awe of" (alternate translation of "*crainte*") Pope John Paul II. However, the revealing of the three secrets of Fatima was "not" so that all "will see" the truth.

Many people have "doubted" the letters of Sister Lucia, as have been released by the Vatican. Many feel that a false document (a "likeness" or a "counterfeit") has been released, appearing so people "will see none" of the real warning. Included in the 20th century history of the Church, since the first apparition at Fatima, May 13, 1917, when the holy "candle" began "burning," to expose a danger (light in the Church) and to conceal that warning (papal seals on the letters), "Holy men" have been replaced by "likenesses" and "figures" unlike those prior to that century.

A true "Saint" became pope in 1978 (August 26), and he began investigating the Church's "budget" (translation of "*boge*") and finances. There was reason to "dread" the result of that audit, and as "feared," the truth was exposed. The Vatican Bank was laundering Sicilian drug money, due to the decline in Catholics in the affluent nations of Christianity. That "Saint" was murdered by those who would later cover up that murder and become the next line of popes (John Paul II and Benedict XVI).

Those would begin naming new "Saints," which would give them the "images" as "Holy men." Those men would cast "doubt" on the Prophecy of the Popes, by Saint Malachy (12th century, first published in 1595) and the Fatima Prophecy; but "none" of the popes seeing those letters and knowing that end "will see that," at least as worthy of acting upon from faith. They were all too busy focusing on the "wallet" and the "purse" of the Church. Because of "that," they will be "swallowed up" and spit out for being lukewarm.

In all, quatrain VIII-80 perfectly predicted the current state of the Roman Catholic Church and the collapsed condition of the Christian world. This one quatrain sums up one of the major themes of *The Prophecies*, where "religions" were one of the stalwarts of the 16th century, one prophesied to become "opposite, diametrically." This quatrain explains that theme by telling how the head of the Church will be corrupted, making everything from the head down a sham. This theme and explanation is then at the root of all the apparitions of the "virgin," in particular the one witnessed at Fatima.

All of the appearances of the Virgin Mary have been to those who are the "innocent ones," and who had been too young, too poor, and too uneducated to hold devout levels of belief in the Christian dogmas of the Roman Catholic Church. All the children were members of the Catholic faith, but most belonged to parents who did not take their children to church regularly. No demands were made on the children, as the "virgin" made requests that were voluntary. All gladly accepted, and followed her instructions wholeheartedly. Anything she said to them that was meant to be revealed was a test of those who lead the Church, to see if they would likewise respond with vigor and delight.

It makes sense to realize, especially as the letters of Sister Lucia have proven, the Vatican has been frozen "From fear" (a sign of a lack of true faith), unable to act because of the claims of a stupid little peasant girl, turned nun. It has been much easier for their "doubt" to explain their failure to respond, as "not" (the primary translation of "*ne*") able to go along with those instructions because of a lack of proof. Quatrain VIII-80 exposes popes as "not" truly "born" (translations of "*ne*" and as "*né*") to serve God, Christ, or the Blessed Virgin, more than themselves.

Chapter 10
The Seventh "*Vierge*" Quatrain

Quatrain VIII-90

The seventh and final quatrain stating the word "*vierge*" is found positioned as the 90th in Centurie VIII. The word "*vierge*" is found placed in line three, meaning its placement makes it be a supporting detail of the main theme of this quatrain. In that quatrain Nostradamus wrote (In the Old French of Nostradamus, followed by my English translation):

> *Quand des croisez un trouvé de sens trouble*
>
> *En lieu du sacre verra un bœuf cornu*
>
> *Par vierge porc son lieu lors sera comble,*
>
> *Par roy plus ordre ne sera soustenu.*
>
> --
>
> When of them crossed ones one found with intelligence trouble
>
> Upon seat of the sacred will see one bull having horns
>
> Through virgin swine its rank then will be summary,
>
> By reason of king more order (of religious men) not will be supported.

Quatrain VIII-90 beings with the word "*Quand*," which can be either an adverb or a conjunction, meaning (briefly) "When" (adverb) or "Seeing that" (conjoining to something stated before). You may not recall, because I did not go deeply into explaining this before, but quatrain III-44 also began line one with the same word. Its main theme stated, "*Quand l'animal à l'homme domestique.*" That can translate as, "When the animal in the man domestic," but rather than go over that quatrain again, I feel it is important to see how a capitalized word is repeated, and how repetition makes its own statement, regardless of the specific word translations.

As a stand-alone word of importance, the word "*Quand*" is indicating a significant event in time. As the first word of a quatrain, introducing all four lines, as well as the main theme statement, "When" something happens is important. The focus is then importantly "At that time," when this quatrain will begin to take effect.

In Randle Cotgrave's 1611 dictionary, the word "*quand*" is said to have translations that mean, "if that, although, howbeit, notwithstandingf, all were it; till, until, or against the time that." By knowing it can convey the sense, "Against the time that," we have a comparison of time, from one event to another, with the two events related. A connection is made between something having already happened and something related that is to happen next. As such, seeing the first word state, "If that," "Although," "Howbeit," and/or "Notwithstanding" (conjunctive translations of "*Quand*"), a statement is made that this quatrain follows another quatrain. That is a statement of order within the quatrains of *The Prophecies*.

By recognizing this statement of ordering, quatrain VIII-90 is immediately known to follow some other quatrain (minimally one). In this book about the messages of the "virgin" in the quatrains of Nostradamus, it should be seen how this is the seventh of seven quatrains I am presenting, where each contains the word "*vierge.*" Quatrain III-44 is another quatrain like quatrain VIII-90. By following a natural order of selection, through "*Centurie*" representation order, both III-44 and VIII-90 can act as continuations of quatrains II-17 and VIII-80, respectively. Still, the seven quatrains may be rearranged and put into a new order, but quatrain III-44 and VIII-90 cannot be the first, because of their first word playing the role as a conjunction.

When Crusaders Sense Trouble

In the first line of quatrain VIII-90, the timing of "When" is connected to the word "*croisez*," where one is again shown a word with a "-z" indicating the plural number. Since the word "*croise*" can also be accented, as "*croisé*," the plural number is again shown connected to a past-tense verb. The word "*croisé*" is the past-tense form of "*croiser*," meaning "to cross, to sign or make the mark of a cross; to lay something across something else; to make an X; or to cross something out in writing."

With these translations, it is important to realize that the word for "cross," as a Christian word indentifying a "crucifix," is "*croix*." The word (unaccented) "*croise*" is the first and third person indicative present of the verb, as "I cross" or "He crosses." The spelling, "*croisez*" is the second-person plural, indicative and imperative, form, as "You cross" or "You cross, please." Because the word connecting "*Quand*" with "*croisez*" is "*des*," a plural preposition-article combination word meaning "of them" or "from those," the unaccented translation would not fit well. This makes "*croisé-z*," as "crossed ones," act as a religious sect marked by a "cross."

Certainly, seeing "*croisé-z*" as "crossed ones" makes the word Christian in nature. As such, it can represent all who wear necklaces and pendants with a "cross." Since all of the quatrains containing the word "*vierge*" have verbiage pointing to the Roman Catholic Church, and the popes of Rome, that line of bishops certainly would fit a description as "crossed ones." One well-known group that also would fit that description would be "Crusaders." The leaders of Europe, with the support and encouragement of Rome, promoted those armed branches of Christianity, whose armor bore the sign of a red cross. Thus, all of this can be read as a time "When of those crossed ones" something is important.

Because the word "*vierge*" appears in line three, where the supporting details are found for the main theme line, it is important to recall how Sister Lucia recalled being shown a vision of the future by the Blessed "Virgin." The vision involved "crossed ones," although not called by that name. She wrote, "[We saw the] the Holy Father … Other Bishops, Priests, men and women Religious going up a steep mountain, at the top of which there was a big Cross." She continued, saying, "[The Holy Father was] on his knees at the foot of the big Cross … [where he] was killed by a group of soldiers who fired bullets and arrows at him, and in the same way there died one after another the other Bishops, Priests, men and women Religious, and various lay people of different ranks and positions."

This is foretelling of an important time, "When to the crossed ones" will come pain, suffering, ruin, and death. The "crossed ones" are "Bishops, Priests, men and women Religious," i.e.: ranking Christians. Lucia's depiction tells of extreme persecution, under a cross. Those shown to her would be killed by "Crusaders" (ones without crosses), with their objective being against Rome. In such a case, "crossed ones" would also be a statement of anger held by those of two opposing parties.

In support of this vision shown to a "virgin" by the "Virgin" Mother, a girl who would later become a "nun," line one continues to state, "one contrived from reason unsettled" (one possibility of translation). From that linear reading, one can get an idea of an issue that will have been "unsettled" or a "hindrance" (translations of "*trouble*"), leading to a time "When" the "trouble" is unavoidable. This will have caused a plan of action, because troubling actions will have been planned and "devised," with some advantages "obtained" (both translation possibilities of "*trouvé*").

When other quatrains have brought up the issue between Christians and Muslims, such a "trouble" is the theft of Palestine and the settlement by Jews being blessed by the Church of Rome. When "Crusaders" is read into "crossed ones" ("*croisé-z*"), that Holy Land has long been the target of Roman pontiffs. Because the Roman Catholic Church has been so persistent over the centuries in its desire to obtain the Holy Land (for itself, not for Jews), its other persistent persecution (of the Jews in Europe) has made the Palestine-Israel issue somewhat of a double-edged sword.

The Church had long been cold about its acceptance of Israel as a recognized international entity, That was, "Until" (alternate translation of "*Quand*") Pope John Paul II made a trip to Israel in March 2000. Pope John Paul II officially recognized Israel's right to exist, by that visit. Pope Benedict then visited Israel in the year 2009, and Antipope Francis recently accepted an invitation to visit Israel, in the year 2013. Muslims can very well see this recognition of Israel as another Rome-supported positioning of "Crusaders" in the Holy Land, only the current occupiers of Jerusalem and Palestine are not Christian militia. The current knights making it safe for Christian pilgrims to visit the land of Jesus are Jewish, armed with Western weaponry and technology.

If that acceptance of Jewish control of the Holy Land was enough to elicit Islamic plans for retribution (as seen in the vision of Sister Lucia), Antipope Francis' announcement of 800 new saints re-ignites the issue of Christian-Muslim hatred. Because Turkish invaders in Otranto, Italy (1480 A.D.) beheaded all of the 800, their new sainthood is a slap at Islam being a cruel religion. That recognition of martyrdom ignores many "Crusades" of the past, where equal atrocities were committed, in the name of Christ. It makes sense that the Church realized that after it beatified the 800 in 1717, leaving them as nameless protectors of the Italian city they died in, as beatified martyrs.

By elevating those martyrs to sainthood, the act has glorified their sacrifices, while indirectly condemned all the Muslim faithful. On the other hand, the Islamic Jihad against the West has been bolstered, since those efforts call for an equal element of self-sacrifice, with willing martyrdom through bombs strapped to children. The acts of popes seem to be designed to anger Islam, whether or not this is planned. Since 1994, when Pope John Paul II began diplomatic a relationship between the Vatican and Israel, three popes have intensified a long-existing "trouble," rather than abate one.

When one remembers the instructions given to Sister Lucia was the re-consecration of Russia, she was told to pass that message on to the pope at a specific time. Since that reconsecration never took place, by constantly keeping those instructions secret and hidden from the public view, Russia is still a factor in the dangers shown to the "virgin" children at Fatima. The Muslims will have the capacity to attack Rome because Russia is atheist and not an ally to the pope. This is how Muslims will have "obtained" or "found" (translation possibilities of "*trouvé*") weapons that can be used to shoot "crossed ones."

The Worship of Ba'als

Line one does not end with any punctuation, meaning there is nothing to pause the main theme from continuing into the secondary theme. While both themes are separate perspectives of one theme, as stated by two separate lines, the lack of interruption by punctuation makes the secondary focus directly relative to the time "When" this "trouble" will befall the "crossed ones," but subsequent to the beginning.

The transition word, the capitalized first word of line two, is "*En*." This preposition means, "In, Into, On, Upon, At," as well has been discussed, "Thereof." Because "*En*" follows line one, the word could then be an indication of something that reflects an important aspect of that mentioned previously. When this last translation ("Thereof") is used as a linkage to the "one found" who offered an "opinion" (alternate translation of "*sens*") that would bring "trouble" or "turmoil," then the significance of capitalization means an important subsequent event or condition is "Thereof" relative.

When that translation fits as a connector to the main theme, the secondary theme can then be read as beginning with the importance of direction, "In, Into, On, Upon, and/or At." This then links to the following words, "*lieu du sacre*," which are translatable as, "place of the sacred." When "*sacre*" is realized as supporting the main theme word "*croisez*," one finds the Christian theme repeated, when an accent mark is added to "*croise*." The word "*sacré*" (with an accent mark) means, "Sacred, sanctified, made holy; received into or invested with religious orders; dedicated, consecrated, or devoted unto religious uses."[180]

Without the accent mark, the word "*sacre*" has far different translation possibilities. Randle Cotgrave listed an unaccented "*sacre*" twice, both as masculine gender words, which differs from the accented versions. When accented, the word "*sacré*" is masculine, while "*sacrée*" is feminine.

The first spelling of "*sacre*" is defined as meaning, "The dedication of a church; & thus the coronation of a prince, or the consecration of a prelate [pope]."[181] The second version was stated to mean, "A saker [Eurasian falcon]; the hawk, and the artillery of the same name; also a ravenous and greedy fellow, one that makes boot of all he can lay his clutches on; an excessive glutton, or gully-gut; and a spend-all, unthrift squanderer, extreme rioter (especially in respect of his belly)."[182] Obviously, this last translation, when used in the context of line two, shows a pope [prelate] importantly "Upon" the "seat of the consecrated" (alternate translation of "*lieu du sacre*"), "At that time" when Rome is experiencing "trouble."

The word "*lieu*" can translate as, "A place; room; seat, rank; stead; also a quality, calling, degree, state; also credit, esteem, reckoning, account; and also a house or dwelling place."[183] This word is not only identifying where the "trouble" will be "found" effecting the "crossed ones," as "In

---

180 From Randle Cotgrave's 1611 French – English Dictionary, published online by Greg Lindahl. (http://www.pbm.com/~lindahl/cotgrave/search/843l.html)
181 From Randle Cotgrave's 1611 French – English Dictionary, published online by Greg Lindahl. (http://www.pbm.com/~lindahl/cotgrave/search/843l.html)
182 Ibid.
183 From Randle Cotgrave's 1611 French – English Dictionary, published online by Greg Lindahl. (http://www.pbm.com/~lindahl/cotgrave/search/581l.html)

house of the sanctified," meaning Vatican City, it is specifically directing one to look "At" the "seat" of the "crossed ones." This is the Holy See, which in Latin is "*Sancta Sedes*," meaning the Holy Seat.

Still, when one looks at who is seated "Upon" the throne of that "place," who holds the highest "rank of the sacred," this is telescoping to the pope. Thus, as a continuation of line one's "trouble" where "one" (from "*un*") will be "found" (from "*trouvé*") "At that time … with judgment" (alternate translations of "*Quand … de sens*"), that "one" causing that "judgment" will be the pope.

The remaining words of line two then state, "*verra un bœuf cornu*," which can translate to say, "will see one bull horned." In this series of words, the word "*un*" is repeated; and although "*un*" is limited in what it can be translated to say ("one, a"), it does not refer to the same "one" twice. The "one" of line one is "Upon" the "seat of the trouble," which that "one" pope "will see." However, the "one" of the secondary theme is what will be coming from outside Rome, which "will see" the "one" "Upon" the "seat." The "one" of the secondary theme will be represented by the "bull horned." This can then be interpreted as saying that one will be angered, armed, and charging, as would a "bull" when "it will see" red.

In the secondary theme of quatrain VI-35, a series of astrological signs appeared to be written. One of those signs was "*Taurus*," but in discussing that quatrain I explained "*Taurus*" was the Latin word for "Bull." I also explained the "Bull" symbolism, due to the importance of capitalization, and explained how it is a symbol used by the European Union. Here, in quatrain VIII-90, the word "*bœuf*" appears, in lower-case French, also meaning "bull," but also "ox" and "beef."

When this is combined with "*cornu*," the adjective meaning "horned," the combination shows a "wild ox," rather than a domesticated animal (a reference found in quatrain III-44). However, when "*bœuf*" is seen as representing Europe (with Rome in Italy, in Europe), one must realize that "*cornu*" is also Latin, used to describe the crescent moon, as the "horns of the moon." The use of Latin always is designed to lead to a higher level meaning.

This realization means that line two states a theme that tells of the "trouble" taking "place At" Rome, "In" Italy, "Upon" Europe. The use of Latin makes that identification. This can then lead one to see how the pope will attract the anger of the Islamic "bull," which will charge with "horns" lowered. The "horns of the bull" is a term used to describe the Crescent Moon, and thus is the sign of Islam. The "horned bull" will then intend to pierce "Into" an enemy long hated. Those "horns" will have been "obtained" (translation of "*trouvé*") from another enemy of Western Europe, Russia.

With the main theme focusing on the history of "Crusades" sponsored by the Roman Catholic Church, the secondary theme then focuses on "When" that "trouble" will be found "In the Holy See," from the horns of enraged Muslims. Because line two also does not end with any punctuation, its flow of thought is continued into line three. Line three is where the supporting details for the main theme are always found, but the lack of punctuation pausing thought makes it clear that the elements of line three are always subsequent and also related to that stated in the secondary theme.

When Swine Trample Places Holy

The important link that line three makes to line two is shown through the capitalized first word, which is the preposition, "*Par*." This word mirrors the importance of "When" (line one's first word) and "Upon" (line two's first word), by stating the importance of, "By, By reason of, Through, For, Of, and On." This preposition also directly links to word two of line three, which is where "*vierge*" is found. Thus, when one is seeing a main theme of "When Crusaders find trouble," with a secondary theme focusing on that time of "trouble" being relative to one "Upon the Holy See," the Church of Rome is identified.

This makes that the Church "Of the Virgin," "Through" the Catholic veneration of her (capitalized use of "*Par*"). This is also "By reason of" so many Roman Catholic cathedrals, basilicas, churches having been named in her honor. This translation and meaning continues the religious themes and supports a main theme as confirming the main focus as being on her Church.

Besides "*vierge*" being a key word in line three, the word following it, "*porc*," is also important to recognize as a symmetrical word. Both "*porc*" and "*bœuf*," as "pork" and "beef" or "swine" and "ox," are representative of domesticated animals. The word "*porc*" means, "pork, hog, swine" (indicating a whole living animal), while also meaning "pork," as a cut of meat (from a dead swine). The French spelling is directly linked to the Latin root, where "*porca*" is a "sow" and "*porcus*" is the masculine word for "pig, hog."[184]

This Latin connection is important in a quatrain with religious (Christian) themes, especially seeing how "*vierge*" supports that as well. The use of Latin then creates a symmetry of opposites, where French and Latin terms of domesticated animals are used. In that case, the use of Latin places a special focus on the word "*porc*."

In the letter of preface to *The Prophecies*, Nostradamus quoted the Apostle Matthew, who quoted Jesus in his Gospel. From that book, Jesus said, "Give not that which is holy ("*sanctum*") unto the dogs, neither cast ye your pearls before swine ("*porcos*" – plural), lest they trample them under their feet, and turn again and rend you." (Matthew 7:6 – King James Version, Cambridge Ed.)[185] As a preface to the quatrains, Nostradamus stated that "dogs" and "swine" would never serve God or Christ as their master, such that those animals become anthropomorphisms of people who would act as such animals. In that way, Nostradamus explained how the dangers of his prophetic future would include "swine" figures. That is what can be understood in line three's use of "*porc*."

In the preface, because Nostradamus was making that quote from the *Holy Bible*, he wrote in Latin. That was (and still is) the language of the Roman Catholic Church's translations of the original Hebrew and Greek texts. Whenever Nostradamus wrote in Latin, in both the letters and quatrains, he did so to make an indirect statement relative to Rome, and in particular to the Roman Church. Since the only use of "swine" in the preface is that one Latin word, "*porcos*," all of the presentations in the quatrains meaning "pork, swine, hog" are related to that prefaced meaning.

In all of the quatrains of *The Prophecies*, quatrain VIII-90 is the only one where the spelling "*porc*" is used. Nostradamus did write the French word "*pourceau*" in two other quatrains (I-64 and III-69),[186] which means the same as "*porc*." That uniqueness and closeness to the Latin spelling makes the use of "*porc*" in quatrain VIII-90 an indication of the Vatican

---

184   From the Notre Dame University "Latin Dictionary and Grammar Aid," under a search for "porc." (http://catholic.archives.nd.edu/cgi-bin/lookup.pl?stem=porc&ending=)
185   From Biblos.com, under search for "Matthew 7:6." (http://bible.cc/matthew/7-6.htm)
186   From the website "Index of the Centuries of Nostradamus," prepared by J. Flanagan, under the heading, "Alphabetical Index of Nostradamus," and sub-headed "N-P Nostradamus Index." (http://alumnus.caltech.edu/~jamesf/nindex/np_index.html)

"swine" (plural).

That connection makes it directly follow "*vierge*" as a natural statement about the Church that reveres Mary the mother of Christ. It does not have any meaning about a "virgin" group of "hogs," nor does it make a statement that the "Virgin" is to be seen as a "swine." It is a reference to "swine" being exposed through the "virgin," which is what happened when Sister Lucia sent a letter to the Vatican stating what the Holy Mother had instructed her to tell the Pope.

Thus, importantly (from capitalization of a preposition) "By reason of" (possible translation of "*Par*") "virgin," meaning an apparition of the "Virgin" Mary to the children of Fatima, a "swine" will have taken "his place." This is known by the trampling underfoot (or at least out of the way, in the archive vault) of the pearls of revelation Sister Lucia provided. Once in "their place," a series of "swine" would ensure the words were "rended," by making them secret and only releasing some version of their message, well after the fact, in parts. Pope John Paul II declared there was no longer any need to fear the warning, as the Soviet Union "rended" itself, saving the Church from that dirty deed.

The remainder of line three states, "*son lieu lors sera comble*," which can translate to say, "his place then will be summary." In line three, one finds the word "*lieu*" is repeated, as it is also stated in line two. This, again, is a form of symmetry, where there is a difference between the two "places."

The masculine gender possessive pronoun, "*son*," precedes "*lieu*," in line three. This makes it appear that the masculine gender noun, "*porc*" ("swine"), is a focus of possession, as "his." This implies the one possessing that "seat" is "sacred," as was stated in line two. However, the general can also be read, as "its seat" or "its reckoning" (both translations of the word "*lieu*"), when linking "*son lieu*" to the word "*porc*." The use of "its" is more in line with how one would identify an animal, regardless of gender.

When each word is read as individually important, with the freedom to relate equally to other words in the text of a quatrain, "*son*," as "his," becomes relative to the "virgin," as a male heir. This means "*his house*" (alternate translation of "*son lieu*") is the Church of Christ, where "his" mother, the "virgin," is venerated. Following the word "*porc*," where a leader of "his house" is metaphorically called a "swine," "By reason of" the "virgin" (from "*Par vierge*"), this "will be" the time when that "house" of God "will be" ended.

Because line three is adding supporting detail to the main theme (line one), one needs to see the timing reflection of "*lors*," relating to "*Quand*." The word "*lors*" translates as, "then, while that, in that time, and/or in that season," such that the first to third support establishes a "When – then" scenario. "When of the crossed ones one contrived with understanding sedition" is established through control of the "Holy See" ("*sacre lieu*"), "then" that "rank will be closed up" (translation possibility of "*lieu ... sera comble*").

This requires one see the multiple sides of the word "*comble*," which is another word that can be accented, as "*comblé*." Whether "*comble*" is seen as a noun, adjective, or a verb form, all meanings are relative to the infinitive verb, "*combler*." The word "*combler*" translates as, "To fill or heap up; also to accomplish, fulfill, satiate; make or close up."[187] The Wiktionary website adds, "to satisfy; to fill (add to the point of full); to fill (to install someone); and to counter."[188]

Thus, the unaccented noun, "*comble*," means, "roof of a building; peak; full measure,"[189] as well as, "fullness, abundance, heaped measure; the chief point of, whole sum of, summary of, or accomplishment of; the roof of a house, etc."[190] Randle Cotgrave also listed the unaccented adjective as meaning, "full to the top, or up to the roof." The accented verb, "*comblé*," is stated to mean, "heaped full of, or filled up with; also fulfilled, accomplished; made or closed up; roofed."

In this regard, the word "accomplished" must be seen as meaning "completed" or "effected," more than as a statement of proficiency. While the "rank" (translation of "*lieu*") of pope has been on that level of accomplishment in times past, as the "chief point of" an institution leading people to Christ, the word "*vierge*" prompts one to see how that "seat" has been "completed" and no longer serving in that capacity. This meaning is deduced from the vision of Fatima, which presented the end of the papacy.

---

187   From Randle Cotgrave's 1611 French – English Dictionary, published online by Greg Lindahl. (http://www.pbm.com/~lindahl/cotgrave/search/215l.html)
188   From the website Wiktionary, under the search term "combler." (http://en.wiktionary.org/wiki/combler)
189   From the website *Wiktionnaire*, under the search term "comble." (http://fr.wiktionary.org/wiki/comble)
190   From Randle Cotgrave's 1611 French – English Dictionary, published online by Greg Lindahl. (http://www.pbm.com/~lindahl/cotgrave/search/215l.html)

When the word "swine" is understood as a sign of this completion, where "the animal in the man" is no better than a "domesticated hog" (combining quatrain III-44 with the information here, in quatrain VIII-90) an overthrow will have taken "place." It makes sense of "Give not that which is holy unto dogs," as "the state of the holy" ("*lieu du sacre,*") is "In" ("*En*") one's heart; and one must also be warned, "Cast not your pearls before swine" because they will trample them underfoot. This is what has been predicted to happen when "swine" are put "In" charge of a "sanctified place," as one's trust in "the man" ("*l'homme,*" from quatrain III-44) and not in God and Christ.

Line three is focusing on the time "When" that prophecy of Jesus will "fulfill" the cycle of one apostolic universal Church, allowing "swine" to take over "his place," the Church of Christ. Additionally, heartless men will be taking over "her place," where the Roman Catholic Church is the church that most worships the "virgin." This will be "When" the times of *The Prophecies* "will be" (translation of "*sera*"), because "at that time" ("*lors*") "swine" will take "their place" ("*son lieu*") in history.

That is to be the "full measure" (translation of "*comble*") of why the End Times theme will come to pass. The "summary" (alternate translation of "*comble*") of "swine" in "abundance" (alternate translation of "*comble*") in a "house of the holy" ("*lieu du sacre*") means there will be no one representing "his rank ... filled up" ("*son lieu ... comble*") as Jesus, filled with the Spirit. There will no longer be "one" ("*un*") truly acting as the Good Shepherd to a flock.

The "chief point of" (alternate translation of "*comble*") the "crossed ones" represents the corruption of the highest dignities of the Church, so all leaders will be "diametrically opposite" the way they are supposed to be. The presence of "swine" as popes means "religions" will become "opposite diametrically" to God's will. "When" that time is "found" (from "*trouvé*"), the prophecy "will be accomplished" and "fulfilled" (translations of "*sera comblé*").

Before moving onto line four, it is important to realize that Christ watches over Christians, just as the Blessed "Virgin" watches over her son's Church. God watches over all beings that breathe air, and people of all religions pay homage to God, in one way or another. This means there is no desire by God to have the world come to an end.

The apparitions of the "virgin" have shown her holding back the arm of punishment, because her desire is to save the world, not have it destroyed. Due to this desire to save the world, Christians recognize that God has spoken through the prophets; and as such, Marian Apparitions are the warnings of God to Catholics, mostly to the children of those who have strayed from the Church. Nostradamus, whose name honors "Our Lady," is unrecognized as a true prophet of God, but the purpose of this writing is to project him as one who is repeating the same messages of warning sent previously, only in a somewhat different manner. All are pointing to the danger signs, for the hope of eliciting faithful changes away from that end.

When one sees how there is no desire to have the Church destroy itself, as warned in the apparition at Fatima, Portugal, God knew a line of popes would fail to act. This does not mean God wanted that to happen, but that God tested the hearts of those who would be popes, by letters from a peasant girl in Portugal. Her small voice said that the pope should be strong and act against a dangerous foe. In this regard, Christ sent the Church a champion to right its direction, in Pope John Paul I. That champion was murdered by supposed holy men, and covered-up out of fear. The reaction of a corrupt Church must be recognized now, if there is to be any chance of making saving acts, at this late stage.

Pope John Paul I took the Holy Seat at the Vatican in 1978. He rose and took the name John Paul, being the first to take two names as one. He also was the first to designate the number "1" after his name, as the first of a line, rather than be unnumbered until a later pope would also take John Paul as his name. John Paul I quite soon realized the Vatican accounting books were out of order, and he immediately ordered an audit. The results were obvious to him, indicating inappropriate practices and inappropriate associations between Vatican clergy and evil people. He ordered changes in the hierarchy of the Church's bank and its monetary controllers; and he planned the removal of those who had no legitimate business with the Church.

John Paul I would do all this in his first 33 days, but he would be silenced. He was murdered, "When of those crossed ones one found" evidence of "sedition."[191] Pope John Paul I discovered that "sedition" and planned to

---

[191] There are books written, and several websites that focus on the details surrounding the death of Pope John Paul I. The website Prose & Poetry has an article entitled, "The Mysterious Death of Pope John Paul I [A Treatise], by Gregory Christiano (2003), which seems to fairly state the facts. Other sites make theories that match what I have stated.

expose it, in order to cleanse that wound and heal the Church. His murder is supported in line three's use of "swine," who Jesus warned would "trample, turn and rend" any who placed the pearls of that which is holy before them.

This means the main theme of quatrain VIII-90 is focusing on the time "When" Pope John Paul I would become pope and "sense trouble," while also being about the times "When" he would be murdered. Upon his murder, "those crossed ones" who were in on the plot would have the "one" John Paul I ("*un*") "found" by a nun, and immediately declared dead by natural causes. To "sense" ("*sens*") the need to keep the actual cause of death (poisoning) from being "found" by Italian authorities, an immediate embalming process was ordered and performed.

No autopsy was ever allowed. Had one been done, the Italian authorities would "reason" to come to the "understanding" (both alternate translation of "*sens*") that a murder had taken place. Instead, a cover-up went "Into place" ("*En lieu*"), citing Vatican City immunity from Italian law. Became of that "hindrance" (alternate translation of "*trouble*") of justice, "judgment" ("*sens*") was manipulated, allowing for "sedition" ("*trouble*").

This whole view of the rise and fall of "one" who would "understand" ("*sens*") the need to act "For" (the capitalized word "*Par*," in line three) the "purity" (seeing "*vierge*" as an adjective, by definition meaning, "pure and natural, uncorrupted, unsullied, or untouched.")[192] of the Church, based on him being a "crossed one" who saw the letter of Sister Lucia as truth. Her words, from the "Virgin" Mary, were pearls of wisdom placed before the "one" who "found" the "meaning" of "trouble" as impossible to avoid.

Still, the actions of Pope John Paul I would upset those established amid the corruption the Church had accepted, if not welcomed. The actions of that "one crossed one" would bring about his end. Thus, the main theme is of all the times "When" popes brought about "trouble" for Catholics, culminating in the final corruption that took place in 1978. This theme is stated in the preface to *The Prophecies*, projecting that some quatrains will tell a story of the important time "When" the Vatican will officially reach that state of being "diametrically opposite." At that time, the Church of Rome will forever onward be controlled by "swine."

---

[192] From the Free Dictionary by Farlex, in a search for "virgin." [Source unclear] (http://www.thefreedictionary.com/Virgin)

Chapter 10: Quatrain VIII-90

The End of a Lineage

Line three ends with a comma, which indicates a pause in time before the next series of words continues the themes. One is separated (comma use) from a developed state "at that time" ("*lors*"), where "one's calling" ("*son lieu*," alternate translation) is no longer felt coming from Christ. That "place will be closed up" (from "*lieu ... sera comblé*"), having "fulfilled" ("*comblé*") its intended service, regardless of whatever pretense seems to keep that "place" in operation. The continuation of information in line four is separated from the prior flow.

Line four states, "*Par roy plus ordre ne sera soustenu.*" This can translate to say, "By king more continuation not will be endured;" but "king" must be seen as the Bishop of Vatican City, due to the Christian themes. It can also represent Christ as "king," whose line of popes owe their elevations into power to him as the Advocate. "Through Christ," "more" will be called to serve as Good Shepherds, in the "order" of the Church of Christ. Without his assistance, "more calling of men will not be supported" (translations of "*plus ordre ne sera soustenu*"). Without any "more" truly dedicated to the "continuation" of the Spirit of Christ, that "house of the holy" will end.

The word "*ordre*" also has the ability to translate as, "order; method, fashion; disposition; a rank, file, row, continuation; due place or seat; fit state or posture; also the calling, degree, or estate of men; also an order, society, or sect of religious men or women; also a company, fellowship, or brotherhood of knights, (termed) of the order and instituted by a sovereign prince."[193] This scope of definition can find use in several ways, with the "brotherhood" and "fellowship" aspects representing "religious order," as well as that "diametrically opposite," the pseudo-religious Masonic style of fraternity. Both stand "For" (translation for "*Par*") influence over the seeker; and the element of "sect of religious men" can be seen as another break away from the original Church of Christ, in Rome. It all develops a view of "method" or "disposition" to Church hierarchy, being more important to one's "calling" than a natural "calling" by the Holy Spirit, being recognized by fellow priests as dedicated to the One God.

Perhaps the most important word of line four is "*soustenu*," which is the present participle of "*soustenir*," meaning, "sustained, supported, up-

---

193   From Randle Cotgrave's 1611 French-English Dictionary, published online by Greg Lindahl. (http://www.pbm.com/~lindahl/cotgrave/search/676r.html)

held, stayed up or born up; also endured, [tolerated], abided; also (in singing) a held note; and [in horse training] a horse reared and kept from coming down to the ground too soon."[194] This word, in all uses, symbolizes the end of the papacy, as prophesied by Saint Malachy.

That prophecy listed the symbolic names all of the popes who would sustain that "religious sect of men." Once the last pope is "fulfilled" ("Peter the Roman," following the current Pope Benedict XVI, as "Glory of the Olive"[195]), there "not will be" any more popes between Benedict XVI and "Peter the Roman" (disregarding all Antipopes who may be named as interims).

According to Saint Malachy, his prophecy states, "In the extreme persecution of the Holy Roman Church, there will sit." This details Peter the Roman, which would be the one Sister Lucia was shown walking up a hill, blessing the dead along the way, until being murdered at the cross, along with all the other "Religious men and women."

Saint Malachy went on to say that Peter the Roman, "will pasture his sheep through many tribulations; and when these things are finished, the city of seven hills [Rome] will be destroyed, and the dreadful judge will judge his people. The end."[196] It is doubtful that "Peter the Roman" will go through the pomp and circumstance of masses waiting around Saint Peter's Square, looking to see what color smoke comes out of the chimney. "Peter the Roman" will be a pope like the original Peter the Apostle of Rome. Neither will be appointed by men.

Along this line of thought, it is important to realize the Vatican's spin on Saint Malachy's list of popes. While Pope John Paul II was serving as the head of a corrupted Church, he put out the disclaimer that (paraphrasing now), "There is nothing to say that the next-to-last name ("Glory of the Olive" – Pope Benedict XVI) will be the next-to-last pope." They knew the last pope's symbolic name, but they suggested that "any number of popes could be between "Glory of the Olive" and "Peter of Rome."

Perhaps that is why Benedict is retired and living in a Vatican villa, along with his Antipope buddy, Francis. They must have wanted to drive home that point by selecting someone from South America, just to get some-

---

194 From Randle Cotgrave's 1611 French-English Dictionary, published online by Greg Lindahl. (http://www.pbm.com/~lindahl/cotgrave/search/881.html)
195 From the Wikipedia article "Prophecy of the Popes." (http://en.wikipedia.org/wiki/Prophecy_of_the_Popes)
196 Ibid.

one to act popish who came from as far away from Rome as possible.

Summary
A Church in Need

Basic Review

Eight times Nostradamus presented some form of the word "virgin" in *The Prophecies*. Each use comes with surrounding verbiage that is relative to a coming destruction, targeting Christianity. This is one of the major themes of *The Prophecies*, where the Church will be one of the causes of the End Times. That will be due to its corrupted state and inability to lead the people towards lives that glorify God and Christ.

As a theme that is prefaced and explained in the letters, then developed in all of the quatrains, a focus on the Virgin Mary can be seen as coming from seven of the 948 quatrains. That element of the whole is not clearly seen at first, because they are not together in one place. When those seven are sepearted from the whole, so they can be seen as one set, a prophecy about a future prophecy comes to light. Still, foretelling of the Blessed Mary's warnings takes on a secondary focus, rather than cast as the primary intent, where the secondary supports the primary.

Each of the eight "virgin" uses link together through a repetition that also exists in the surrounding words. This is more than simply seven quatrains linked by one common word that is found stated once in each quatrain's four lines of words. The one use of "virgin" found in the letter to Henry II becomes one keyword in a series of segments of words presenting other keywords. When each quatrain that contains the word "virgin" is placed into the context created by several quatrains, especially after optimum ordering has been established, a prophetic story is told. The grander the scope one gains, the more difficult it is to focus on one word as having such a profound effect, uniting the other references to it.

There can be no denying that *The Prophecies* is a prophetic vision of terrible times. Simply from the repeated uses of words, such as "war," "famine," "plague," and "death, an unwanted future is developed. Likewise, the prophecy known as *The Apocalypse of John* also uses those words in depicting a horrid future. Because both prophets used highly metamorphic wording, the generality of destruction and pain strongly felt makes it difficult to grasp and nail down exactly what will happen, much less when. This is the manner and style of God's prophets; and because one believes God speaks through the words of prophets, one must believe each word from a prophet originated from God, not the mind of a man.

Nostradamus explained in his letter to his king that *The Prophecies* had something to do with the lineage found throughout the *Holy Bible*. Nostradamus began telling of Adam, and at a later point he wrote, "redeemer Jesus Christ, born of the unique virgin" ("*redempteur Jesus Christ, nay du unique vierge*"). One can see how those words can indicate redemption from Christ coming uniquely from the virgin mother of Jesus.

As an explanation for *The Prophecies*, those words say Jesus delivered a prophecy to Nostradamus, through His spirit. Our Lady of Fatima would then repeat this truth in another unique manner. To read the French that way, "*nay*" takes on the English meaning, "indeed, in truth," and "but also," rather than a form of "*né*," meaning, "born."

Due to the letters "*y*" and "*i*" being interchangeable so often in Nostradamus' text, one can read "*nay*" as "*nai*." In Old French, the word "*nai*" was a version of the word "*nef*," meaning "ship," but also accepted metaphor meaning, "the body of a church" (as is the word "nave," in English). This makes "*nay du unique vierge*" translate equally to state, "ship of the special virgin." When one sees the word "*Christ*" immediately preceding the word "*nay*," this is the "bark" (barque or barchetta) of Saint Peter, or the Church of Christ in Rome, dedicated to Jesus as Christ and "with the unique" veneration to, thus the protection "of the unique virgin" mother of Jesus.

Since the explanation in the letter to Henry II leads one to expect to find the Church of Rome as a key element in one's delivery to heaven, the warning of *The Prophecies* is then relative to the dangers that Church will present towards that redemption. The virgin will then play a role in safeguarding that trust held by the people, in the Church and its pope, through her appearance to children in Europe. She appears to those whose parents have fallen away from the Church, leaving the future of the Church at risk. The Marian apparitions of the 19th and 20th centuries were unique ways to forewarn the Bark of Saint Peter of collapse.

Through the wording of the seven quatrains containing the word "*vierge*," one can realize how Nostradamus prophesied those warnings by Mary, the mother of Christ. Each use of "virgin" is repeating the implication made in the letter to Henry, with the surrounding words in each quatrain detailing aspects of the church and the degree of danger to that institution. Those dangers can be expressed as coming from it, to those who have put their trust in its connection to Christ; and they can be detailing dangers brought upon itself and its faithful, from those who detest what the Church stands for.

In quatrain II-17, the main theme states, "*du temple de la vierge vestale*," meaning "to the church of the virgin pure." That quatrain's main theme is then supported by the use of "*d'Ethne*," meaning "of Gentile people," and "*vignes*," which refers to the "vines" of which Jesus spoke about in parables. The purpose of the Virgin Mary is to preserve the purity of her son's Church, and to insure that those of varying ethnicities remain fruitful through that influence.

Quatrain III-44 shows the word "virgin" as a supporting detail to a main theme that focuses on the domestication of man, away from its animal nature. This is a role the Church plays. Line three depicts "A lightning bolt in nun" ("*Le foudre à vierge*"), which is reminiscent of the ecstasy of Saint Teresa of Avilla, whose cloistered prayer led her to experience the Holy Spirit as the golden spear of an angel piercing her heart. This intent will keep the animal instinct at bay. However, in the case of "the animal in the man" taking control (from "*l'animal à l'homme*"), then the lightning becomes a vehicle of "punishments" (from line two's "*peines*"). This is an act that "will be so hurtful" (from line three's "*sera si malefique*"). The use of "virgin" relates this evil to those leading the Church.

In quatrain III-84, "*vierge*" is once again found in line three, supporting a main theme that states "There [in a] great city" ("*La grand cité*"). The city should be protected by the Blessed Virgin, but instead the city is "desolated" (from "*desoleé*" ending line one) and the "virgin violated" (from "*vierge violee*" ending line three). Some themes of John's *Apocalypse* are reflected in line four, where Nostradamus wrote, "By weapon, fire, plague" (from "*Par fer, feu, peste*"). The vision of Fatima is found mirrored when Nostradamus wrote, "canon people will die" (from *canon people mourra*"). This death prophesies the Church's end, and line two's use of "one alone" (from "*un seul*") represents the last pope.

Quatrain IV-35 offers the plural number for "virgin," making it appear to be more representative of "nuns." This word is found in the main theme statement (line one), and it is followed by the present participle word, "betraying," preceded by a statement of "fire consumed." This matches the visions presented in the last quatrain, where a violation becomes synonymous with betrayal. Death to those who follow Church law (stated in quatrain III-84) can be seen further explained by the words of quatrain IV-35, where in line three one finds "Lightning" and "weapon" (as "*Foudre à fer*") as the cause of death and fire (double meaning of "*feu*"). This matches the vision Our Lady of Fatima allowed Sister Lucia and her cousins (all "virgins") to see. That vision foretold of the end of the Church and the murder of the pope and his followers.

The only capitalized version of "virgin" appears in line two of quatrain VI-35. It appears amid language that appears to be one thing, while being realized as something else. The capitalization, as "*la Vierge*," following a string of Latin words synonymous with astrological sign names gives the appearance of stating the astrological sign Virgo. The main theme, once the word "*Rion*" is read as "*Noir*" (meaning "Black") places focus on Christianity, with Islam and Russian atheism nearby, geographically and historically. The use of Virgin is supported in line four's presentation of "letter hidden with the candle," which references the papal refusal to address the Blessed Virgin's warnings of Fatima.

Quatrains VIII-80 and VIII-90 are where the final two presentations of "virgin" are found. *Centurie VIII* was not published until 1566, or eight years after the letter explaining "born of the unique virgin" was sent to King Henry II of France. Henry would die in 1559, the year following receipt of Nostradamus' explanation; but approval to print the last three Centuries (VIII, IX, and X) came just before Nostradamus' death. Demand for the letter meant none of the king's wise men, including his religious advisors from Rome, could understand anything of merit about the quatrains. The letter explaining them made even less sense, but amid the words that seemed to be lunacy were clear statements indicating intentional confusion, by design.

Since quatrains VIII-80 and VIII-90 fit the theme of the other quatrains containing the word "*vierge*," they (and all the 300 quatrains in the "last" three Centuries) were written prior to the letter to Henry being penned. That supports the theory that a predetermined order exists for all the quatrains, so the presentation order of publication is another design of confusion. Nostradamus explained the "unique virgin" as being somehow relevant to *The Prophecies* in the letter to the king (1558). One can then assume that the letter explained ten Centuries of quatrains, prior to the release and publication of the final 300. Due to the death of the king, the Church would play a larger role in the approval of Nostradamus' final versions going to print, with the letter sent to Henry acting as a second preface.

Quatrain VIII-80 has a main theme that focuses on a bloodline between a "widow him & virgin," which would become the line of kings that would rule Europe. That line would begin in southern France. The candle is repeated in this quatrain, after telling of the "likenesses" of holy ones, who symbolically using the dregs of wine in communion. This is yet another quatrain that paints a picture of a Church that fails the people. It will be found doing "hurtful deeds," pretending to be the "medium" for the spirit of Christ.

In the final quatrain that presents the word "*vierge*," VIII-90 states a main theme that is relative to the "crossed ones." This is a reference to Crusaders, as well as all Christians. That Christian theme is then furthered by stating, "In place of the holy," which is both Rome (the home of the Church) and Jerusalem (the quest of the Church). Line three supports "trouble" (stated in the main theme) by saying it will have been placed "By swine." They are identified by the reference to the "virgin," the protector of the Roman Church. Thus, the word "swine" is a symbolic statement about the pope, the "king" (line four) where "order [of knights] not will be supported."

All of these references to one word wrap themselves around a theme that is Christian, such that the "virgin" is symbolic of the Roman Catholic Church. The seven quatrains restate and add details to the visions of Fatima, as the prophetic warning of the Blessed Virgin, Our Lady of Fatima. That prophecy matches the one of John's *Apocalypse*, as the times when the Church will be a disservice to those following Christ. The verbiage of death and destruction that John wrote of metaphorically can likewise be seen reflected in the use of lightning, fire, lances, and swords by Nostradamus. Sister Lucia said the pope would be shot by bullets and arrows, which was a combination of modern and archaic forms of warfare. This death will come as a city is in ruin and dead line the streets.

The point of this book has been to show disassociated quatrains, coming from different places in the chapters of *The Prophecies*, having a more purposeful meaning when joined together. The one word, *"vierge,"* becomes their link. While I have presented the seven quatrains in the order of their appearance, from *Centurie Tierce* [III] to *Centurie Huitième* [VIII], that order may be tweaked so there is a better continuity. I leave that work to the reader to find. Still, in the order presented the theme of the diametrically opposite turn of the Church away from God, towards ruin, can be seen advancing in stages.

The aspect of "virgin" then fills one role of support for a main theme for the whole of *The Prophecies*. It tells a story of one failure on the part of the Church, which will reflect its complete turn away from God. It presents the Church of Rome in a position diametrically opposite of its original intent and purpose. This failure is based on its refusal to act on a divine prophecy presented to Portuguese children, once that prophecy will have been turned over to the Church. It is a story of the last 100 years of that institution, and a story of the disgraceful state it will have fallen into at the end.

The Slope of Failure

Since "to err is human," we all experience failure. Because humans lead churches, churches also fail. In chapter 37 of the Book of Ezekiel, one finds written in verses 1 through 14 a synopsis of the failure of the House of Israel, which was the "Church" of God. Ezekiel wrote:

> "The hand of the Lord came upon me and brought me out in the Spirit of the Lord, and set me down in the midst of the valley; and it was full of bones. Then He caused me to pass by them all around, and behold, there were very many in the open valley; and indeed they were very dry. And He said to me, "Son of man, can these bones live?" So I answered, "O Lord GOD, YOU KNOW." Again he said

to me, "Prophesy to these bones, and say to them, 'O dry bones, hear the word of the Lord! Thus says the Lord God to these bones: "Surely I will cause breath to enter into you, and you shall live. I will put sinews on you and bring flesh upon you, cover you with skin and put breath in you; and you shall live. Then you shall know that I am the LORD."'" So I prophesied as I was commanded; and as I prophesied, there was a noise, and suddenly a rattling; and the bones came together, bone to bone. Indeed, as I looked, the sinews and the flesh came upon them, and the skin covered them over; but there was no breath in them. Also He said to me, "Prophesy to the breath, prophesy, son of man, and say to the breath, 'Thus says the Lord God: "Come from the four winds, O breath, and breathe on these slain, that they may live."'" So I prophesied as He commanded me, and breath came into them, and they lived, and stood upon their feet, an exceedingly great army. Then He said to me, "Son of man, these bones are the whole house of Israel. They indeed say, 'Our bones are dry, our hope is lost, and we ourselves are cut off!' Therefore prophesy and say to them, 'Thus says the Lord God: "Behold, O My people, I will open your graves and cause you to come up from your graves, and bring you into the land of Israel. Then you shall know that I am the Lord, when I have opened your graves, O My people, and brought you up from your graves. I will put My Spirit in you, and you shall live, and I will place you in your own land. Then you shall know that I, the Lord, have spoken *it* and performed it," says the LORD.'"

The setting of Ezekiel was the impending collapse of that Church of God. God chose the descendants of Jacob for a reason that is explained in the Old Testament of the *Holy Bible*. Through Jacob, from Isaac, and from Abraham, was a bloodline that is traced back to Adam. David was of this lineage, as was Jesus, who was born of the Virgin Mary. In this sense, Mary was "unique" because she contributed her DNA to the Son of God, born of a woman. Nostradamus explained this lineage in his letter to Henry II, albeit in a nebulous manner. This means *The Prophecies* relates to the Church of God, just as does the prophecy of the *Book of Ezekiel*.

The history, contained in the Torah, goes to great lengths detailing this lineage. The patriarchs establish a genetic link from Adam to the Tribes of Israel, but the focus changes to show a drifting away from God. Their turns away from God shows the people relying on flawed kings and false prophets to guide them, with a desire to live like other peoples enjoying earthly delights, more than sacrificing for a heavenly reward. The Old Testament stories lead to need for a series of true prophets, such as Ezekiel, rising due to a commitment to reason God chose them, possessing genetic predispositions to hear God's voice. Thus, the dried bones of Ezekiel, more than the people of Israel, are the words God's People memorized, but did not follow. This passage from Ezekiel shows God telling His prophet to speak life to the words written, so the people can remember their past failures and realize a need to turn and face God once again.

When one reads this selection from the *Book of Ezekiel*, it then becomes important to see the dried bones of the Old Testament as being just like the quatrains of *The Prophecies*. There are very many quatrains, as 948 survive to make up the ten Centuries. There are other writings believed to have been by Nostradamus (quatrains, sixtains, presages, etc.), found after his death that have been presented in publications after his lifetime. When one reads them all, they are very dry, in the sense that they are void of language that makes them easily understood. What seems understandable on the surface can be found much deeper and fuller, when guided to see that new level of meaning. The *Holy Bible* is the same way, in the books of both the Old and New Testaments. Thus, if the parallel question were to be asked, "Can these quatrains have deep meaning?" the answer is the same. "God knows," meaning human brains are too feeble to see with their eyes and minds alone.

To hear God tell someone, "Prophesy to these quatrains, and hear the word of the LORD!" This says, "Make deep sense from the words that no one can understand." Through the breath of God, the Holy Spirit, one can speak in the tongue of Nostradamus, a divine prophet, and add the sinew to words that are bare bones of holy thought. They come to life, not so one person can seem wise and intelligent, but so one person will let all know they have risen because of the LORD.

When the passage says, "So, I prophesied and the bones came together, bone to bone," this is how all of the quatrains come together, from a disassembled order of fragments, to a whole entity that allows a lucid story to unfold. This is how the seven quatrains of this book have been joined together. They fit because they were made to be together. Still, for as much as I can look and see this remarkable transformation, there is no life in them if others cannot see this transformation.

As Ezekiel went on, writing, "Prophesy to the breath, prophesy, son of man, and say to the breath, 'Thus says the Lord God: "Come from the four winds, O breath, and breathe on these slain, that they may live." The "breath" is the Holy Spirit. The Holy Spirit is more than the breath of life, which comes at birth. It is the rebirth of that birth spirit to a resurrected state. To "prophesy to the breath" means to be filled with the understanding of holy prophecy, from the whispers of the Holy Spirit.

I have written step-by-step breakdowns of those whispers. I wrote them as they came to me. I explain how meaning comes so others can understand for themselves how the words of each quatrain come together, in ways that did not have life prior. It is not my intelligence that leads me, such that if my explanations appeal only to one's intelligence, then I am not allowed to breathe life into the words written by the man Nostradamus. It is my heart-felt emotional connection to the Holy Spirit that leads my mind to explain, so that others will also be emotionally affected and receive the spirit of my words. I write so others will allow the Holy Spirit to enter them. Prophetic words inspired by Christ, the Redeemer, suddenly have a wealth of meaning. When that connection is made, then others will see the life that previously did not appear.

The word "virgin" is the thread that runs throughout this book that I have now written. That one word creates one line of thought from which other dried bones dangle: One word, in a valley of 948 quatrains and two letters, repeated eight times; eight words among well over 25,000 words; and eight lines amid well over 4,000 lines.

The word "virgin" is related to the Church, which is what God told Ezekiel. God said, "Son of man, these bones are the whole house of Israel. They indeed say, 'Our bones are dry, our hope is lost, and we ourselves are cut off!'" The house of Israel, those chosen by God to be His priests, has become the Church of Christ. Through the "virgin," that Church was born; and the story of *The Prophecies* is just as the dream of Ezekiel, about hope being lost.

God told Ezekiel, "I will put My Spirit in you, and you shall live." This means the ability to understand the words of the *Holy Bible* comes from God's Spirit. It also means being able to understand the words of *The Prophecies* of Nostradamus comes from the same source. My explanations are not the only way to be so filled with renewed life, but understanding Nostradamus' prophecy is renewed life in those who are more inclined to believe through a source that is not affiliated with a Church that has been "cut off" from God and Christ.

A Thread of Sinew

In some Christian churches, each Sunday a lectionary is predetermined. This includes the Roman Catholic Church, the Lutheran Church, the Episcopal-Anglican churches, and the Methodist Church, to name a few. There is a set three-year schedule of Biblical readings, generally selecting one Old Testament passage, a Psalm, an Epistle from the New Testament, and a reading from one of the four Gospels. The Gospel is the cornerstone, as a fixed entity, while some options are made available for each parish to choose which readings will accompany Christ's lesson from the Gospel.

From this lectionary, a priest or minister prepares a sermon for each Sunday service. In this preparation, some meditation and contemplation, some prayer and reflection, should be put into how each reading links to the others. This means a thread exists that connects all of the readings to a central theme. This means people long before saw the sinew that attached those bones together; however, some times the theme is more obvious than at other times.

Frequently, the individual readings will seem unconnected. This can end up taking too much of the rector's time to prepare a sermon properly, based on the totality of the readings. For that reason, many pastors prepare a sermon only referencing the Gospel. Too often, the meaning from the links to the Old Testament and Epistle readings are missed or ignored.

This is a disservice to the faithful in the congregation. Those who come to church each week are the sheep, with the pastor serving the role as good shepherd. The point of a church is to spread the Holy Spirit, more than recite some readings from a book deemed holy. Since God chose a people who would serve Him, as priests to the One God, the development of temples and synagogues served the purpose of training those priests. The minister was called "rabbi," meaning "teacher." When Jesus came to announce he was the one God had promised, the Messiah, the Savior, he was not sent to set up a new system for training new priests to prepare speeches.

The spreading of the Gospel meant letting everyone know the "Good News!" This specifically meant going to all the places where Jews (Hebraic peoples scattered to the four corners of the earth) had settled. The Good News, of course, was the announcement that God's promised Messiah had arrived, which was a promise to the priests of the One God, those chosen people of Abraham, Isaac, and Jacob. The good news was not about a new church being formed, one exclusively for Gentiles, but one that allowed new blood to become one with those descendants of Israel, those who then believed the Gospel.

This was when the Apostles, filled with the Holy Spirit, went out to spread the word that Christ (the Greek word for Messiah) had come, died, resurrected, and ascended. It was time to act as the priests God had prepared them to be, from which their faith had kept them prepared to accept the Gospel. Just as the Spirit of the risen Christ walked the road from Jerusalem to Emmaus, accompanying two followers of Jesus of Nazareth in a form they did not recognize, so too must today's priests speak as Jesus to the flocks.

Jesus explained to his companions the prophecies in the books of Moses, the psalms of David, and the books of the prophets. They knew all of those writings, but each lesson he taught amazed them with new enlightenment. They received the spirit of belief in Christ because, as Jews, they knew those books and songs, but they never once had seen the links of the past to the present. Because they were Jews, they became Christians, through receipt of the spirit.

There is a difference between receiving the spirit and being filled with the Holy Spirit. To receive the spirit, one must accept that Jesus was the Messiah. As the Christ of God, the teachings of Jesus were the instructions one must follow, faithfully, because of that spirit of belief. Through this discipline, which comes from learning the links between the books of God's Covenant and the history of Jesus, one can then be raised to the highest level allowed to human beings – that of being filled with the Holy Spirit. Through belief in Christ, the Spirit of Jesus will advocate for his followers, so that God will make a link with those individually, so each individual can ascend to the level of a Christ-like existence. This state is what produces saints and truly holy men and women.

For this metamorphosis to take place, the standard practice of the Jewish synagogue had to be amended. In addition to singing the songs of praise to God, a rote practice that surrounds one with the mantra of God, and reciting passages from the Torah and books of the prophets for discussion, the Apostles introduced a connecting link to the life and teachings of Jesus. This addition produced the New Covenant of Christ, as a compliment to the Old Covenant between God and his chosen priests. One cannot exist without the other. A priest to the One God must be devout to the Law of God, while also following the model of Jesus, in faith and acts, so each priest is filled with the Holy Spirit, for the purpose of filling others with the same beliefs and talents.

As a ritual that is symbolic to this purpose, and as a model demonstrated by Jesus to his disciples, the New Covenant of Christ incorporates the sacrament of Communion. This is the recognition of the remembrance of Christ, through taking in his body and blood, as symbolized by the consumption of bread and wine. This must be realized as a symbolic gesture of faith, one recognizing what is required by each disciple of Christ to become filled with the Holy Spirit. A symbolic gesture is not to be mistaken for a real act denoting one's progress towards that end.

The body of Christ, which is consumed for the remembrance of his life on earth, represents the Old Testament prophecies of Jesus, as well as the New Testament recounts of his teachings. This means one must consume and digest that knowledge first, as a sign of faith in Jesus as the Messiah. One must have knowledge of the words proving God always intended Christ to come as he did, well before his arrival. One cannot walk the road to Emmaus and be amazed at the links between the elements and the whole, if one has not learned the whole and the elements. The body of Christ is the Holy Word of God.

The blood of Christ, which is poured out for the remission of sins (Matthew), shed for many (Mark), and for you (Luke), is the new covenant. This represents the time when one will be filled with the Holy Spirit, through Christ, from God (the trinity), being reborn with unrelenting faith. It comes after one has consumed the body of Christ, not before.

Just as the consumption of wine, a drink of fermented spirit, causes one to feel elevated, happy, and free, those physical symptoms only mimic the spiritual changes that come from receiving the spirit of faith in Jesus as Christ. One cannot touch the hearts of others by being in a drunken state, as the disciples were mistaken for on the Day of Pentecost. Thus, the blood of Christ is the Holy Sprit of God cursing through one's being, raising one to act as Jesus. Each individual must become a pure sacrifice to God, a reenactment of Jesus, the Son of Man, flesh born of a woman.

The Church of Rome, founded by the Apostle Peter, was originally an institution where Jews, who believed their Messiah had been delivered, relished this new covenant. Many of those early Christians sacrificed their lives, dying for their beliefs just as Jesus had done, and as would all of the Apostles. This level of commitment, of faith, of belief in the body and blood of Christ, does not come from eating a piece of bread and then drinking some wine. It comes from true dedication to a life of sacrifice, where the remission of sins, the letting go of one's distraction to the material plane, and thus the forgiveness and pardon of past sins takes hold. This only occurs when one's body and soul are submissive to God, allowing the Holy Spirit to take over.

As all Christians are in varying states of reception of the spirit and dedication to a life of piety, as priests with different level of experience acting for the One God, ritualistic rites become the bond for all. Those of all ranks can then come together and confirm their support for one another in this quest to be a model of Christ. That is why Christians recite:

> "The LORD be with you. We lift up our hearts to the LORD. Let us give thanks to the LORD our God. It is right to give Him thanks and praise. It is right, and a good and a joyful thing, always and everywhere to give thanks to you, Father Almighty, creator of heaven and earth."

Likewise, it is right, a good and joyful thing, always and everywhere to demonstrate that thanks by consuming the body of Christ and allowing a pouring out of his blood within ours. The true church of Christ, the real temple of God is within us, heart-centered, spiritually (heaven) and physically (earth) manifesting throughout our presence.

Failure to maintain a church on this individual level is the reason external churches go astray. By projecting that responsibility onto an institution (a Church), and then onto the man who leads that institution (a priest, minister, bishop, or pope), one has repeated the error of Israel, when it sought to have kings and be like other nations.

That projection leads those few in power to experience a power over others, seemingly of a spiritual nature but solely on the material plane. It leads to bad shepherds being given responsibility over the souls of lost sheep, and trust placed in the hands of those who are untrustworthy. To counter that failure of royal rulers, the kings of Israel needed prophets close by. Eventually those too were corrupted or killed. Today, prophets do not enjoy a position that puts them close to the ears of our world leaders (Christians).

The people sitting in the pews are not taught the lessons that link the Law to the Light, so that each individual is empowered to find Christ, God, and the Holy Spirit alone, then thank God by passing that gift onto others. The spread of the Church of Christ (not the incorporated entity, but the true meaning of the words) came from the spread of the Holy Spirit. The spread of Roman Catholicism came from imperialism that modeled the Roman Empire, at the point of a spear and the edge of a sword. The empowerment of the people was never the intent, and people, like Martin Luther, began pointing that out, commencing the breakup and downward slide of that church.

This degeneration has continued over the centuries and this corrupted form of the church is quite visible in today's headlines. The splintered denominations, having taken rise in that fall, are led by the minds of individuals (and collective minds of small groups), which fuel their hearts to act religious. Still, a church that has failed to spread the Holy Spirit as the central purpose of gathering, to discuss Christ and the prophecies of his coming (and coming again), has led to more disagreement and disillusionment than faith in a church, not truly believing the individuals are indeed living lives that model Christ.

Because the leaders of the churches have neglected the people by not serving the body of Christ in each service, through group discussion and questioned learning, the people are unprepared to go out alone, as true priests of the One God. Without the proper training and community support, they are unable to fully bring God into their hearts and use Christ as their model, through the Holy Spirit. For every step towards the remission of sins, they take steps backwards, unable to resist the temptations of the material realm. Finding more immediate comforts from earthly pleasures and delights, more and more people turn away from the churches, and thus away from God.

This is the reality of the seven churches, to which John was told to write letters. His instructions were to tell them they were failures in some regard, with those failures negating whatever good they had maintained. John, as the prophet Apostle shown the first post-Jesus version of the End Times, was writing to today's churches in those letters. Regardless of how seven ancient churches might have experienced shortcomings, in Christ's eyes, during John's time on earth, the importance lies in how the Church of Christ will play a global role, throughout its subsequent history.

The role of an Apostle of Christ, as a true Bishop guiding many churches, is to write letters letting the faithful know their shortcomings and errors. This is done in support of their individual quest for a greater reward. Therefore, John was serving in that capacity by writing a book that would be preserved for all times, to counsel all Christians as long as the Church of Christ continued.

Nostradamus was shown, as he explained in his letter of preface, the times when the Church of Rome will have reached its End. A church for Christ was seen to have shifted into a diametrically opposite position, which is a turn that will have evolved over many centuries of time. Instead of serving God, through Christ, at the time of its End the Church will be found supporting evil over good. This reality has intensified over the past 100 years (1914 – 2013), during times of great wars and increased sufferings by the people of the world, when the Church has repeatedly cowered down in the face of adversity. It has acted against the Will of God.

The Prophecies can then be seen as a renewal of the prophecy shown to John. The Church of Rome reflects all of the symptoms of the seven churches named by Christ in his appearance before John. Still, Nostradamus used the term "religions," such that the Roman Catholic Church is not the only degraded form of religion. The seven churches reflect the Jewish people, who have rejected Jesus as Christ. They reflect the different forms of the Orthodox Church, who have their faults and failures spreading the Holy Spirit. All of the denominations created out of protest against the Church of Rome are likewise reflected in John's letters. John foresaw a time of great danger to all Christianity, preceding the great End, and Nostradamus was led to detail that failure of the religions (including Islam) and the war releasing deadly forces upon the earth. All of this is the main focus of *The Revelation of John*, as it is the main focus of Nostradamus' work, with all relative to the negative influence of churches.

The appearances of the Virgin Mary also follow this prophetic line. The Roman Catholic Church has increasingly been warned by her appearances during the 19th and 20th centuries. Her warnings have been given to children (sons and daughters), rather than young men visionaries (Nostradamus) and old men dreamers (John). Mother Mary has repeatedly warned that the Church must change its course or face dire consequences. In her vision of the future, shown to the children of Fatima, that theme once again supports the prophecies of John and Nostradamus.

Because all are saying the same thing, with the prophets of the Old Testament also adding support to End Times visions and warnings, the message is unchanging. The prophecy of John makes it clear that God's judgment will come because the people will not be asking to be led by God, due to the failures of institutions. Nostradamus not only confirms this turn away from God by the religions (Church), but also the royalty (the European kings descended from a bloodline of Jesus) and the sects (the non-religious philosophical influences of mankind). All will have turned away from God. Due to the scope of this turn, the Blessed Virgin appeared in tears at La Salette, France. She expressed sorrow that the Church was filled more with people of cold hearts and feeble minds, than by the faithful filled with the Holy Spirit.

Her Son's Church

One has to understand the nature of a mother to understand the protection the "unique virgin" has provided for the Church of Rome. Mothers typically want the best for their children and they take an interest in the institutions their children attend: schools, athletic organizations, hobby clubs, home interests, etc. Mothers, due to holding forming bodies in their wombs, have an emotional attachment to those bodies, their children. That closeness creates an intuitive link between the minds of mothers and that of their offspring.

The Church is a physical body that represents Mary's child, the Son of God. As a body, it is an extension of Jesus. It evolved from Jewish synagogues, where Jews believing their Messiah had been delivered ("born of the unique virgin") became Christian. In the book of Matthew, Jesus is quoted as having said, "For where two or three are gathered together in my name, there am I in the midst of them." This is not a requirement that specific dogma be followed, only that when Christians gather (in small numbers) that is a Church of Christ.

The Roman Catholic Church has gone well beyond that small size element, thriving throughout the centuries by focusing on the large. That "big picture" approach is not concerned as much with the individual's relationship with God, as it is with the relationship Christ has to the institution representing all who gather in Christ's name. Therefore, it is natural for the spirit of Mary, the mother of Jesus, to take a personal interest in that Church of Christ, while realizing how Mary has a closer relationship with the Roman Catholic Church, than she does with the Orthodox churches in the east.

The Roman Catholic Church's sphere of influence, and thus the higher role of significance Mary enjoys, has been primarily with Western Europe, and through colonization, the spread of Christianity around the world. That church is most reflective of one that models the Roman Empire, more than Jesus the Son of God.

The Roman church's European reach included the Holy Roman Empire (Central Europe, as the Austro-Hungarian dynasty's faith in Christ), but the Protestant reforms caused many to step away from veneration of the Virgin Mary. The Central European Church is therefore more in line with that held by the Orthodox Churches of Eastern Europe, including Russia and Greece (Constantinople). The strongest base for the Roman Catholic Church is in Italy, France, and Spain, the areas of the Romance languages. Thus, the Virgin Mary is the venerated protector of that body of Christ.

The reverence shown to the Blessed Virgin by the Roman Catholic Church in Western Europe, in my opinion, has much to do with the landing of the three Maries on the coast of France (then known as Gaul). Although the mother of Christ was not among those passengers, that raft represented the first Church of Christ in Western Europe. Mary Magdalene accompanied Mary Salomé, Mary Jacobé, Joseph of Arimathea, Lazarus (the brother of Mary Jacobé), and either an Egyptian servant girl or an infant child named Sarah. That landing, set out on a raft without a sail, which traveled from North Africa (Egypt), became the seeding for the true church of Western Europe. One would expect that arrival to be by divine design, in the hands of God, serving some purpose well beyond the immediate. The lineage they began would not only demonstrate Christianity to Western Europe, it would eventually unify the nations of Western Europe under royal bloodlines. Those kings and queens would represent a Church of Christ collectively, as powerful as the Roman Catholic Church.

Two male Apostles, Peter and Paul, had direct ties to Rome, with the Roman Church fulfilling Jesus' prophecy that Peter would build the cornerstone to Christ. While both Apostles have been deemed saints, and Peter recognized as the first pope of the Church, they both are recognized more for their actions while living. They are known for sowing Christianity, more than for their guidance and protection of the institution of the Church. In this regard, the Virgin Mary holds a special place.

In fact, all of the early saints were known for their spreading the Gospel to the four corners of the earth, going to places where the children of Israel had been scattered. Paul was the one Apostle who had Roman citizenship, and he was the one who advocated that Gentiles be welcomed into the Church of Christ. The Church would cease to be synagogues, under the guidance of a Holy Temple, but an evolving scattering of Jews and Gentiles who believed in Christ as their Savior. The Apostles, as the first bishops for the new Church, supported those new churches; however, they would die martyrs, leaving others who had been filled by the Holy Spirit to move into the positions of leadership. This model is what blended with the Roman Church of Christ, founded by Peter, later blending into a model of the Roman Empire, leaving an Emperor-like pope at the top.

This is not the way the Church initially began in pagan Europe, in the places where the Roman Empire had spread its outreach. Regions of Britannia, Gaul, and Iberia (Western Europe) where still in opposition to Roman rule and had maintained a strength that ensured their independence and safety. It was into those regions that direct followers of Christ spread (the three Maries), becoming absorbed into the fabric of those European societies. Everyone was allowed to maintain their religious customs, with Christian settlements being closely related to Jewish settlements. Thus, the earliest Church of Christ was not about forced domination over people, by the sword. It was established separately; and the affect those settlements had on others was through those settlers being living examples of Christianity.

The Christianization of Western Europe was then much slower taking hold. This is because Christianity is a way of life, much more than a dogmatic religion, where memorization of and obedience to fixed laws becomes the primary objective. The goal of Christianity is many people living together, all filled with the Spirit of God. In that way, they can each support one another in a lifestyle that models Christ, developing close-knit societies that live as Jesus lived.

The Holy Temple of Jerusalem had become a model of corruption by the time Jesus walked the earth. The advent of the Roman Catholic Church would also succumb to that same model of corruption. Both Churches were originally conceived from pure intentions, the Covenant between God and the children of Israel, and the covenant between Christ and those accepting the Son of God. However, both would struggle to maintain that state of goodness, and their corruptions reflect a stance for one thing and a life reflecting quite another thing.

The legend of six people arriving on the coast of Gaul, on a raft with no sail, carrying five first-hand followers of Jesus, all closely related with him and deeply influenced by him, is the insemination of Christianity into Western Europe. Their lore tells how each of the five separated and went to different places along the coast of what is today southeastern France. They were accepted into those pagan societies and recognized for their holiness. They stayed apart from those whose ways were not Jewish, but they assisted the local populations when asked. They influenced those outsiders by a way of living right, rather than by telling them they were all Gentile sinners who needed to be saved. This is the right way for a Church to operate, and this style is what Nostradamus was told would change for the worse, becoming completely opposite, diametrically.

This change is what has brought about the necessity for divine intervention. Nostradamus was chosen as a prophet, like John. Then the spirit of the mother of Christ made her maternal presence be felt by innocent children, who were without good shepherds to guide their beliefs. Nostradamus wrote in his explanation letter to his king that The Prophecies involved the Biblical lineage, from Adam to Jesus. He stated his writings were about "the times of our savior," which can also state, "the times of our protector," or "the times of our defender."

To clarify this "time," Nostradamus then wrote, "redeemer Jesus Christ," or "deliverer Jesus Christ," where "Jesus," as "Messiah," would be the "redeemer" promised to the children of Israel. He also will be the "redeemer" of those who believe the man "Jesus" was indeed the "Christ." This becomes all who follow God, through Christ, such that Christianity is the way of life to redemption. Still, when "*redempteur*" is read as "the deliverer," stating the mother of "Jesus," who is the "Christ" of God, "Christ Jesus" was then "born" of a woman, "to the unique virgin."

Still, the element of birth is present in the story shown Nostradamus, such that a past event will be reflected in the future. For all times hence, one's redemption is relative to accepting "Jesus" as "Christ," meaning one is "born" anew, in the Holy Spirit. When one has received "of" this Spirit, then one is led "to the special" life led by "Christ." In this sense, each of us has been redeemed of our sins, making us renewed as "virgins."

This means the Virgin Mary acts as "our protector" in the "times of our" future, those told of in *The Prophecies*. As the "deliverer" of "Jesus," the "Christ" for the world, she has been "born" to hold this "unique" and "singular" responsibility as protector of all seeking this virginal state of sinlessness. This is symbolically demonstrated when she appears to children, innocent "virgins," acting as the "only" saint attempting to redeem the Church, representing an external manifestation of the Holy Spirit.

Mary instructs those innocent ones she appears before to carry warning to the representatives of the Church, who are responsible for acting as good shepherds to the faithful. In the process of her apparitions, the Blessed Virgin has created miracles, healed the sick, and provided hope for generations of believers through pilgrimages to those sites. That connection has led to her veneration; but she has also set the Church of Rome on notice that the all-seeing eye of God knows their wrongdoings. Christ played that same role when he appeared in a dream telling John to write letters to the churches.

The true history of the Christian movement has been suppressed and altered over the past centuries, by the Roman Catholic Church. The drifting of five followers of Jesus to France, those who knew the man personally, Jews believing the Messiah had indeed been delivered, symbolizes the natural spread of the Gospel. Like a seed being planted, slowly spreading and bearing fruit, like the formation of a child in the womb, this is way a church develops and remains true to its roots. The growth of the Roman church has been forced upon prisoners, who would eventually rise up against that enemy, striking it down.

That is the story of *The Prophecies*, but that story was also told during the eighteenth century, when the royal families of Western Europe would lose their influence over the people, along with some of their lives. Today, ridicule is placed on the idea that human beings can declare themselves rulers by birthright, profiting from the people submitting to those claims. A few living royal lifestyles, while many of the people suffer, is no longer deemed acceptable (since the French Revolution). The erasure of the history that the holy blood of Jesus penetrated Europe, giving rise to a lineage that would serve the Lord - the model of Arthur and the Knights of the Round Table - leaves Europeans (all Westerners) forgetful of how it all came to be.

The rise of the Cathar people in southwestern France can be attributed to the seed planted in *Saintes-Maries-de-la-Mer*, not long after Jesus ascended into heaven. That population was called Gnostic by the Church of Rome, meaning they did not follow the Church's official interpretation of the *Holy Bible*. The whole scope of the holy books written by those filled with the Holy Spirit, the true followers of Christ, had been limited through censorship; and all who believed differently than Church doctrine allowed were condemned as heretics. Because the Cathars grew to numbers that threatened the rule of Rome, they were exterminated in what was called a Crusade. That title is fitting, because hired knights declared war on innocent Christians; but the Albigensean Crusade was actually the Church's first exercise in genocide. It was symbolic of Christians being thrown to the lions in the Roman Coliseum, for the entertainment of the Emperor and guests.

By the time of that extermination, the royal bloodlines had been established and were already unifying France, Spain, England, and others, into the nations recognized geographically today. The Church of Rome would exercise its influence over those kings, in a manner that would be designed to use national powers as the military arm of the religion called Christianity. The Inquisitions targeted those of different faiths still thriving in Europe, with Jews and Muslims (Moors) given the option of conversion or deportation, before they would be murdered as the Cathar people were. The Moors would be defeated by the sword and mostly sent back into North Africa.

Summary

The Church of Rome explained the waves of plague that befell Europe during those days of genocide and forced conversion as caused by Jews. They presented an evil element of that race (not religious Jews of Judaism) as trying to kill innocent Christians. This aspect of hatred has become so deeply drilled into the Western psyche that anti-Semitism has often risen (like the plague) without warning or viable explanation.

The primary reason a prophet like Nostradamus struggles for respect as a prophet of God is the Church has summarily rejected his name. Their influence has caused a deep-seated fear of Nostradamus by Christians, primarily because he practiced astrology. The Church deemed that art evil, primarily because they could not master its use to their benefit, but also because only Jews and Muslims practiced it.

The non-religious Jews are the militant arm of Judaism. They found sanctuary in Geneva when it was a city-state. Because the Church of Rome has been at war with Judaism, the bankers of Geneva have been at war with Christianity. Geneva has been the breeding ground of philosophers who have been the black knights threatening Camelot. They are the moneychangers who financed the rebellions against England (the American Revolution) and France (the French Revolution). When the kings of Europe were no longer ruling over nations, the influence of the Roman Catholic Church was eradicated and the Church became powerless.

This influence for change and revolution extended through all of Europe, culminating with the overthrow of the Czar of Russia in 1917. Geneva was also the covert origin of mind-centered schools, such as those that would spawn Freemasonry and Rosicrucianism. Although those schools of thought have been banned to members of its clergy, by papal decree, those influences have infiltrated the Catholic faithful and led them away from the Church.

Just as the Spirit of Christ appeared to John of Patmos and told him to write letters to the seven churches, telling him to note how each had done good deeds, the Virgin Mary's spirit has informed the Church that not all has been lost. Her call is for change. Nostradamus' prophecies likewise tell what will happen if nothing is done to stop evil from being in control. All prophesy that Christians must take steps towards God and stop moving away from Him.

This is just as the tale of Arthur shows near that story's end. We are shown a distraught king unable to rise up against a kingdom rapidly falling apart. Arthur represents a king without a sword, as a Church of Christ without the Holy Spirit. Camelot represents a land without a king, paralleling Christendom without Christ. This state is that foreseen, and against which the Blessed Virgin warns. She has appeared to wake up Christianity from the fog, into which the Church has fallen. She orders a quest to seek the Holy Spirit, for one last stand, good against evil.

This is the element of redemption found in the seven quatrains developed in this book. The apparitions of the "virgin," particularly those at Fatima, Portugal, in 1917, showed what would happen should nothing be done to stop that desolation. The whole of *The Prophecies* is a story of what will bring about the end of the world, should nothing be done to prevent that end. While the whole story details the horrors of that demise, just as *The Revelation of John* is mostly focused on tragedy, the purpose of prophecy is not to have the prophecy fulfilled.

Nostradamus develops three subplots, from the general theme of the influences of good turning into influences of evil. They involve the deterioration of the churches, the rulers, and the sects. Thus, the element of the church's fall is detailed in roughly a third of the quatrains (300 or so). This fall will target the one institution seen as being responsible for the negative light that has been cast upon Christians, which is the Church of Rome.

The seven quatrains that link together by the use of the word "virgin" act as the forewarning to the detail of the whole story. The seven quatrains can be read as a preface to the end of the Church. Nostradamus' vision matches the vision shown to Sister Lucia by Our Lady of Fatima, in greater detail.

The quest for the Holy Spirit cannot be a collective reward. All may seek, but only individuals may find. Neither churches nor kings can absolve us of any sins, theirs that we allow, and many others we independently, warmly embrace. In a time when our traditionally respected influences have dissolved into bad shepherds, pied pipers leading us toward the great abyss and eventual spiritual ruin, it is up to each one of us to make the decision to change. Only through a return to Christ will God forgive us, individually, our sins.

The Holy Spirit is in the words of *The Prophecies* and I have attempted to demonstrate that presence through explaining the meanings of some words. I do not expect that every possibility I have brought forth is the primary meaning, with some, admittedly, being conjecture. I do not ask that anyone believe what I write, only to take what I write and test it for truth. As I claim to be led by the Holy Spirit, those testing should ask for guidance from the same source. Receive the spirit.

The Holy Spirit is just as present in the books of the *Holy Bible*, such that the systems I have used for explaining *The Prophecies* can be applied to those passages as well. All prophecy comes from the same one source, through an infinite number of prophets. The benefit of prophecy comes from believing God has spoken, that He has spoken to us personally through others we do not know. I can only pray that others will be able to absorb this work to a point that it helps them reach out and ask God to confirm His meaning to them.

Nostradamus & Our Lady of Fatima

www.ingramcontent.com/pod-product-compliance
Lightning Source LLC
Chambersburg PA
CBHW031244290426
44109CB00012B/433